Advance Praise For
Dark Daze & Foggy Nights

"*Dark Daze & Foggy Nights* shows insight into the mind of a police investigator when dealing with a complex case that delves into the horrific serial rapes of many women. The reader will learn the traumatic consequences that will lead this officer into the darkest time of his life as he suffers for the pain and emotional distress of the victims. This is a provocative read and brings a good perspective into the life of a police officer."

—Floy Turner,
Special Agent Florida Department
of Law Enforcement (Retired) and
Best-Selling Author, *Behind Her Miami Badge*

"In this compelling pager-turner, Investigator-detective Edward S. Scott offers rare insights into how sexual assaults continue to plague communities of all sizes. As someone who has written about sexual assault and has been an advocate at a rape crisis center, I'm all too aware that sexual assaults of all kinds too often go unreported. These are the crimes that tend to fall through the cracks of justice. Without Scott and the survivors, the rapist, well-known in the community, would still be among us, free to victimize even more women. Scott actually listened to the multiple accusers, most of whom hadn't filed police reports. He allowed their trauma to affect him and change his life, and not always for the better. *Dark Daze & Foggy Nights* is an excellent book."

—Virginia McCullough,
Award-winning Author of Women's Fiction and Romance

"*Dark Days & Foggy Nights* is authentic and brutally honest. Edward S. Scott does an outstanding job of capturing the essence of the police investigation and the heart of a true public servant in telling this amazing story. In my thirty-three years in a police uniform, working a patrol beat to narcotics investigations, I have seldom read such accurate descriptions of policing and the nuances that make up a driven public servant who puts him/herself in harm's way. Scott breathes life into this incredible story from the firsthand perspective of a working police investigator."

—Joseph E. Mosca,
Sergeant (Retired), Florida Highway Patrol and
Author of *Scorpion Win*d: A Trooper John Stella Novel

"*Dark Daze & Foggy Nights* is a riveting true crime drama by first time author, Edward S. Scott, who takes readers into the nether world of bars, single women, drink-spiking and serial rape all at the hands of one denizen of this world. This is not a "just the facts" book, but a gritty story of a world, that once you enter it is hard to exit until that story is over. This is a walk on the road of good versus evil. Be prepared to be mesmerized."

—Steve Daniels,
High-Risk Parole Agent (Retired)
and True Crime Author

DARK DAZE & FOGGY NIGHTS

Edward S. Scott

DARK DAZE & FOGGY NIGHTS

*An Untold Story
of Breaking the Silence*

Edward S. Scott

Written Dreams Publishing

Green Bay, WI

Publisher/Executive Editor: Brittiany Koren
Cover Art Designer: Ed Vincent/ENC Graphics
Interior Layout Designer: Amit Dey
Ebook Layout Designer: Amit Dey

Category: True Crime Memoir
Description: The true story of a public safety investigator's side of a sexual assault case.
Hard Cover ISBN: 978-1-951375-67-6
Paperback ISBN: 978-1-951375-68-3
Ebook ISBN: 978-1-951375-70-6
LOC Catalogue Data: Applied for.

First Edition published by Written Dreams Publishing in January, 2022.
Ebook Edition published by Written Dreams Publishing in January, 2022.

Green Bay, WI

To the courageous women that selflessly chose to come forward to pursue justice against Marcus Somerhalder, to the confused and broken women who have yet broken the silence against their assailants, to Katie DeNiel who never recovered from the consequences of his actions, and to my amazing daughter Raya Hope who will need to find her path and protect herself against narcissistic sociopaths in this cruel but beautiful world.

Every 68 seconds, a person is sexually assaulted. If you or someone you know has been sexually assaulted, contact your local police department or find resources at RAINN (Rape, Assault & Incest National Network). Call 1-800-656-HOPE (4673) or visit https://www.rainn.org.

AKA A NOTE FROM HOPE

When I reported my assault to the police, believe it or not, it was a difficult decision because I really didn't know the details of what happened to me that night; I only knew for certain that I had been sexually assaulted. Despite my lack of recollection, I had to report what I could. I knew it was an important first step in reclaiming my power. I admit, every step after that first one was even harder to take and too far apart from the last.

For a long time, I was angry and very suspicious of men. More than that, I became overly sensitive when I experienced men measuring us women by our looks and bodies rather than our minds, skills, and personalities—I hated it. Those feelings of anger have faded, but still, after all these years, I can't help but slip back into that mindset when I hear someone minimize sexual assault. Please don't. You're not helping. When you trivialize sexual assault, it influences those who hear you to do the same, which is only perpetuating rape culture and the idea that "don't get yourself raped" is more pervasive than the proper teaching— "don't rape someone."

I know false accusations happen, but they aren't prevalent. It's better to believe and support first because the truth isn't always so easy to find. Furthermore, the search for that truth should happen while respecting the privacy of everyone involved, including the accused, because the repercussions of quick judgement and assumptions can be detrimental to so many.

Now more than ever, people are talking about sexual assault and the dialogue has been eye-opening. It makes me wonder, with so many voices now speaking up, how it's taken this long to break down these walls. The answer doesn't matter, but it's given me hope. I feel it more strongly every time I see a man—or anyone, honestly—empathize, understand, and take a sexual assault claim seriously. There are many supporters and believers out there, but there needs to be more, and let me tell you why:

Victims are lonely, afraid, and so very confused.

After my assault, my mindset around strangers who were drinking changed dramatically. I used to think drunk people were foolish but harmless for the most part, but after Marcus, my naïve trust in the goodness of others was gone. I tried to keep going out with friends so I could go back to feeling "normal," but instead, I felt like a target; I felt vulnerable.

When there was a drink in my hand—sometimes even when there wasn't—I was worried there were predators watching and waiting for their chance to get to me, and it haunted me. I worried about being drugged again. I worried about being raped again. I'd see other women who were drunk or alone and became hyper-vigilant about making sure they were safe.

Those were all huge anxiety triggers because, first of all, my original report against Marcus was dismissed as hearsay, and if that wasn't terrible enough, his assault on me disrupted my confidence in so many ways. Because I wasn't sure what happened, I was forced to question myself. "Do I have a drinking problem? Is it so bad that I ignore my limits? Do I have issues with self-control when I drink and get to a point where I totally disregard my convictions?" Then, there were all those questions every person who's ever been sexually assaulted asks themselves. "Is it my fault this happened to me?"

I questioned everything about who I was, I doubted my judgement, and deep down, I began doubting that people truly cared about one another. It's a terrible thing to lose faith in humanity.

My family and friends who knew what happened supported me the best they could, but I was a wreck inside. I really believed I would eventually work through my emotions on my own, but it didn't happen for me. I became a very poor student at college and had to repeat classes, which forced my student debt to grow. I became a pretty lousy employee—indifferent and low-energy. I remember feeling like a screw-up with very little motivation. I just felt *defeated*, and for longer than I'd like to admit, I just didn't care. I wish I would have had more guidance on how to defeat my demons because I was too big a mess to seek out the help for myself.

It wasn't until years later, when Marcus Somerhalder's case went public, that I found out I wasn't alone.

I didn't need to be all that involved in the case as it happened, so I didn't know how many victims had come forward against him. I wish I had known about them sooner. I think it would have helped me to know how closely their statements corroborated mine; I would have loved to know that their stories *validated* mine. Maybe, I wouldn't have felt so alone.

I'm glad Marcus Somerhalder was charged, convicted, and is off the streets, and I've tried not to think about him while he's been in jail. In fact, I've tried to forget about him entirely, but it's hard to ignore my concern about his eventual release. I'm not confident he's going to be cured of being a serial rapist while incarcerated. I don't have a lot of faith that the parole system will be enough to prevent him from reoffending. I'm glad he's a registered sex offender, but, yeah, that loss of faith in humanity is especially delicate when it comes to Marcus Somerhalder eventually being allowed to walk the same streets as me again. Personally and selfishly, I don't want to see him in my town.

I've learned that a trauma like sexual assault lasts ages; it can seem like you'll never overcome it, which is discouraging because it's probably the last thing you want defining who you are. The feeling of being a target has faded, but I'm still overly cautious in public. It's a reality that we never really know what people are capable of—especially when no one else is watching, so I'd rather be prepared.

Healing is slow and painful. It takes time, so show yourself grace. What helped me heal the most was listening to God's word—it's where I find peace and how I recognize the "current me" is the best version of myself so far, with the best version yet to come. No matter how you heal, don't be afraid to rely on faith, family, friends, and know there are resources out there made specifically for you.

To sum it all up, if you're a victim of assault, please find someone to talk to. Supportive family and friends are invaluable.

If the first person you tell is too uncomfortable to listen, find someone else. You deserve to be heard. Tell your story. If you feel shame, try not to fear it. The shame we feel as victims loses power each time our story is aired-out. You're not alone, so find other people who can relate. Hearing your story helps them feel less alone, just like it will for you, and that's invaluable. Trust me.

To the other women who helped solidify Marcus Somerhalder's reputation as a serial rapist: knowing how courageous you were throughout this case has replenished my own courage and it feels authentic—like the bravery found in numbers. I'm so grateful for your courage to come forward. It means that like myself, you believed your story—no matter how terrible—could make a difference. Thank you!

—Hope Alby

AKA THE REASON

What I, Edward S. Scott AKA Scott Schermitzler, do for a living requires a certain level of empathy to help people through some of the darkest moments of their lives, so, from the very inception of a sexual violence case that landed on my desk, the victims were the very highest of my priorities. As an investigator, I couldn't relate to what they'd been through completely, but I understood their feelings of embarrassment, guilt, and shame. So, if nothing else, I understood what was floating around in their heads. I was as close to this case as any one of them—if not closer—by the end of it. In their weakest moments, I calmed them as they heaved and sobbed through every feeling that accompanied the betrayal they'd suffered. And I suffered alongside them. With each and every comforting coo, they'd feel a bit better, but I'd slip a little further into despair. It was worth it.

That despair fueled a different fire—one that invoked a passion to fight desperately to get their assaulter, Marcus Somerhalder, behind bars. He had exposed them and callously harmed them; the very thought that videos so distressing in nature remain in existence and kept on file as evidence against their attacker, caused colossal stress and anxiety for the victims. That knowledge made it imperative that the district attorney and I do everything in our power to keep those young women and the grotesque videos out of a crowded courtroom.

Each and every time those videos were watched—the victims exposed—those women felt assaulted all over again. Marcus is serving a lesser sentence, but he'll remain a registered sex offender until the day he dies. Unfortunately, it wasn't enough for some of the heroic women.

It wasn't until I reached out to them many years later that I realized how deep those emotional wounds had gone. I was taken aback and darkly amazed by how wholly the selfish, vulgar acts of one man could devastate down to the very core of so many lives. Some of the women have yet to, and will likely never, get over the pain and turmoil he caused.

We can never predict what direction our lives will take us, and none of us are ever in total control of the path we end up on. These women had their paths drastically changed in the most tragic way by the events that precipitated this book. I fully acknowledge what they went through; it is not my intent to exploit their suffering but to celebrate their strength and bravery in bringing Marcus to justice.

I'm telling this tale with the sincerest of intentions—that so many will benefit, and maybe even learn, from it. I think it's in the public's interest to know this story of abuse and betrayal because it's important for society to understand horrific things like this really do happen. And, when they do, we need to *empower, support, and encourage* victims to come forward. We, as a society, can hold sexual predators and sociopaths accountable for their actions. If we don't know what they're doing in the shadows, their sicknesses will evolve (often dangerously), thus making us, bystanders and victims alike, enablers through our silence.

There's a true need to reach out to victims and let them know they aren't alone in how they feel. They suffer the effects of PTSD in addition to their struggles with guilt and shame, also the devastation of trust and self-confidence as well. We can never go back and change their pasts, but we certainly can provide hope for their futures.

To the best of my knowledge, the events described in this book are correct and accurate. In good faith, and because of how strongly I feel about protecting the victim's privacy and reputation, I offered to change the names of all of the women involved in this sexual violence case. Imagine my surprise (and pride) when some of the women and their families not only approved but actually encouraged me to use their *real* names.

The last thing I would ever want to do is make these courageous women victims again. Each of the women mentioned in this book is truly amazing; they unselfishly put themselves and their reputations on the line to save others from becoming victims.

As important as this is to me, they also want to play a vital role in empowering women to take control. I've been in awe of their commitment and sacrifice, but this puts them at an even higher level of admiration. They're no longer willing to submit to events and feelings that were never their fault. I truly believe their unselfish commitment in helping me put an end to Marcus's sexual rampage saved lives, and with this story, our hope is it will save many more…

Remember: you're only a victim if you allow abusers and oppressors to have that power over you. Speak out—take your power back.

INTRODUCTION...

AKA INTO THE LION'S DEN

It was in August of 2003, as I chatted with a fellow Ashwaubenon Public Safety Department investigator, that I learned Marcus Somerhalder was the only assailant named in an official sexual assault complaint.

I knew this man personally. He was an acquaintance—more or less a friend, I suppose, so I felt compelled to take on the case with the full intention of proving him innocent.

I had met Marcus through my longest and most trusted friend, Skinny, who was the current manager of Marcus's bar, the Velvet Room. They had known each other for quite a few years, and despite knowing he was fairly good friends with Marcus, it was obvious I had no choice but to attempt to utilize Skinny as my first *point of interest*.

This meant I would be faced with a double-edged sword, of sorts; it was great that I knew someone who was so close to the alleged assaulter, but that relationship created a need for delicacy in how I approached Skinny on the subject. I had to make sure I delivered what I knew in a way that didn't make him run straight to Marcus, which would inevitably break the case wide open. I was pretty confident his loyalty to Marcus didn't trump *our* lifelong friendship. I was a shoe-in, if we were playing favorites, but I've learned it's never safe to assume.

Thoughts on how to play the whole situation were forefront in my mind in the hours before I made contact with Skinny. The majority of that thinking happened while I surveilled the Velvet Room to make sure Marcus wasn't there.

I admit, I might have even dragged the surveillance out a little longer than necessary as I allowed my fear of confronting Skinny to get the better of me. I was definitely ruminating it all, but it really was that complicated in my mind. I didn't want to act until I was sure of my approach.

It finally came down to the realization that there was absolutely no way of knowing how Skinny would react. I had no choice but to roll on into the Velvet Room and question him. I'd play the situation like I'd done so many times before—trust my instincts. I'd find a balance between not giving him too much information and getting his honest take on Marcus's love life.

On the sexual assault report, there were four names listed as being involved: Marcus, Faith, Alisa, and Piper. I was fairly confident Skinny would be familiar with all of them. Skinny seemed to be familiar with *everyone*, so I couldn't have asked for a better informant...in theory.

It would severely jeopardize the case in the worst possible way if Skinny ratted me out to Marcus, who had no idea he was even being investigated for a sexual assault. The ripple effect would most certainly put my integrity as an investigator into question as well. I couldn't let that happen. I had to make the best-case scenario be the only one; Skinny was going to stay hush about the whole thing and provide information that proved Marcus was either innocent or guilty.

To hell with it all. Come what may, it had to be done.

It was mid-afternoon by the time I, in a feigned-casual manner, made my way into the Velvet Room to see Skinny. The place wasn't open yet, but the doors were unlocked. As I slid through the second set of doors, Skinny looked up from his work. He was surprised to see me at that time of day but didn't ask why I had come by. So, I took a seat at the bar while he cleaned up behind it. I ordered a soda on the rocks, and in true old-pal fashion, we small-talked about what was going on in our lives.

It wasn't long before the conversation began to trickle, so knowing we were alone, I decided to casually start talking about Marcus's current girlfriend, Faith.

"Is Marcus still seeing that Faith girl?" I asked.

"Yeah, Scott, why?" Skinny wondered.

I ignored his question and continued. "Do they get along pretty well? Have they been having any problems? Also, do you know if Marcus is a drug user?" I winced after blurting the last question out.

Skinny stopped what he was doing to give me a sideways look.

I took a nervous chug of my soda to chase away the immediate thought that the conversation was going to take a negative turn (I wasn't being nearly as subtle as I'd planned), but he merely said, "There are *always* problems because Marcus *always* keeps his options open, and no, Marcus is a huge anti-drug guy. Doesn't touch any of that stuff."

Curious, I asked, "What do you mean, exactly, when you say there are *always* problems?"

"Well, I'm sure you've noticed the guy is forever being swarmed by women. It's baffling, man. He doesn't even treat any of them all that well, and they still keep coming back."

"So, there's a lot of exes out there… Do you know if he's having issues with any of them?" At that point, I got the impression Skinny was starting to catch on to what I was throwing, and his answers became exactly what I was looking for.

"Scott, this guy has women who downright hate him. I'm not even kidding. They've told me all sorts of crap about him. Some of it pretty bad, too. A couple of them say they think Marcus drugged them. Can you believe that shit?"

The hair on the back of my neck rose to attention, my interest was piqued, and my suspicions rose to a new level. I watched as Skinny's demeanor shifted from carefree to troubled. His brow furrowed, and he was emitting a strong vibe of disapproval regarding Marcus's womanizing ways. He shook his head and went back to wiping the bar, and I immediately started to worry he regretted saying so much.

Beyond the report I'd read the day before, I'd never even heard a whisper about this side of Marcus. This was disconcerting news to me.

My thoughts flickered to the hopeful probability that these were just untrue, unsupported, and unreported accusations. In fact, Skinny had undoubtedly heard them uttered from the mouths of drunken, jealous women. Maybe they were angered by a bitter breakup or lack of interest from Marcus? At that point I couldn't say, but I knew I wanted this investigation to be fair and without bias, so in honor of keeping an open mind, I had to consider the flipside—what if there *was* more?

Maybe Marcus had a very dark, secretive, evil side to him.

I was all ears.

I'd never have imagined Skinny would have a bad thing to say about this guy, but as we chatted more, I could tell he was fairly confident his sources had been telling the truth. Add the fact he didn't seem at all bothered by me asking about it. If Skinny was willing to keep talking, I was willing to keep listening. Maybe they weren't as close as I'd thought.

I was quickly becoming more optimistic that I would be able to confide in Skinny about the investigation. I knew Skinny would be honest with me and respected my position as a law enforcement officer, but I hadn't quite worked up the gumption to confess the reason for all of the odd questions, or where I was going with the conversation. I was still a little worried he'd rat me out. I decided it would be best to divert the focus for a bit and allowed the conversation to drift into another subject until I was ready.

But it was eating me alive…

I sat there, trying to continue on with the small talk, but it all felt so mundane compared to what I really wanted to say. I guess I *was* ready.

Before I crawled out of my skin in discomfort, I took a leap of faith and asked him if I could trust him to keep something confidential.

Once again, Skinny stopped what he was doing and slid along the back of the bar to get closer to me. He glanced first to the back of the bar, then to the front, and despite us obviously being alone, said in a hushed tone, "Of course, what?"

Skinny has always had a very relaxed and casual demeanor, but he knew I had something very important to tell him and was clearly excited to hear it. He leaned over the bar toward me in anticipation. Although I still had some nagging fears about how he'd process the information, I had to stuff them down. He'd helped me with other minor investigations in the past, so I had to believe I could trust him this time, too, no matter how close to home it hit.

"Okay, Skinny," I started, "you know I like Marcus, and I would never want him to be unjustly charged for something he didn't do—"

"Whoa, whoa, whoa." Skinny's eyes shot to the size of dinner plates. "Are you serious? Someone went to the police about Marcus?" He continued to look me square in the eyes—completely silent—waiting to hear more.

I stared back at him. "Well…"

CHAPTER 1

FOR EXAMPLE. . .

AKA THE BURRITO

I've always seen myself as a pretty normal guy—if that means anything these days—with a very complex and exciting job. A job that's given me many unbelievably great experiences and opportunities, yet it almost kills me on a regular basis. It's been 25 years since I got my start in public safety, and as much as it feels like it was just yesterday, it feels like an eon ago as well.

As an eighteen-year-old, I started in this line of work in 1991. I was blissfully ignorant as to who I was as a human being or how this job would affect my life. I had no idea what an important role I would play, how many lives I would affect throughout my career, or the decisions I would make within that career—who ever does? All I knew was that being a paid on-call firefighter and EMT seemed like a really cool idea. The action and thrill were keenly intriguing to me and sucked me in.

But I learned there was a certain feeling of accomplishment and satisfaction that came with helping people in need, and I thrived on it. It soon became clear I was made for this racket, so I aggressively pursued what eventually became a unique career in public safety.

People who work in law enforcement, EMS, and firefighting are definitely of a different breed, and I say that with utmost endearment toward them. There isn't any other way to say it, except that when tragedy looms and the world crashes down around unfortunate people, there *needs* to be people in the world who can pick up the pieces—men and women who can walk into danger, seemingly without fear. People who can then go home, hug their kids, mow the lawn, wash the dishes, and in general, move ahead like the horrors they saw never happened.

I remember one event in particular that will put it into perspective.

It was on a sunny day in May 2001 when my friend and paramedic partner for the shift, Don, and I pulled the ambulance out of the station. It had been a rather uneventful morning, so we made our way over to Eddie Peppers, a local gas station/Mexican joint for lunch.

We ordered two of the biggest, sloppiest burritos they could cook up for us. The cashier was making small talk as she rang up our order, and asked in a sarcastic yet playful voice, "So, have you had any plane crashes recently?" She chuckled, making light of the two recent plane crashes that had occurred in our village within the last few months. Before that, we hadn't had a plane go down in our jurisdiction for over ten years, so to have two so close together was uncanny.

Of course, we laughed and shook our heads. "No such luck, ma'am," I'd said.

It couldn't have been more than a minute after we grabbed our burritos when the radio crackled to life and alerted us to respond to a possible plane crash at Green Bay's Austin Straubel Airport.

Don and I shot looks of disbelief at each other before we bolted out to our rig with burritos in tow. I tried to think along the lines that it was more likely someone was falsely reporting an incident to see the big red trucks roll. Like the woman behind the counter.

As we raced through Ashwaubenon and got closer to the airport, confirmation came through that a small plane had indeed gone down in the northeast corner of the airfield. Airport public safety let us in at the gate and escorted us to the tattered remains of the single engine plane that had taken a nasty nosedive into the grassy field adjacent to the tarmac.

We parked a short distance away from the downed plane, jumped out of the ambulance with med kits in hand, and began making our way over to the crash site to check for signs of life. With every step we took toward the accident, our hopes someone had survived diminished. By the time we reached the wreckage, every single one of those hopes were scattered in the grass behind us.

Sadly, the pilot had been transected, his internal organs and intestines exposed across the cockpit. The injuries were incompatible with life, and needless to say, he had no pulse. Beyond what you see, hear, and feel in a situation like this, there are also a myriad of smells that tend to accompany it. When exposed, the intestinal area on most living things on this planet have a very unpleasant aroma. Unfortunately, this truth encompasses us humans as well. It was a horrific and intensely grim scene. The only comfort I recall feeling was the surety that the man had most certainly died on impact without suffering.

I make it a point whenever I'm in situations like that to say a little prayer and ask God to be with the deceased and care for their family. It helps me settle my personal feelings, which is paramount, because on the most traumatic calls, there isn't time to dwell on emotions or sorrow. We had a job to do.

We gave our heads a shake, then moved on quickly to secure the area and make notifications to the medical examiner and the airport officials. There was nothing more we could do for this unfortunate soul.

Don and I returned to the ambulance, took a few moments to debrief each other, then—while we waited for the coroner to arrive—dove right into the sloppy burritos we'd left resting on the dash of the ambulance.

As we began devouring our food in delicious silence, I looked at Don, who had remnants of burrito on his face. It occurred to me then we were truly cut from a different cloth than most people. The realization hit me like a brick square in the forehead. Yes, a different breed entirely. Who could possibly enjoy eating anything, let alone a sloppy beef burrito, after witnessing a scene like that?

Surely, we meant no disrespect to the poor fellow or his unknowing family. Surely, we felt terrible about such a tragic situation. How could we, in good conscience and ease of appetite, eat those greasy, cheesy, meaty, sloppy burritos while a pile of fresh human flesh and guts had been exposed in front of our very eyes?

The truth is, we really did feel terrible. We wondered about who the man was and how much his family would grieve and miss him. We wished we wouldn't have had to see such a tragedy. I wouldn't wish anything about that situation on anyone.

As we finished our last bites, we looked toward the airport fence about 150 yards to the east, and to our surprise, saw a local news truck and a reporter capturing video of the crash. I don't know how they do it, but it's a usual occurrence for the news trucks to arrive at accident and crime scenes faster than most officers. We all know they have scanners, but none of us have ever figured out how they *always* seem to be in the right place at the right time.

At any rate, our first thoughts were of hoping the video footage on the local news wouldn't reveal the two responding paramedics disrespectfully chomping on burritos at the scene of a devastating airplane crash.

Everyone in the business probably understands what I mean. I'm betting doctors and nurses get it, too, but it would be difficult to explain to my friends and family why we were eating instead of trying to save that man. I'm certain they'd think it was demented, gross, or even disrespectful, but that wouldn't be the truth.

That evening, Don and I watched the news. We were visible in the front of the ambulance, but thankfully, it didn't reveal the grotesque aftermath of human remains nor our equally grotesque burrito-splattered faces.

Some of the traumas I've experienced throughout my professional career have faded into the shadows of my psyche, and I'm thankful they have. But after nearly twenty-five years, the burrito story remains vivid in my mind— the sight and scents of that day revisit me on occasion as well. To survive in this line of business, learning to cope with tragedy is a necessity; if you don't or can't, the job will systematically break you down until you can't effectively do it anymore. Beyond that quick little prayer I said when I first arrived on scene that day, eating burritos seemed like the next normal thing for us to do. After a sight like that, *normal* was what we needed.

When you're used to dealing with everyone else's issues, problems, and tragedies, it's easy to start sinking into your own dark little world. Camaraderie and a good laugh can be like reset buttons after dealing with tragedy, and more often than not, the remedy to alleviating our heartache and anguish.

I went to work with a smile on my face every day. I smiled because I wanted to be sure I was setting the right tone and instilling the right attitude in the newer officers. Sure, I'm saddened by the nature of the beast that is my job, and sometimes frustrated by administrative work issues. I still need to provide and promote a pleasant, friendly, and humorous environment to keep morale where it should be.

Humor, especially.

Public safety folks are known for having sick senses of humor, but it's our sense of humor that prevents us from getting sick ourselves— in the head and the heart. If the general public knew the things we talked about in the station, they'd most certainly be appalled by the content. They wouldn't find a grain of hilarity in what they heard, but if they dealt in the business of tragedy on a regular basis, I think they'd completely understand the compulsion for our unusual senses of humor. I'm certain they would embrace it and promote its presence just like we do. We must appreciate and celebrate the good times and the good people we have in our lives because you never know when it'll all come to an end.

Every once in a while, I find myself starting to sink into disparity and depression and need to quickly check myself to prevent it from growing into something much more difficult to handle. Or worse yet, having the occasional bouts of depression and self-pity start affecting my relationship with my wife and kids.

I don't think—*I know*—I'm not alone in my fight against occasional depression in the public safety field. Dealing with the negativities of society in a community you truly care about is challenging; it would be impossible not to fall into a "funk" every so often. It's how you deal with it that's crucial in not letting it kill your energy and human spirit. When I start feeling the effects, so much so that I have a hard time showing up at work with a smile, I always go back to my faith in God.

Beyond my faith, it also helps to remind myself that we're only short-timers here on Earth. I'm grateful for each day I have, each breath I take, and each moment I get to spend with my family. Life is fragile and can be taken from you in a split second. Whether you like it or not, when the big guy pulls your number, it's your time to go. When it happens, you'll only have yourself and your faith, whatever that may be.

When I see others get worked-up by the minor inconveniences of daily life, I have to tune it out, so I don't get sucked in. I've seen so many people's happy and prosperous lives get cut down in a blink of an eye that it's made me nearly oblivious to the petty problems of everyday life. I don't want to fret about minor issues anymore—we have more than enough to worry about in this line of work.

There's nothing simple about being a cop in today's world. It's a big, complicated job living in an infinite loop of caring for others and yourself, while trying to avoid attracting any more negative public scrutiny. We quite literally must have a smile on our face while trying to make the correct, spur-of-the-moment choices in harrowing situations. If we don't, we face the harsh judgements of the public and media. It's not fair—it's the sad truth, and it's only getting worse.

This job has always asked the same of us; it's always asked us to give more than most people ever could. The burdens have changed with the demands and stigmas society are putting on police officers. It makes me wonder and worry how we'll ever attract high quality, qualified, educated, ethical people to become officers of the law.

Many years ago, I would've encouraged and been proud if my children wanted to serve and protect the community as law enforcement officers, but these days I would never want my kids to enter such an unhealthy, volatile, and scary occupation. I hate to have such a negative tone because this profession has given me the opportunity to do some remarkable things. I've helped thousands of people, and it's shaped me into who I am and what I perceive as important in life.

What we really need the world to recognize of police officers is, that above the normal responsibilities of taking care of our own families, we're also the family counselor in other people's domestic situations. Beyond even that, we're social workers, lawyers, referees, caretakers, mechanics, mentors, and sometimes even MMA fighters. We love what we do. If we didn't, none of us would have made it through the first year…

The first murder scene…

The first horrific car accident…

The first time being the messenger who tells the parents their child is never coming home…

The list goes on. The ones who are still serving just keep adding to it. They continue on, despite being hated by so many, being called every stereotypical name in the book, and they smile the whole time they're doing it. Well, no they don't, but they sure as hell wish they could.

I'm infinitely glad I was not only a police officer during my 25 years. I loved working all three facets of public safety (police, fire, and EMS). I don't know if I could've only been a law enforcement officer. I loved the shot of adrenaline, the exhilaration, and the profound sense of responsibility I felt when hopping into the ambulance and firetruck. It's an unbelievable feeling to have confidence in your ability to think clearly in desperate situations. I know the situations I'm rushing into are going to be handled intelligently by my team and I, and I believe it's important to know this should not be misconstrued as arrogance. First responders need to have confidence in their actions and abilities. They need to make quick, clear, and concise decisions—this job takes a certain kind of person. Not everyone can do it or handle it. Yeah, we're a different breed.

But with that said, knowing all that's expected of us, all we can do, need to do, need to cope with, and what drives us to wake up every day and keep doing it…sometimes, there's a case that hits just a little too close to home. One that doesn't fade away into the background like we've trained our brain so diligently to do with cases such as this. It lingers in the forefront of your psyche to torment you because there are reminders of it *everywhere*—behind you and up ahead.

This book is a story not directly about me, but rather about a lot of beautiful people and one ugly soul. It's complicated, definitely sordid, and the true story of a nefarious man who had everything, but because of his unquenchable desire for sexual power and control, he lost everything. This is the case that hurdled me into the one and only professional situation that *truly* hemorrhaged into my personal life. There have been a few that bled down, of course, but this is the one that left me unable to simply winnow away how I felt.

It's important I tell this story because it's the only one that left me feeling victimized; the best way to shake off the demons of what I saw and heard throughout the investigation. They've clawed at my temples for far too long.

My work on this case raised me up onto a high professional pedestal as it plunged me into a very dark world I didn't recognize as my own. It's taken me years to sort through it all, and now, I want the world to know and celebrate the true heroes of this story...

And lastly, I have to tell it so I can heal, and to help the many, many victims of sexual assault realize how strong they are when they raise their voices against the actions of their aggressors.

CHAPTER 2

THE HUMBLE BEGINNINGS OF. . .

AKA QUE SERA SERA

As soon as this story became personal, it boiled out of my professional cauldron and into the fires of my everyday life. This transition mutated the case from being classified in my psyche as an investigation like any other, into one that involved feelings damn near impossible to ignore. To understand the impact this case had on me we should start at the beginning. Knowing where I come from, the kind of person I am, and how I got to where I am now will be vital in telling the story properly.

My life began humbly on a sunny day in late-September, 1971 when I was born to two of the kindest people this world has ever known. I realize there are billions of people on the planet, and I'm sure a good number of them insist the same about their own parents, but to be fair, they've probably never met mine.

My mom is as close to being a saint as any mortal could possibly be. Even when life went full-on sideways, she remained unselfish, empathetic, and optimistic. Her parents were the same way, so she comes by it honestly. She gives everyone the benefit of the doubt and as her parents passed that on to her, she did the same for me. Mom taught me that everyone is inherently good inside and deserving of trust and respect—until they aren't. In my line of work, this mentality is constantly marred and remolded—an exhausting automatic response to wanting to stay alive, I suppose. It's difficult to trust a man with a gun just because he promises not to shoot.

Mom supported us boys through thick and thin, and with the eventual arrival of my youngest brother, it must have been one heck of a challenge in a house surrounded by boys—not that we ever heard her complain. Her all-around loveliness permeated the roughest and toughest souls—boy, did my dad ever luck-out.

Growing up, Dad was fairly strict with us, but he was gone a lot for work and play. This left Mom to do her best to discipline us boys, and for the most part, we didn't give her too much trouble. God forbid though, if we pushed her too far and she told our father. Don't get me wrong. Neither one of my parents ever beat us, but I still feared my dad as much as I loved him. His wrath—even the thought or threat of it—was enough to put us in tears or straighten us up in a hurry. Of course, just as we sometimes pushed Mom far enough to bring Dad into the disciplinarian mix, there were also occasions when we pushed Dad a little too far, too. Not often, but enough to learn not to make the same mistakes twice, or we were the recipients of a red bottom. Spanking isn't considered a valuable parental tool anymore, but when I was growing up it was simply a consequence to our stupidest actions.

Thankfully, my brothers and I have grown out of the necessity for my parents to play good cop/bad cop, but back when they did, Dad was *always* the bad cop. Being a former U.S. Marine, it was a stance that seemed to come naturally to him; he was sometimes stoic and stern, and other times, he went a bit nuclear. Still, he always remained fair. We knew without question he loved us even though he never said it out loud. I was alright with that. Besides, I think Mom loved being the one to make everything better. I don't know if she could have found the gumption to be the bad cop. To this day, she's always been a comforting presence and quick to tell us she loves us.

We always felt loved by both of them, but until my late twenties, I was much closer to my mother. As I got older, my relationship with my dad has opened up, and now he's a great resource and friend. I'd say I'm just as close to him as I am with my mom. They live only three houses down the street from me and we help each other on a daily basis. I would never want to disappoint either one of them.

*   *   *

My older brother was born in Orange County, California while my father was stationed there. About a year and a half later, we moved on from the OC to Appleton, Wisconsin, where I was born. I can't say I remember all that much about living in Appleton. At the tender age of three, my parents packed us up and shuffled us 30 minutes north to Ashwaubenon—one of the many smaller communities that encircle the metropolis of Green Bay.

At a little over 104,000 people living within its city limits, Green Bay isn't all that big. Even once you factor in the villages, towns, and other small cities that cozy up to Green Bay's borders, the grand population only slides to just above 300,000 people—a trifling number compared to some of the denser American cities. While Green Bay is definitely small, the lively middle-class village of Ashwaubenon—with its current population of approximately 17,000 (only 2,500 more residents than when my parents brought us here in the mid-1970s)—could be likened to a pinhead on a porcupine quill. But this little town doesn't suffer its size at all; there are a great many benefits to living here.

On any given day, you can expect to see someone you know while running daily errands. It's not unusual to leave your doors unlocked, and sometimes, even your keys in your car overnight. Crime is minimal with only the occasional petty theft or egged car as a result of a lovers' quarrel gone wrong getting written into the police logs. Everyone seems to know everyone, and it's an ideal place to work and raise a family.

One thing about Ashwaubenon that's made us feel like our village is a little more important than any of the others is our direct connection to the Green Bay Packers. The famed and historic Lambeau Field is cut right out of the southern edge of Green Bay, but all of the Packers' practice fields are within Ashwaubenon's village limits. This means the players have to travel a few hundred yards to get from their locker room to the practice fields. So, for as long as I can remember, it was a tradition throughout the football season for all of us kids—with bikes in tow—to muster near the Packers' locker room before practices. It was there we'd wait in hope that one of our favorite players would commandeer our bikes for transportation to the practice fields.

In my youth, a guy by the name of Bart Starr was the coach, and I had players like James Lofton, John Jefferson, Lynn Dickey, and Jan Stenerud ride my bike. It was a chance for us little guys to rub elbows with football celebrities and feel important. Back in the '70s, there would only be twenty or thirty bicycles lined up before and after practice, so you could afford to be a little picky about which player you wanted to ride your bike. I really dreaded the occasions when the 300-plus pound linemen would eye up my meek Omni ten speed, toss me their helmet, and take off down the hill toward the practice field. The extreme tension the weight put on my rims was almost tangible, and I swear more than once, I could see them bending. Several times, as I ran alongside one of those men, I worried my bike was going to end up as scrap metal. Even worse than that, what if the wheels crumpled under his colossal weight, and he went flying over the handlebars? Would I be to blame? I mean, they picked up some impressive speed heading down that hill. Add the fact that some guys were so big you couldn't even see the bikes underneath them—there was just no telling if they would make it to their destination in one piece. I know it was probably an irrational concern, but I was a kid, and as much as I loved my bike, I loved my favorite footballers even more.

It's things like that which lead me to say I definitely had a pleasant childhood in this modest little football-loving Midwest community. Winters were cold, but no one cared—wouldn't have mattered if we did; we were shooed out the door to play or trapped in school all day anyway, so the colder months seemed to blow by quickly enough.

My parents liked to travel, so in the summer months, we often had opportunities to broaden our horizons while vacationing at all sorts of places throughout the U.S. Our adventures—sometimes by car and other times by air—took us to California, Mt. Rushmore, Deadwood in South Dakota, and many trips to Florida.

Looking back on my childhood, I really am fortunate to have grown up in the time that I did. Life seemed to move at a slower pace, people were more social, and us kids, well, we weren't coddled into thinking mediocrity was the same as excelling. We were expected to work hard for our successes and the things we wanted. So, in my early teens, my brother and I earned our spare money by working a neighborhood paper route for the *Green Bay Press-Gazette*. Rain or shine, that paper was delivered. My mom helped us sometimes, but for the most part, we were pretty much on our own.

I got to know most of the people in my area and the neighborhood's vibe. I could pretty much predict when certain people would be home or away. I got to know who the slobs were, who the crabby ones were, and the clean freaks. An important asset for any paperboy was to know whose yard I could cut across and which ones I shouldn't. Needless to say, I learned mighty fast!

I knew everyone from the young couple that had just moved in to the old folks who had lived there for so long the village streets were named after them. I really enjoyed the familiarity I had within my community as a youngster. As I grew up and became a public safety officer within that same community, it proved advantageous most of the time.

Besides delivering every day after school and weekend mornings before 8 a.m. (for minimal pay), as a paperboy I also had to collect payment from the customer. In those days, there was no question as to whether or not it was safe or appropriate for a twelve-year-old to knock on the doors of strange homes and demand payment—it was simply expected. So, that's what we did. I don't remember ever worrying that someone would steal my money, assault, kidnap, or kill me, and I don't think my parents did, either. People were rude and didn't want to pay, but our parents sure as hell didn't have the same worries parents have these days. No, my parents didn't worry. They expected us to always be committed to the job and provide good customer service, and that's probably what helped build my strong commitment to solid work ethic.

It's a shame that commitment to hard work didn't leach into my school career. I wasn't overly intellectual—a mediocre student at best—and was never all that put-out by the fact. I had an excess of energy for sports and absolutely thrived on competition. Whether it was pitching fastballs or pitching quarters with buddies, I was willing to partake in a little action and keen to come out on top.

I always knew I wanted to do something important with my life, but I had no idea what that would be, or which direction fate would pull me.

So, from the time I was fifteen and able to work, up until my high school graduation at seventeen, I muddled along without interest through several jobs in grocery and retail. To my parents' relief, I never found my niche in either of those industries. Yet, even after graduation, I still hadn't concluded where my place was in the world, or what I should do with my life. Unlike so many of my peers, I had no clear direction or career ambitions.

As I recall—instead of trying to figure it out—I pleasantly distracted myself with the occasional underage drinking party, gambled a little, played a lot of amateur baseball, and generally had a lot of fun. There wasn't a heck of a lot to do in the Green Bay area back then. When I wasn't working, I drank copious amounts of cheap beer and played a lot of poker with friends—a fact I'm certain my parents remain ignorant of today. Until they read this, of course.

Even in my teen years, I had a lot of respect for my humble, god-loving parents, and I can't help but wonder how they'll react when they read about what actually went on. They know I turned out fine—maybe even exceeded their expectations, but I'm certain they would have questioned my future had they known what I was up to.

It was nothing on a Friday or Saturday night to win or lose $50 – $100 playing guts or draw poker, or a little dice game called Ship, Captain, Crew while downing a twelve-pack of Busch Lite. Somehow, I was always able to walk home harmlessly and secretly crawl into bed with my parents being none the wiser that I was a completely shitfaced-drunk punk who had just lost a week's earnings. I mean, they were pretty meager earnings from bagging groceries at the local market, but I regularly blew it all.

None of my friends were into drugs, but I had more than a few opportunities to try pot if I'd wanted to. Any time it was around or offered, I'd laugh it off and excuse myself from the area—it just wasn't my jam. To me, drinking alcohol was no big deal because everyone was doing it, but the drug scene was a whole different level. I didn't want to have anything to do with it. I can honestly say I've never tried any sort of illegal or illicit drugs, nor have I ever used any prescription medications for anything other than what they were intended for. I'm proud of that fact, but I almost wish I would have tried THC at least once to see what the big deal is. I mean, there's an entire culture carved out of the love of this stuff that I have no real idea about.

Alas, until I retire, I guarantee I won't find out. Despite my happy ignorance of drug inebriations, I managed to do every other stupid thing my friends were doing. Unfortunately, my friends were usually up to something fun, ridiculous, and occasionally, illegal. It was never anything too extreme and more or less harmless—the product of idle minds who had nothing better to do with their time. It was fun for a while, but it soon became clear it was time to find a purpose in life before I was sucked in a direction I would regret.

In 1991, I was eighteen and dating a gal who babysat for the captain of the local public safety department. On a whim, I decided to apply for a paid on-call firefighter position, and I guess she put in a good word for me because I got the job. Had an extensive background investigation revealed the shocking (but also impressive) amount of beer I had consumed as a minor, I probably wouldn't have even been considered. Lucky for me, things were a little different back then. It was easier to hide your skeletons, and thus, I began working as a paid on-call firefighter for the little village of Ashwaubenon, Wisconsin.

For all practical purposes, it was really a volunteer gig because the minimal per-call wage they offered was hardly enough to put gas in my car. This didn't really bother me though. It wasn't about the money—it was about having a direction and purpose in life. I soon realized I needed to stay on the right side of the law and not give in to the typical, routine peer pressure that had previously occupied my life.

Now keep in mind, I had just turned eighteen, really had no idea where the bear shits in the woods and had a relatively sheltered childhood. I was just a kid, but that didn't stop me from jumping into the opportunity head first. A firefighter? How cool a gig was that? Especially considering where I'd left my friends—still colluding shenanigans, playing cards, and drinking away their meager earnings. To make it even more boss (to coin a '90s phrase), not long after I completed my firefighter training, the department offered to pay for my Emergency Medical Technician training. I jumped at the opportunity, took every class they offered me throughout that year, and by the time I turned nineteen, I was a certified firefighter and EMT. Being a firefighter alone is pretty impressive—my buddies agreed—but being a firefighter/EMT at the age of nineteen was supremely cool to me.

Throughout that time, I spent as many hours as I could on the ambulance and firetruck, and at the Brown County Veterans Memorial Arena to gain knowledge and experience in the public safety field. I carried a pager and wore it all the time because there was no way I was going to miss out on a big fire or crash. I signed myself up for EMS ride time a few times a week, and practically vibrated with enthusiasm waiting for each shift to start. And with that pager on my hip, I responded to every single fire call that came in if I was available.

I remember one time when I had to drive by an active house fire in my neighborhood to get my gear from the fire station. I responded in the fire truck with the rest of the guys, but I have to say, it was a pretty rough feeling to see it happening and just drive by.

Back then, the firetrucks only had room for two guys to ride inside the cab, while all of the other firefighters rode outside. I honestly believe if it wasn't for the automatic adrenaline injection we got just from being on call, I'm pretty sure we would have frozen solid to the side of the truck. It was damn cold tearing down those icy roads during Green Bay's cold winters. It was especially hard at night when going suddenly from your nice warm bed to riding exposed to the elements on the back of a noisy firetruck. It was a rush I eventually grew to know extremely well.

I occasionally hung out at the primary public safety station with the full-timers. In the beginning, they seemed larger than life. They were heroic and great, and I almost felt like a pretender in their presence. I admired and looked up to them as role models—which they were, but more importantly, they were real people that did their job because they cared about people and their community.

I got to know them well and I'm pretty sure they liked me as well. It probably helped I was a keener, and made it a point to do as they asked and do it well. I would check equipment or clean up the trucks because I wanted them to recognize how eager I was to earn the right to be the first into the fire or the guy on the nozzle. I understood my humble position at that point and never overstepped boundaries, but they knew how badly I wanted a bigger piece of the pie.

It took a couple of years before my ass-kissing…I mean *eagerness*, finally paid off. Those guys, even though they eventually became my professional peers, will always be larger than life to me. I couldn't have asked for a better work family.

While I was spending my spare time at the public safety station, I was also maintaining a full-time job as a nighttime grocery store department manager and loss prevention agent. To this day, I can't figure out how I was able to do all that and still be a full-time student at Northeast Wisconsin Technical College working on my police science degree. It was a crazy schedule and my sleep definitely suffered, but I kept going. Even though it wasn't easy, I enjoyed the stress and excitement of being busy. Any extra time I had was usually devoted to a number of different women I dated, playing amateur baseball, or spending time with my family. I suspect that had my schedule not been so hectic, I would've had a lot more time to get back into the same old trouble with my friends.

I discovered a lot about myself throughout this time. First of all, the feelings of true purpose and the pride in my accomplishments were something I had never felt before. To be fast-thinking, dependable, and confident in my role was only enhanced by the realization that this job regularly put me in a position where these strong character traits were utilized in crucial life and death situations—I thrived on that knowledge. It felt awesome. Second, I had always been an adrenaline junky, but I realized that not only did I revel in the pressure and intense stress, I almost *yearned* for it. Third and last, but certainly not least, when I was caring for someone in their time of need, I was happy. All of this is what eventually steered me into the career direction I would choose and the man I would become.

I still remember one of the first emergency medical calls I went on. It was one that really put things into perspective and still haunts me to this day. I was asleep at home when the Plectron pager (which was about the size of a small television) sitting near my bed went crazy at 2 a.m. I sprang from my bed with my heart pounding; I threw on my department-issued public safety jumpsuit and awaited the call information.

In the cold, dark early morning hours, a car had crashed on Highway 172 with injuries. Now, "with injuries" was very general information, but it was all I got. It could have meant a bump on the head or several mangled bloody bodies strewn about the highway. It didn't matter either way—it meant I was on my way to help someone and potentially make a difference.

At the time, I still lived with my parents, and I often think back and wonder how my job must've affected their sleep patterns. They never complained, but as bad as I feel about it now, it didn't matter back then. I hurried through the house—probably sounding like a herd of elephants— while I scrambled for the keys to my shabby Plymouth Turismo, ripped it into gear, and headed out toward the highway.

The wreck was only a short distance from my house, so it didn't take more than a couple of minutes to get to the crash site. Parking on the side of the road well out of the way, I quickly ran across the traffic lanes and stood there alone, looking at the chaos in front of me, the distant sound of several sirens in the background. I could hear screaming coming from the inside of a car. It had heavy front-end damage, and from the position of it, I could tell it had obviously rear-ended a van that was parked in the middle of the highway. Scene safety was, and still is, a top priority in this line of work, but I couldn't standby and wait for support. I had to help immediately.

I made my way to where the screaming was coming from and found a young man sitting behind the wheel. He was conscious, bleeding, and spewing all sorts of colorful profanities. As I approached the passenger door to gain access, I smelled a scent I can still recall to this day—an odor I've smelled hundreds of times since then—alcohol saturated blood mixed with gas and oil. Until the day I die, I'll still be able to recall the smell just by thinking about it.

I looked down and saw a severed leg with a women's tennis shoe still neatly tied on. It wasn't just any tennis shoe, either. It was the same as the brand-new pink and white Nike tennis shoes my mother had recently purchased for herself. A sudden rush of panic coursed through me as I moved around the car to take a look in front of it. On the ground, a middle-aged woman who was missing her right leg lay unconscious in a large pool of blood and fluids from the crushed vehicle.

All I could do was stand there and stare. To this day, I'm not sure where that time went, but I know I was completely void of all five of my senses and utterly paralyzed in place. Thankfully, and not a moment too soon, the sirens blaring in the background became forefront—the cavalry had arrived.

It seemed as if every police officer in the county and two rescue squads magically appeared in an instant. My wits suddenly came rushing back to me as I did the quick calculation in my head to determine that Mom was safe at home, and this was *not* her lying in bloody oil. But for those brief few moments, tragedy had struck me, and I was rendered helpless in shock.

With the help of my fellow first responders, we found out the intoxicated female thought it would be a good idea to stop in the middle of the highway and get out to fetch something from the rear of her van. The young man in the car (who was also intoxicated), not anticipating anyone would be so foolish as to stop there, didn't see her or her van, and drove full-force into the back of it. She was crushed between the two vehicles and lost her leg— she's lucky that was all she lost. I clearly recall placing that bloody, mangled leg on the cot next to the unconscious woman before she was quickly taken away in the ambulance.

Although this accident didn't end with a fatality, and I didn't know either one of the victims, this wasn't the sort of event I could just forget. The moment those pink and white Nike tennis shoes tricked my mind into considering it might be my mom on the ground was enough to sear the whole thing deep into my psyche. I recall the whole incident on a regular basis because it made me question whether I should carry on in this line of work, or get the hell out before I was scarred for life. I worried—expected— that one day it would be someone I knew lying on the road bleeding out, or shot, or…something.

The thought process that kept me at it was confidence—I'm so damn good at this job. If someone I love needed fast-thinking, reliable, intelligent care, I would be there for them, and I could be the difference between them living or dying. I've seen a lot of gruesome scenes since that accident. I'm still glad it's me that's seen so much because I know how to handle it. It isn't easy, but I know how to keep my head on straight.

I didn't stick with being an EMT. In 1992, at the tender age of twenty, I graduated from NWTC with an Associate's Degree in Police Science and went on to become a full-time public safety officer for the Village of Ashwaubenon.

Being a public safety officer meant I was a hero of all safety trades. I was a police officer, firefighter, and medical responder all at once. With great power comes great responsibility, and you can bet that a twenty-year-old public safety officer's every move was under the microscope.

I was expected to be an honest, trustworthy, and hardworking servant to the community. Considering the satisfaction I got from doing my job, it was easy for me to keep my nose clean. It also put a significant amount of pressure on me to grow up fast.

I'd set my goals high and decided I would someday be chief of the awesome and unique Ashwaubenon department. If that meant slightly distancing myself from some of my old friends, well, that was what I was going to do. I had every intention of becoming the best paramedic, firefighter, and officer the department and community had ever seen. Being young, energetic, and sporting a pretty impressive reach-for-the-stars attitude, nothing was going to stop me.

*   *   *

For the next few years, I put my nose to the grindstone and focused on my career. Within that time, I was fortunate enough to meet a nice gal. She was supportive, and although she worried about me when I was working, she never seemed to be overly stressed out about my job. She was pretty all right. So in 1995, at the age of twenty-five, we got married.

In early-1997, I proudly added being a paramedic to my résumé, and a few months after that, my chest swelled even more as we welcomed our first son. It was such a busy time in my life.

I occasionally found time to see my old friends, but it wasn't more than once every couple of months. The one friend I saw more than all the others was Skinny, who, despite his nickname, was a tall, hefty, behemoth of a man. We'd been best buds since elementary school, and although we were nothing alike, our friendship had remained steadfast. Making time to hang out with him here and there was the one last connection I had to my youth.

We got together when we could—even played softball together for a few years, but, in time, I just couldn't fit that into my schedule, either. I was busy learning how to be a great cop and trying like hell to figure out how to be a good husband and father. Skinny was a bachelor entrenched in the bar industry and always in the midst of a good time. At least, that's how I saw it back then.

In the late-1990s things were going great for me—I seemed to have the world by the balls. My second son joined the familial party at the tail end of 1999, and I pretty much thought I had it made. The only way I could've brought my life any closer to being a fairy tale is if I'd learned to talk to animals. I had great friends, a nice house, a wonderful wife, and two little boys I adored more than anything. My career was taking off and I was making a positive impact within the community. Everything about my job was incredible; I got to carry a gun, drive fast cars, save lives, and take care of people during times of turmoil and tragedy.

I was proud that friends and family would look to me for advice and confide in me on a regular basis. At one point, we even had a local news station come to our house to do a story on the lifestyle and risks of being a public safety family. Not to mention, in the two years since I'd become a paramedic, I'd also managed to become a SWAT member, a firearms/tactical rifle instructor, a Field Training Officer, a crime prevention officer, a gang officer, a motorcycle officer, an Explorer advisor, and was in the process of getting promoted to investigator status. Yeah, things were good—maybe too good.

Ah, c'mon…

I can admit now that just because I felt like I could do no wrong sure as hell didn't mean I was doing everything right. While all of these wonderful things were happening, my long list of triumphs grew and my successes were celebrated. I was completely oblivious to the fact that my relationship was languishing—no matter how obvious it probably was to everyone else.

Looking back at my life, this had to be one of the biggest and most difficult lessons I have ever learned. I had so much good going for me at work, and so much respect and admiration from others while at work, I unknowingly let it negatively affect my relationship with my wife.

I would work twenty-four hours straight dealing in every kind of situation and tragedy you can imagine; in most cases, I was the savior, the protector, the counselor, and the one that had to make things right for others. I felt important and incredibly necessary while I was at work, but that changed in an instant the second I walked through the door of my own home. There were countless occasions when I came home from work, beat up and exhausted, to a nagging wife telling me what I should or shouldn't be doing.

It was a difficult transition from work to home, and one I resented instead of taking in stride. I can definitely admit I was shitty at making the complex paradigm shift from hero to humbled and understanding husband/father. To be fair, I'm not sure I had enough synapses firing by the end of my day to even accomplish it. Still an excuse, but there's definitely some truth to it.

In a single shift I might respond to a horrific deadly traffic crash, then fight to subdue an enraged husband after he found his wife in bed with another man, then do CPR on a middle-aged father while his wife and kids desperately scream for me to do more. Follow that up with going home to my wife only to have her tell me to take out the garbage, clean the house, and don't forget to pick up the spaghetti sauce for supper. It just didn't seem right to me that I should have to listen to her tell me I had to take care of all of these petty chores when I was so used to dealing with *real* tragedies and issues.

No one would make Captain America do the dishes after saving the world, would they?

Yeah, yeah, I know I'm no Captain America, but it really was hard to wrap my wearied brain around how normal her requests were. Needless to say, I didn't deal with it well. In a very short amount of time, I stopped feeling appreciated at home entirely. I felt lost and constantly taken for granted.

My two young boys remained my highest priority, but my wife and I started to drift apart. We tried counseling but couldn't come anywhere near to agreeing on the important stuff. Before long we were separated, and the inevitable divorce was quick to follow.

It wasn't until many years later I realized how wrong I was. I should've learned to cope better. There wasn't a single moment while my wife and I crumbled apart that I saw myself as selfish or egotistical, but I obviously needed to open my damn eyes.

In this profession especially, one should never inadvertently let their ego get the best of them. Police officers get accused of it all the time, and I know it's definitely true of some. There's a bit of a God complex that comes with the territory, and it really needs to be brought into check. I learned the hard way I had to set professional and personal goals to always stay humble. I knew firsthand if I didn't, it would destroy my world again. Maybe this is good advice for everyone. Learn how to rein yourself back whenever you start thinking you're more important than you really are. You're never more or less important than anyone else out there—we're all just different.

There's a quote by a very intelligent man by the name of Dr. Rick Rigsby about pride and ego that I truly believe in. I live by this sentiment now.

But in 1999, not all that long after my youngest son was born, my journey as a single father began. I took care of my very little boys from the time I finished my twenty-four-hour shift at 7:00 a.m. through the majority of my forty-eight-hour downtime. To be exact, I was a full-time dad until 5:00 p.m. the day before my next shift began, so it wasn't truly downtime at all. I enjoyed it, but there was never any real time for me to relax. I was extremely busy, and it was also hard to make ends meet from a time and financial standpoint. Somehow, I managed.

Up to this point in my life, I had invested a substantial amount of time maturing within my career. This was the first time I had to put a real conscious effort into maturing as a grown man. I found out how difficult, yet how rewarding, it was to be a good dad.

My ex-wife and I agreed that while we may not always agree with each other, we had to be amicable for the boys' sake. They were, and always remain, our highest priority. It was our job to make sure there was never any question in their minds as to whether or not they were loved. They were too young to ever think they could be at fault for what happened to their parents' relationship, but we still made sure they knew it wasn't. The boys were never used as pawns in our post-marriage lives— we likened that tactic to abuse. I can say with complete confidence that's the reason my boys have grown to be respectable, caring young men with a lot going for them.

Just because a family is broken, doesn't in any way, mean it's bad. It just means separated parents need to work a little harder to create a healthy relationship balance for their kids. With enough effort—and it might take a lot—you need to show mutual respect toward each other. Without that in place, you simply can't raise well-adjusted kids. You aren't doing them any favors when you as parents are vying for their affections. Kids don't need to have a favorite parent. They need to have love and respect for their parents, and we teach them that by example. I thank God my ex-wife is a good woman and an excellent mother. We both understood this concept and the importance of it as we raised our boys together apart.

It was complicated getting back into dating, but I did okay. I went out with my fair share of women and had several steady girlfriends. Even more than that, it was exciting to get back out and see what my single friends were doing. When I didn't have my sons overnight, I was able to hang out with my old boys again—not the same old shenanigans, though. We'd go out for a few drinks or play golf or softball. Nothing like the beer-drinking poker nights we used to have, but still a damn-fine good time.

Occasionally, I'd head down to the bar scene to see Skinny and have a drink while he worked around me. It didn't take long before I got to know a lot of the people in Skinny's circle of bar patrons, bouncers, and co-workers. They were interesting real people and I enjoyed fraternizing with them. It was easy, laid-back fun, and considering how chaotic my life had been, it was a much-needed break.

Most of them had no idea I was a local cop. Had they known, I doubt the majority of them would have even talked to me. People tend to party differently when they know a copper is in the mix. The ones who knew who I was and what I did for a living weren't at all bothered by it. We'd sit around with drinks in our hands, and they'd bounce hypothetical questions off me—sometimes it was tavern-related legal questions or about traffic law. I'd do my best to give them good answers.

It was in the summer of 2000 that Skinny was approached by Marcus Somerhalder and his business associate, Mike. They wanted him to be a part of their joint venture to start up an upscale bar on Washington Street they were going to call the Velvet Room. Skinny had known Marcus for a few years by then as they'd worked together at Brewbaker's Pub in Green Bay. Skinny also knew Marcus was an intelligent and savvy bar manager, so from the get-go, he was all-in.

I didn't know Mike at all, but I'd known of Marcus for almost as long as Skinny had. He and I had never become close, but he knew I'd patronized his bars in the past and would definitely be spending some time and money in his soon-to-be, upscale lounge. We knew each other well enough to buy each other drinks, hang out at some of the same events and make small talk, but that's about as far as it went. For the most part, I liked the guy and the circle of friends he hung around with—most of them in the bar industry, as well.

From the outside looking in, Marcus was a guy who seemed to have everything going for him. He was well-versed in the hospitality business and had what it took to be a successful businessman: he was charming, highly social, women thought he was good-looking—he must have been because they were always flocking to him. He had the kind of charisma that everyone wanted to have and wanted to be around.

I certainly wasn't jealous or envious. He seemed like a good guy to know, and I had no reason not to like him. Skinny, on the other hand, really liked Marcus. He didn't mind working hard for him; so, in my mind, if Skinny thought the guy was cool, it was probably a good indication that Marcus was a pretty all right guy.

Beyond agreeing to help Mike and Marcus get the place up and running, Skinny also agreed to manage it. He'd been in the business long enough to know how to run a smooth ship, and from Marcus's point of view, Skinny had learned from the best. I was happy for my old pal; it seemed like he was moving up in the world.

When they bought the business that would eventually become the Velvet Room, it was a tired, dark old tavern in sore need of updating. Mike was a super guy that had no real interest in slinging drinks or working in the bar, but he sure did enjoy the bar scene itself. He had spent years working in construction, and once he became bored of his trade, he cashed out of it and decided to become an investor. His construction background made him a good partner for Marcus, especially with regard to the Velvet Room—the building needed a substantial remodel to bring it into this century and reinvent it as a dance night club.

Mike was fully capable of doing all of the work himself but welcomed Skinny's handyman skills. The two of them were close friends, so any time I stopped by, I walked into them having a pretty good time. They worked together tirelessly to polish the old space into a shiny new penny while keeping renovation costs down.

I used to find myself checking in on their project on a regular basis, and in doing so, got to know Marcus and Mike a little better. I remember the one time I stopped by while they were working on constructing the new dance stage I was quickly put to work. I had nothing better to do that night, so I had no problem pitching in on their construction project while sucking down a few beers. It's kind of ironic now that I think about it—I helped build the place that I eventually helped destroy.

CHAPTER 3

IN ASHWAUBENON, I'M AN OFFICER, PARAMEDIC, FIREFIGHTER, AND BUDDY. . .

AKA YEAH, IT'S COOL IF YOU CALL ME BATMAN, I CAN BE BROODING

In the United States, there are many Public Safety Departments, but only a handful of them do things the way we did them here in Ashwaubenon, Wisconsin.

Our department currently has about fifty sworn public safety officers. Each shift runs twenty-four hours straight, followed by forty-eight hours off. Within that twenty-four-hour shift, we're police officers for eight hours, and for the remaining sixteen hours, we're first responders for fire, rescue, and medical emergency calls. As a lieutenant, this usually allows for an interesting sixteen hours because I have to accompany every fire call and any critical EMS calls.

Since the age of twenty-one, I've worked every third day, which translates into an entire third of my life. That's a long time in a career that's tough on the body and mind.

We usually get very little sleep throughout our shifts, and as much as I'd like to say we get used to it, I don't think any of us ever do. Knowing that alarm could go off at any second to thrust you into a stressful, serious, and dangerous situation can make it difficult to relax enough to fall asleep. It's amazing we don't suffer trauma from the fiercely interrupted REM cycles alone! One second, you're dreaming about chilling in the hot tub at the back of your limo and the next, you're trying to vault out of the sunken divot in an old twin bed to throw your standard issue uniform over your tired bones. So, yeah, sometimes you've got to be completely bagged to justify taking a nap.

Whether you get any sleep throughout your shift or not, any one of our jobs is too much to handle for a full twenty-four-hour shift, and I personally enjoy switching it up. This was especially true for me as an officer in my first five years on the force.

After earning my badge, it took no time at all for it to become glaringly obvious there were some definite drawbacks to working as a law enforcement officer in my hometown. Ashwaubenon is the only home I've known since I was three years old. Back when my parents settled into the older section of the village, near the banks of the Fox River, the population was smaller. People knew each other—neighbors were friends, and life was simpler. At least, that's how my parents recall it. I suppose I remember it that way, too, but not with nearly as much nostalgia. I don't remember a time when I couldn't walk down any street in Ashwaubenon without seeing a familiar face, though. That said, I didn't foresee how much my village familiarity would backfire on me when I moved into the public safety profession. If I thought I knew just about everyone in the village before I joined the force, then the population must have doubled the day I graduated!

In the first years of my career, it seemed like everyone I pulled over and every disturbance I was dispatched to, involved a friend or family member of someone I knew. The (sarcastically speaking) best part of that? They all knew me, too, and every single one of them expected me to give them a break. I was everyone's "buddy." Damn, did I ever get sick of being called buddy.

It made it extremely difficult because I had a job to do, and it was important—necessary—for me to be fair. By the time I was done dealing with them, most of them didn't see me as their buddy anymore. Oh well, Batman doesn't have many friends while in uniform, either.

Beyond those wanting out of their misdemeanors, I can't even recall the number of times I've seen people I know arrested or, worse yet, killed in horrifying accidents or suicides. It's hard enough when it happens to perfect strangers, but when it's someone you know, love, grew up with… well, that creates an emotional conundrum that some people in this line of business have a difficult time sorting through. No matter how hard you try, sometimes that stern and logical emotional barrier comes crashing down.

For instance, a darker day of mine was when one of my parents' closest friends—with nothing I could do to save him—died of cancer in my arms. Only a shadow of the taut professionalism I try so hard to uphold remained visible that day, but I don't regret it was me there with him at the end.

Times like those are awful, but the emotional repercussions aren't hard to manage when compared against many others. There are events that have hit me harder, not because what happened was more gory or terrible or painful, but because the tragedy trenched deeper than I was able to reach into my emotional-self. There have been situations where I've questioned my confidence in my professional abilities and my personal convictions. I've experienced times when a call has paralleled a personal experience from my past, and I've had to pause for a moment to ensure I was focused on the "here and now."

This becomes especially true when a fellow public safety comrade falls in the line of duty. You do what you're trained to do in the moment, but afterward, you wonder if you did it right. Did you miss a step that would have made a drastic, positive difference? Did you hesitate?

The aftermath of situations like this usually involves professional comradery, where we lean on one another within the office/hall to cope. But someone needs to remain strong and focused. One person has to keep their head on straight so business moves along as usual, and as a supervisor, that job often fell on me. Delaying your emotional response until everyone else has been taken care of is sometimes exactly what I needed to do.

One of the most vivid experiences I've had in this category happened on July 22, 2017 just as I'd finished up my police shift. Despite the off and on heavy rain throughout most of the evening, it had been a typical eight hours full of retail thefts, vehicle crashes, domestic disturbances, and random misdemeanors. I was happy to be turning it over to the next lieutenant.

I remember greeting him and the night officers as they prepped their rain gear and squad cars. As I stood at my station locker removing my police gear—which seemed to weigh a thousand pounds on my exhausted body—the radio began buzzing about a minor car fire on the stretch of highway our southern border shares with the City of De Pere. I tuned-in to catch clearer details, because depending on the exact location, it would likely be my engine that responded.

The way it was sounding, it was going to end up in De Pere's fire response area. Even if we missed out on this call, I knew well the kind of action this sort of weather usually ushered in after dark and was prepared for a busy nightshift between the ambulance and firetruck. I continued changing over uniforms, suspecting it would be highly unlikely I'd be getting any shut-eye during this shift.

We sent along two officers, Wudtke and Murphy, to assist state troopers with traffic control while De Pere's first responders handled the crash-site. Once our guys got there, they determined we wouldn't be needed for the call. We dropped our guard a little—even considered napping, but the thought only lasted a moment before the station rescue tones began to blare.

As it turned out, a separate vehicle vs. pedestrian crash had just happened in the same area. The information was vague, but dispatch warned it might be an officer that was down. With officers and troopers scattered all along the highway to slow traffic around the car fire, dispatch was having a hell of a time verifying details. I had my police radio in hand and stared at it anxiously as dispatch continued their attempts to gain clarity. The caller reported hitting something but wasn't sure what—so damn vague.

Despite the confusion, it was clear my rescue squad and I needed to prep and roll out. The adrenaline coursed through my veins, but this was unlike any call I had ever experienced before—this was potentially one of our own in need. We were scared shitless, well, maybe not shitless, but it was definitely a different caliber of pucker-pinching anxiety than we were used to.

While en route, more information trickled in, but it still remained limited. We finally got confirmation that it was *indeed* one of our own, and he was unconscious. We still didn't know who it was. We had no idea if it was a state trooper, a De Pere officer, or one of our Ashwaubenon guys, Wudtke or Murphy.

We were hauntingly quiet as we banged around in the back of the ambulance, our brows furrowed deeply in concentration and concern. With quick, steady hands, we prepped IVs and any other equipment we might need to save a life. The focus each task required allowed us the time needed to mentally prepare for whatever it was we were about to face, but truth be told, it wasn't helping. The fact that the dispatcher still couldn't give us definitive information over the radio was wholly disconcerting.

As we pulled up to the scene, it was obvious where the fallen officer was. A fellowship of officers, sheriffs, deputies, and troopers encircled their comrade, blocking him from view.

I vividly remember the sole of my boot hitting the rain-slicked highway before the ambulance had even come to a complete stop. Not sure why I remember that so clearly, but for whatever reason, it still sticks out in my mind.

I ran toward the chaos. As I did so, I saw the standard issue black boots and dark pants on the ground amidst a frantic group of lawmen. On second glance, one of the boots looked severely askew, confirming there was serious trauma involved.

As my team of medics and I approached, the gathering opened to let us through. I stopped dead in my tracks and gasped as my eyes focused on the Ashwaubenon Department of Public Safety emblem stitched to the unconscious man's shoulder. I'd known both Wudtke and Murphy for some time—it couldn't have been more than twenty minutes since I'd greeted both officers in the station. The thought of losing either one of them was chilling. With that thought running through my brain, it took some special effort to focus on who the man under that face of blood was.

Murphy. Those pork chop sideburns were irrefutable evidence.

The rain started to come down in sheets as if the heavens opened up to get a better look at the scene. We didn't have time to pay the weather any mind. My team worked to get Murphy immobilized on the cot as I ran back to the ambulance.

Cracking open the back doors, I peered in at one of my medics who was working meticulously to hang a second bag of IV. "It's Murphy," I said as I jumped in. The medic let out a heavy sigh, but with the cot carrying Murphy rolling close on my heels, there was no time for any other reaction—emotion had to wait.

Murphy was in rough shape. He had head injuries I would normally relate to terrible and dismal outcomes. We hoisted him into the ambulance, and as we did, the entire crew took a millisecond to reflect and check ourselves before the physical, mental, and emotional challenge we had in front of us began. With that, the professional autopilot kicked in, and we got to work. Only seconds later, the sirens screamed our presence down the highway toward the ER.

The rain slammed against the windshield as the driver pushed the rescue vehicle as fast as she could. Even at the machine's hulking weight, I could see her struggling to keep the damn thing from hydroplaning across the highway. I kept my balance at the foot of the cot as I took the cutting sheers to Murphy's pants, exposing his severely fractured leg. Everything about the situation seemed so unfair. I shouldn't have had to cut those pants—the very same style I was wearing—off of that man. He should've still been out there in the rain, cold and wet, but healthy as he directed traffic away from someone else's tragedy.

It was a whole new feeling for me; it felt like a kick in the ass. I knew it would feel even worse once the adrenaline wore off.

We carefully monitored Murphy's airway and level of consciousness, the whole time working to stabilize him and the compound fracture of his left leg. I think we probably told him to "hang on" and "fight" a million times. The repetition, like a mantra, benefitted us all. We were certain he could hear us, but based on his injuries, we had no idea if he understood a thing we said. It didn't matter, really; his heartbeat was steady and we were going to continue doing everything we could to make sure he survived.

Getting Murphy to the hospital alive was only the beginning of my challenges that night. It was my shift, my guys, and my responsibility to make things right. Even though he was a grown man, I couldn't help but see Murphy like a son—someone I couldn't leave until I was assured he was in the very best hands. My first priority was staying with Murphy until his wife arrived.

His wife.

Good God was I ever at a loss for what was I going to say when she arrived at the hospital. To make it worse, Murphy and his wife, Heidi, had two very young daughters. It was horrifying to even think about the possibility of them losing their daddy.

An officer was sent to the Murphy residence with the unfortunate heartbreaking job of notifying Heidi of the accident. Just like the rest of us, the officer was unsure of Murphy's condition or prognosis and didn't want to speculate, which makes informing next of kin exceptionally difficult. All you can do is stand there, the harbinger of horrible life-changing news— useless in assuaging their worry, heartache, and fears. It's so hard to stay strong when you're in the presence of such despair.

I advised the staff to let me know as soon as Heidi arrived. I wanted to be the one to tell her about Murphy's current condition and support her the best I could. Needless to say, that was one of the most onerous challenges I have ever had.

I considered how it would be if it were my wife in this situation—what would she want to hear from my supervisor if I was fighting for my life? It was important for me to get it right and be there for her in this shitty time of need.

Upon her arrival, I met with her in the family lounge. Despite running through what I would say to her in my head over and over again, I still stuttered and bumbled as I tried to get the words out. There was no easy way to tell her that no one knew if her husband would survive his injuries.

I escorted Heidi to her unconscious husband as he was being prepped for surgery, and like her, I wasn't going to leave his side until I had to. It was important Heidi knew that both she and Murphy were a part of our public safety family, and we would be there to support them throughout this difficult time. So, I stayed there with Heidi until Murphy was out of surgery.

In the end, it was determined that the driver who hit Murphy was intoxicated. As a result of the accident, Murphy suffered life-threatening injuries including a traumatic brain injury and a severe fracture to his left leg. After two successful surgeries, seventeen days in the hospital—three of them in the ICU—he was able to walk out of the hospital. His survival is nothing short of a miracle. His road to recovery was extremely long, but he persevered, and amazingly, was able to be back to work just over six months later.

After it was all said and done, it was important that I followed up with everyone that accompanied me that terrible rainy night. I had to make sure they were all okay. None of us are totally immune in these situations. Like eating the burrito at the plane crash, or the Nike shoe on the severed leg, some events leave lasting and vivid imprints on us.

The one commonality in every story I've told so far is that I've always had closure. No matter the event or the outcome—even as a leader consoling my officers—me supporting them is them supporting me. I was able to sort through my feelings and emotions as I helped them sort through theirs, then move on.

It's a great system, but it doesn't always work.

After paying my dues for nigh on ten years, in June of 2002, I was promoted to the position of investigator. I wouldn't have complained if the standard job attire consisted of the long trench and gumshoe fedora—Humphrey Bogart style, but to my (secret) dismay, there wasn't any change in uniform.

I suppose that isn't true; there were a lot of occasions where I masqueraded in plainclothes while tapping shoulders for info on investigations.

The hours weren't any kind of regular. I worked typical office hours where I wrote reports and scrounged for details on whatever cases I had on my desk. I still went out on calls, too. Most of what I did on the more complicated investigations usually took me away from the station. I loved getting out there to sniff for clues, and I was damn good at it. In the time I worked as an investigator, I helped put to sleep hundreds, if not thousands, of cases.

But on August 19th, 2003, when the biggest case I've ever had reared its ugly head, I had no idea just how little those thousands of cases of experience would prepare me to deal with the appalling machinations of Marcus Somerhalder.

It had been a normal workday for me in the investigative unit. I had attended a briefing, taken care of jail lockup paperwork, and continued on with the day by sifting through and following-up on a number of open cases. There was never a shortage of work to do. If I remember correctly, there were about thirty cases on my desk at the time; all of them required follow-up with suspects and witnesses, and none of them very exciting. No excitement, that is, unless you absolutely love looking into minor criminal acts and ordinance violations…which I don't. Nevertheless, if they were important to someone else, that made them very important to me. I just didn't have to be happy about it.

My fellow investigative partners had been enjoying a similar day: each trying to chip away at the piles of cases on their respective desks. Sometime in the late afternoon, I was made aware that Investigator Lawler was at one of the local hospitals working on a potential sexual assault case. Despite the fact that the majority of sexual assault cases are never reported, we still manage to investigate plenty of them, so, sadly, it wasn't an unusual thing. Nothing about this one seemed any different from the norm, but that all changed when Investigator Lawler got back to the station and showed me her initial report.

My mind was absolutely blown when I saw the suspect's name: Marcus Somerhalder. I was *very* familiar with that name.

Before I read the report, I paused. Surely, it was a mistake. The Marcus I knew didn't seem like the kind of guy whose name you'd see on the cover of a sexual assault file. I thought maybe it was just one of his ex-girlfriends seeking revenge against him. Break-ups can get pretty ugly sometimes. Trust me, I know.

Despite knowing I wouldn't like what I read (not that I ever did, I suppose), I cracked the manila folder open and read through the report carefully. I was taken aback by its contents.

The report read something like this:

In the early morning hours of August 19, 2003, Marcus invited Alisa, Piper, and his girlfriend, Faith, back to his apartment located on Holmgren Way in the Village of Ashwaubenon. At some point thereafter, all three women had passed out or fallen asleep, and while in those varying states, Marcus allegedly took advantage of Alisa.

Alisa also reported she didn't believe she'd drank enough to be so inebriated that she wouldn't have woken up while being sexually assaulted.

This sounded to me like it doubled as a loose allegation of drugging.

Now, let's take a step back so I can explain a little about why the information threw me for such a loop.

You'll recall Marcus Somerhalder's name. I mentioned he was a good friend and long-time employer to my best friend, Skinny. So, by this time, although Marcus and I hadn't grown into what I'd call chums, we'd been casual friends for years. He'd always been good to Skinny, and I'd happily spent the last few years patronizing his various bars and pubs to catch up with Skinny or throw back a few relaxing beers. I'd even been known to party with the guy on occasion. So, despite my suspicions regarding the validity of the report, it was imperative that I kept an open mind. That's my job—look at the case from every angle to protect those who need protecting and bring justice to those who break the law. Parallel to the importance of believing the victim, I also felt it was part of my job, professionally and as a friend, to find out if Marcus was being framed.

I can admit I'd seen hints of the man Lawler's report was describing in the sexual assault case, but at that point, I hadn't ever seen anything definitive to tag him as a sexual deviant. Sure, there was guy talk—what guys don't exchange embellished accounts of their sexual conquests?

From what I'd seen of Marcus, there was no doubt he was a player. He was charismatic and had an amazing talent for oozing charm when he wanted to. The man knew exactly what to say to the women to make them feel special, especially when he wanted something from them. He was a bit of a cad in my opinion, but the guy didn't seem to care, and the women didn't seem to notice. A guy like Marcus shined like a new silver dollar in a jar of tarnished pennies; he could have any woman he wanted. As soon as they saw he was a young, attractive, witty—not to mention successful—business owner, they were hooked and fighting for his attention. He always had gorgeous women around him; each one probably vying to be the eventual Mrs. Somerhalder. It was fascinating and sickening to watch all at the same time. Why the hell would a guy like him need to force a girl to have sex with him?

I advised Investigator Lawler to follow up with Alisa but not to pursue anything else in reference to this case until I could dig a little deeper. I wanted to arm myself with as many details as I could find. After all, Marcus trusted me and had no reason to think I would be investigating him. I felt compelled to figure out how much of it was factually true. But something inside told me—whether I wanted to believe it or not—that Marcus might be capable of these kinds of atrocities, so I used that intuition to jump feet-first into investigating.

I wasn't taking on the case to protect Marcus—I wouldn't do that for anyone. Not to mention, if he was innocent, he didn't need protecting. My intention was to make sure he was treated without bias, and make sure this wasn't a witch hunt against a person I considered a friend.

Marcus's main circle of friends were people I was familiar with, so I knew I wouldn't have any trouble locating people who would be willing to talk to me. The guy seemed to know everyone, so I figured it was inevitable someone would be able to shed some light on the accusations. If I was lucky, one of them would clear things up toot sweet, and I'd be done with these shenanigans altogether.

Considering I knew the accused, there was a chance my involvement in the case would be seen as an egregious conflict of interest, but there was no real evidence of anything yet. The case wouldn't go any further standing on the information we'd received so far. I fully expected it to be deemed by the DA's office as another "He said, she said" case, see it buried under a mountain of other cases waiting to be reviewed, then finally dismissed. So, I figured I might as well do something along the lines of getting some answers to hurry along the process. Someone had to, and I was in a position to do just that.

I knew it would take some secret, off-duty digging, but I was certain no one would bat an eye at me speaking with people in Marcus's inner circle of friends and patrons. I was already seen as a good guy within the crowd and hoped I could inconspicuously pry into Marcus's love life without people realizing I was in the middle of a covert information gathering mission. I knew Marcus and his girlfriend, Faith, but I wasn't familiar with Alisa or Piper. I also knew my best resource at this point would be my good buddy, Skinny.

CHAPTER 4

AND SO IT BEGINS. . .

AKA YOU THINK YOU KNOW A GUY

Skinny is my longest and one of the best friends I've ever had—we've got some great history together. We've known each other since we were four years old, and that (not that I'm keeping track) is a long damn time. Considering all the people who have come in and out of my life over the years, Skinny's friendship has been a constant, even when he wasn't a regular presence.

Like me, Skinny grew up in Ashwaubenon. Our houses couldn't have been more than 200 yards from each other, so neither one of us was hard for the other to find. Within our neighborhood, he and I had a group of about eight friends that we hung out with on a regular basis. We got into all sorts of trouble as a little posse. While we remained a close crew throughout the years, Skinny and I were definitely the closest, especially through adolescence and into our early adulthood years.

We lived in the older part of the village known to many local youth as "the other side of the tracks." It was a bit of a melodramatic title if you ask me. Our parents weren't super wealthy, but rather the textbook middle-class, hard-working type. It wasn't that there were bad people or even poor people living east of Ashwaubenon's Ashland Avenue tracks, nor was it slummy in any way; it was simply a little lower income than the norm for the village. The kids in school that didn't live in this little corner of the village seemed to have nicer clothes and bigger houses. Once we hit high school, those same kids had nicer cars than we did, too. We might have envied them a little bit back then, but I honestly don't think we suffered by not having the same shiny things as them.

Most summer days throughout our elementary school years were spent tearing around on our bikes through the neighborhood. Save for the occasional stop at the house whose mom had gone grocery shopping most recently, we didn't spend much time indoors. The rain didn't stop us, either—there really wasn't anything to do inside, and I think because of that, me, Skinny, and our little group of friends had a great childhood.

I don't envy what parents these days need to do to entertain their kids throughout the summer months. *Everything* is planned. Gone are the days when kids were shooed out the door and expected to find their own fun. Until we got to our teenage years and added girls to the mix, there were never any plans, we just flew by the seat of our pants.

The whole idea that neighborhoods aren't as safe as they used to be because people are more dangerous nowadays just isn't right. I worked those streets. I know it isn't the case at all. Take it from me, you're not doing your kid any favors by keeping them "safe" indoors in front of a TV screen. Oh, and don't even get me started on play dates…

I digress.

Going to the same school and being in the same grade gave us a lot of opportunity to get to know each other well. Despite Skinny being a few months older than me, I was definitely the more mature one. He was fearless, laidback, and carefree, and I was more focused and driven. I'm pretty sure nothing much has changed for either of us in those regards—we had strong, but polar opposite, personalities. A balance was born of those diversities, and it's probably what's kept us friends for so long. Yin and yang kind of stuff, if you feel like getting deep about it.

Other than an occasional stupid squabble between friends and vacations that stole us from town, Skinny and I saw each other daily until we graduated from high school. He took the leap into adulthood when he started going to college, but it was a short-lived endeavor. He was far more interested in the party life and tended to enjoy the action of being out and about on the bar scene.

I was already walking the path to become who I am today, and that career choice saw me begin to drift away from some of my friends out of an obvious conflict of interest. Don't get me wrong. They were all still great guys, and I continued to hang out with them occasionally, but I could no longer do all the things I used to do with them. The parallel interests we shared were veering off into our own paths, and, for me especially, it didn't make sense to hang out in bars as often as we did.

By the mid-nineties, Skinny was a permanent fixture in the bar scene around Green Bay. He was pretty much a jack of all trades after paying his dues as a bouncer, bartender, and cook; the guy was even a bar manager at a number of the establishments he worked at. Skinny loved what he did, and he was pretty damn good at it, too, but I'm certain it wasn't always sunshine and roses.

I think I was a little jealous of his lifestyle and I'm pretty sure he was a little envious of mine. Well, with the exception of that time he got shot in the arm while bouncing at a downtown Green Bay bar. Seems ironic that he's been shot and I haven't been, doesn't it? I plan on keeping that irony fully intact.

The reason I felt this way about his life was because he was constantly surrounded by people having fun, and a good majority of that population were beautiful women. He got to know people from all walks of life, including some of our favorite footballers from the Green Bay Packers and local celebrities. Lastly, and this one's kind of a kicker, he got to stay up late and sleep in—the cherry on top?—he never had to vault out of bed and throw on an apron to sling drinks. Flip that coin, and my life probably looked pretty good to Skinny; I owned my own home, had a family, job stability, and earned a great wage, so we were at completely different ends of the career and life spectrum.

Beyond knowing how to do every job inside and out of those doors, it seemed as if Skinny knew everyone who came in and out of them as well. At his prime, there weren't very many people on the bar scene who didn't know Skinny. Like me, he was everyone's "buddy." He knew what every single one of those barflies wanted when they walked through his doors, and like the ace of spades, everyone loved him and were thrilled to see him. I have no doubt in my mind that it was Skinny's obvious and oozing talent for the industry that launched him directly onto Marcus Somerhalder's radar. What bar owner wouldn't want a guy like Skinny on the payroll?

So, I couldn't have been more pleased he was working for Marcus at the time. As the manager of the Velvet Room, he was privy to the comings and goings of employees and patrons alike. After reading Investigator Lawler's report, I honestly thought I'd hit the jackpot. This was going to be a quick and easy case. I'd have a chat with Skinny, he was going to have enough info that I could either process Marcus for being a pervert or put the whole damn case to bed, and I'd move on to the next.

I didn't have much time to sit on my hands because I had to act fast before news of Alisa's accusation made it back to Marcus. It happens all the time, and all it does is create problems like threats, fighting, fleeing, destruction of evidence and property, and a whole gamut of other general crap that makes an investigator's job that much harder to do.

Jumbled up in all the excitement of having an automatic inside source in Skinny was the true and genuine fear that my old pal would turn on me and inform Marcus of what was going on. The terrible possibility of that happening made stepping over the threshold into the Velvet Room that day one of the most stressful steps I've ever taken. I might add, it was definitely one of the most life-changing steps of my life as well.

I can't even describe the relief I felt when, after hearing some of what I had gone to the Velvet Room to talk to him about, Skinny confessed that he'd listened to many complaints involving Marcus. I didn't know if I could trust Skinny. All I had to go on was our history, but when he told me his boss had women who "downright hate him," I started to feel like everything would be okay.

When I finally spilled the beans by saying, "You know I like Marcus, and I would never want him to be unjustly charged for something he didn't do—" there was no going back. It was almost a relief to have removed the option of worrying about whether or not I should tell Skinny about the investigation, so I pushed through.

Keeping it causal, I asked him if he had any idea who Piper and Alisa (the two women mentioned directly in the complaint against Marcus) were.

"Nope, I don't think so. Should I know who they are?" he asked me.

"Well, no. I was just wondering if you did."

I could see it in Skinny's eyes and body language, the guy was bursting with curiosity, so I explained what I'd found in Lawler's manila folder a mere 24 hours earlier. I suggested it could be someone—an angry ex or scorned woman—trying to set Marcus up for sexual assault, which is why I had asked if he knew Piper or Alisa.

"Skinny, I *need* to find out if these women's allegations are true, but I also want to make sure Marcus has a fair investigation," I explained. "I have to remain impartial to find the truth—this is an extremely serious matter."

Well, that was that. I'd pretty much spilled the beans. There would be no more dancing around it—it was out.

I wondered what he was thinking, and in fear of his response, blurted out some of the specific accusations that I'd read in the manila file, then said, "Skinny, I can't stress how imperative it is to Marcus's guilt or innocence that this not get out to anyone."

Skinny just stood there shaking his head.

I couldn't get a read on what was going through his head at that point, but I'm certain it was a very personal struggle for him. I waited impatiently for a response, hopeful he still trusted me.

I could sense his initial reluctance, but in a very confident manner he said, "Yeah, yeah, you can trust me, Scott. Lay it on me, man. What do you need to know? I'm pretty sure I know some stuff, and I can talk to people and get more information for you."

I had no doubt he would be true to his word.

It was time to find out if there was any floor to this case. There was a chance Skinny's info would leave me floating, but I severely doubted it. I mean, beyond what he'd already said, leaking the fact that he had a lot of useful information was pretty damn telling.

I wasted no time and started digging into Skinny's vast knowledge of the bar scene. I snatched my pen out of my jacket pocket and searched the bar for something to write on. My napkin coaster was the closest thing I could find. I slipped it out from under my glass as Skinny robotically pulled another one from under the bar and plopped my drink on top of it.

First things first. "So, you said there's a bunch of women who think they've been drugged by Marcus—can you gimme names?" I asked.

"The one off the top of my head is Sasha," he said. "I haven't seen her in a while, though. She's kinda like me—been working in the bars and clubs for years, but I don't know where she's at now." He went on give me the rundown of what she had told him. Skinny also seemed to think she wouldn't be interested in cooperating and suggested she might not even admit it happened in the first place.

Furthermore, from what he knew of her situation with Marcus, Sasha hadn't reported it to the cops, which wasn't the best news, but hopefully it wouldn't matter. "Well, if I find her, I'll do everything in my power to get a statement out of her," I said confidently.

Skinny knocked me back down a notch by insisting once again I'd have a hard time doing so. "Like I said, Scott, I don't think she'll be all that interested in dealing with the police. She was pretty firm against it when I told her she should tell you guys, but good luck, I guess," he said.

Curious and heartbreaking. Every victim has a reason that justifies their silence.

So, it was going to be a damn-near miracle if I got Sasha to help me in any way. Even with that knowledge, I knew I had to try to find her.

"Anyone else? Any info, names—whatever you can give me will help," I chattered away at him.

Skinny pondered the situation for a few minutes as he continued to wipe the bar in the same spot he'd been wiping for the last half hour. I could tell the wheels in his head were turning.

Finally, he stopped wiping the bar, looked me square in the eye and said, "Scott, there are lots of them. I've been working for this guy for a long time, and we know a lot of the same people."

I could tell he was still a little nervous talking about it.

"I'm telling ya, man. That's just the tip of the iceberg. I've heard a lot of stories."

I was all ears at that point and let Skinny talk without interruption. He was quick to fill me in on the fact that the complaints weren't only from co-workers, but friends of his, and regular bar patrons. Skinny's a likable guy and people seem to feel safe around him, so it was easy to understand why these women had confided in him.

He elaborated on Marcus's alleged indecent sexual habits as I frantically tried to scratch down notes on my napkin coaster. He even told me Marcus would tell the waitresses to take their tops off—working in their bras would get them more tips. Sheesh.

I still hadn't finished jotting down the notes I had been trying to take on Sasha and was quickly running out of room. Apparently, some of the women had told Skinny that Marcus had forced himself on them. And some had told Skinny they'd been in situations alone with Marcus where they felt dizzy, as if they'd been drugged. Many women even told him they had flashes of Marcus having sex with them while they swayed in and out of intoxicated consciousness.

Holy shit. I couldn't believe what I was hearing.

"Hey, weren't you there that day Mike and me found those naked pictures of Faith on the Velvet Room's camera?" he said, picking up the conversation again after a brief pause.

"Those didn't look like they were forced though, Skinny, and she's his girlfriend."

"Yeah." He agreed. "But I know he likes taking pictures of the girls he's with. Pretty kinky, if you ask me."

Kinky? Maybe. Did that mean Marcus was guilty? Probably not. A bunch of women who "downright hate him"? Stories about suspected rape and drugging? Well, those things made me strongly consider there just might have been some legitimacy to Alisa's accusation. This was the kind of psychopathic horror story you heard on *Dateline*, not while sitting on a barstool in Green Bay, Wisconsin.

Knowing my profession, I wondered why Skinny had never said anything to me before, and as badly as I wanted to know the answer, it wasn't what was truly important in that moment. Two things trumped it:

1. Good God, how many women are we actually talking about here?
2. I need names, and I need them now.

Of course, beyond those two questions at the forefront of my mind, there were now a multitude of other questions that needed to be asked.

How would I find them and even if I did, how would I get them to confide in a cop? Like I said, they all had their reasons for not reporting the incidents in the first place.

And another big question: did Marcus *really* drug and sexually assault any or all of these women?

Skinny was having a hard time remembering all of their names but was at least able to give me a few—better than nothing. He told me he would think on it a bit to remember the others who'd shared their experiences with him.

I wasn't too worried. Along with the first names he remembered, he also gave me a pretty good idea of where I might be able to find them. It wasn't any kind of solid lead, and it was going to be an interesting process trying to locate them all, but it was a start.

All in all, Skinny clearly wasn't surprised by the sexual assault accusation like I'd originally thought he would be. Considering how many women he'd heard from, it was my guess he was more surprised one of them had finally gone to the police about it. Despite that, I could tell there was a hint of reluctance in helping me find truth in the accusations. It probably felt like he was stabbing his boss/friend in the back, so I reiterated how important what he was doing was.

Not to mention, I wasn't dumb to the fact that there could be some heavy repercussions for Skinny, too.

It was time for me to get the hell out of there and get to work. I reminded Skinny one more time about how important it was to keep this whole thing confidential and to get in touch right away if he remembered any more information or names. Lastly, I made one more point of mentioning that my integrity as a detective was hinged on how this investigation went down. Just in case.

I got a nod and a "you bet" from my pal. I left the Velvet Room, thankful of Skinny and confused and concerned for Marcus.

I made my way back to the station, sat at my desk, closed my eyes, and contemplated what my next moves would be. First on the agenda should have been to process the information from Skinny, but I was absolutely vibrating with anxious energy. At the same time, I felt overwhelmed at the thought of the challenges that lay ahead of me.

My hopes of a simple resolution had diminished with every word that had come out of Skinny's mouth, but I knew I had to try and maintain optimism that our pal wasn't a devious sexual predator. Maybe Marcus was the victim of the backlash that comes from being a player. It was seeming pretty unlikely, though, and I started to strongly consider he might be involved in the bullshit I was hearing.

What baffled me even more than anything else I'd learned in the last 24 hours was this: if everything Skinny said about these women being drugged and sexually assaulted by Marcus was true, why had *none* of them reported it to the police? Was it that the potential victims were scared of Marcus—was he threatening them somehow? Did they assume they wouldn't be believed? Based on what Skinny said, they seemed pretty sure something had happened without their consent, but maybe they didn't think they should report it if they weren't irrefutably certain.

Perhaps they were embarrassed? Maybe they were blaming themselves for getting into that situation in the first place?

Or, back to thinking optimistically for Marcus, maybe there really was some sort of jealous conspiracy to hurt his reputation.

One thing was certain, I wasn't leaving my office that evening without doing something with Skinny's information.

So, I sat there, trying to calm down and clear my mind. Focus eluded me for the longest time.

Eventually, I settled enough to wrap my brain around the information and what I needed to do with it. I calmly asked myself the question I felt needed answering the most. "Never mind feelings—innocence or guilt—where does this investigation need to start?"

As soon as I said it, I knew my answer...

CHAPTER 5

TOO MUCH HEARTBREAK. . .

AKA TUMBLING DOWN THE RABBIT HOLE

In any other case that rolls through the door, the first step is to check into the local case records to see if any of the people involved have a criminal history or any similar cases on file. Why that didn't jump immediately into my head, well, I don't know. Considering I'd already been stewing over the fact that if Marcus Somerhalder had acted so heinously toward so many women, how had his name never come up before?

Or had it?

Not that it was all that long ago in the big picture of life, but, back then, record sharing wasn't as efficient as it is today. Databases between neighboring stations like De Pere, Green Bay, Bellevue, etc. weren't connected like they are today. You could still find the info you needed, but it took a lot more digging to find it.

I was quite taken aback when I discovered that another woman had reported a similar incident in the summer of 2002—almost exactly a year apart.

The report was made out of the De Pere Police department and read almost identically to the one presently on Investigator Lawler's desk. The suspect was listed as one Marcus Somerhalder, and it was another accusation of a date rape type incident.

Well, well, well…

The digital file stated the victim, a young woman by the name of Hope, was out for her birthday when, at approximately 1:30 a.m., Marcus invited her to the bar he owned in De Pere called My Place for some after-hours drinks.

My Place Café—I knew it well. It doesn't exist by the same name anymore, which is probably for the best. I'd hung out there on more than a few occasions in my newly single days. It was a keen stand-alone stone building nestled in downtown De Pere, and I think it's worth taking a moment to note that it also had an apartment above it. You could access the apartment from both inside the pub, and from an outside staircase that led up from the alleyway to a raised patio. If you didn't mind having your home as your work and vice versa, it was pretty much perfect.

Apparently, it suited Marcus well.

*   *   *

Hope reported she'd only had a couple of drinks, then couldn't recall anything else up until she woke up naked in Marcus's bed with him on top of her. She began kicking him and telling him to leave her alone. Her next recollection was Marcus waking her up at 11 a.m. the next morning. Hope reported her hips were sore and her tampon, including the attached string, were pushed so far up inside her vagina that she had an extremely difficult time removing it.

As I read on, I found out that, unfortunately, the case was never prosecuted. The file declared that due to a lack of evidence or supporting witnesses, the case floundered before being tossed as a "he said, she said" debacle, and was closed. Marcus walked away without charges. I'm certain I would've heard about it if it had gone to trial.

Once again, I found myself sitting at my desk trying to process this information. I was stunned. To have never heard or suspected anything of Marcus like the alleged accusations I'd been recently inundated with was absolutely blowing my mind. Being an officer in the Green Bay area—who some would compare to the safe and sleepy fictitious town of Mayberry—you would think I'd have heard about that case in one way or another, but I hadn't.

To make matters worse for Marcus, both the case files I was now aware of involved unwanted sex while the woman was allegedly passed out or sleeping. This was very concerning because these two very similar stories came from two independent sources. And, Skinny had mentioned the use of possible date rape drugs with other young ladies.

Alternately, it would also read the same if these two women were in cahoots—maybe they were pals?

Let's just say, for the sake of argument, Hope and Alisa are friends. Hope's got a bit of a thing for Marcus, and finally gets him for a night. She digs him, but any further advances beyond that one night of fun are spurned. In retaliation, she decides she's going to set up Marcus, but the courts see through the ruse—she's obviously crying wolf, so the case is dismissed.

Farfetched, I know, but it's where my head was at. Now, watch me throw this bit into the mix. This honest-to-God ran through my mind as a possibility.

It's been some time since Alisa's best friend, Hope, tried to set up Marcus with a bogus sexual assault rap, and both are still miffed about how the whole thing went down. They've watched Marcus party it up with all sorts of beautiful women and it's tearing Hope apart. So, Alisa decides she's going to go ahead and try to set Marcus up because the jerk deserves it for what he did to her friend...

Yeah, yeah...seems like more work than it's worth. You'd be right if you said it, but I really wanted everything I'd found out to just go away.

The truth is, by that point, I didn't think it was a coincidence these women were claiming similar stories.

It was looking like Marcus genuinely had some secrets to be uncovered. If the accusation turned out to be true, Marcus needed to be stopped and he needed real help. I still had a few niggling doubts—at least, I wanted to have them. Either way, I was determined and motivated to unveil the truth.

Skinny had provided me with a short list of women who had come to him with stories of being victimized by Marcus, so, over the next few weeks, I slowly began the tedious job of tracking them down.

I sat at my desk during the day, working my normal cases, so out of necessity, I had to dedicate the few free evenings in my week to seeking out the women I'd scribbled onto my napkin. Skinny had given me a good idea where some of the women could be found, but seeing as I only had first names for most of them, it wasn't an easy process. He'd also mentioned most of them still worked in the bar industry, which meant that while I was gumshoeing from my desk, they were sleeping. By the time I was off the clock and could navigate my way to an establishment of interest, they were on the clock and not all that accessible for delicate conversation.

As daunting as my task was, I still managed to find that "sneaking" into these bars with my important, hidden motive felt exciting and was rewarding work. Whether I was able to talk to anyone or find any leads there or not, at least I was making a solid effort to get somewhere with the case. Well, for the most part—a couple of those places were so damn scary, I shouldn't have been in them alone. I was more worried about my life than I was about trying to talk to anyone.

One of the first contacts I sought to shed some insight into Marcus's alleged demented exploits was Sasha Colby. She was a gorgeous, intelligent twenty-something who aspired to someday go back to school to work in the medical field. In the meantime, she was happily working in the service industry and had been doing so since the tender age of eighteen.

A woman like her could probably do anything she put her mind to, but she'd learned early on in her service career there was plenty of excitement and money to be had in the bar business—if you knew what you were doing, which of course, she did. I couldn't help but appreciate that kind of drive.

Every bar owner knows you have to be present to make money. If you're not there, your profits are either sliding discreetly into your help's pocket or jovially over the bar in the form of complimentary drinks for chums, pals, and crushes; unless, of course, you had someone like Sasha working. The girl was a natural. She'd worked the Green Bay nightclub circuit and had an excellent reputation among the patrons and bar owners. Sasha had earned the respect of all of her past employers as an eager and trustworthy barkeep. She loved it in Green Bay, and as a result of that, worked hard to afford the life that kept her there.

I tracked Sasha down to a classy little bar/restaurant called the Ten O'One Club in downtown Green Bay, where she was managing and tending bar for her current boyfriend. I began visiting the place on a regular basis with the intention of establishing familiarity. Sometimes I would head over there while off duty, but there was also an occasion or two when I had time while on the clock, though I was never in uniform. I wanted her to think I was a laidback, easy guy. I could sense she wasn't fond of cops. A sentiment not uncommon in the bar scene.

Like so many others I'd tried to extract information from, she'd probably been negatively affected at one point or another by an officer or some kind of adverse event that included many of them. There wasn't a barkeep around who hadn't seen their share of police intervention.

I didn't have much luck with her as the club was a fairly hopping place, so creating any kind of ease regarding my presence was slow-going.

It had been nearly a month since the case had been brought to my attention and although I'd located Sasha and a woman named Theresa, so far, I really hadn't made much progress with either of them. Between Skinny and I, we were quietly and inconspicuously acquiring information, which was difficult considering we were only approaching people we could trust to keep the investigation quiet.

I guess it was kind of okay that things were moving as they were. It's not like I had been resting on my laurels. At the time, I was the youngest investigator my station had ever had, and I was described as a bloodhound when it came to the cases on my desk. I was full of energy and motivated to take on just about anything. I couldn't find it in myself to turn down a case that had leads and I rarely didn't get my man.

With only three investigators working in my department, it meant we all had heavy caseloads. I usually had thirty to forty open cases I was working on at any given time—difficult to keep organized, but easy to stay busy.

So, to keep me on my toes, no more than two weeks after Marcus Somerhalder's case dawned, the second major case of 2003 landed on my desk. It was an awful, bloody disgusting, and very, very heart-wrenching case, but it was meant to be on my desk. I could handle it.

It was a sunny, warm afternoon on Wednesday, September 3 when I got a page from the station while at home with my two little boys. I stopped what I was doing to call in and was given a quick rundown of the situation.

The brief initial report was that of a two-year-old boy who had presumably fallen down the steps at his mother's duplex on Cormier Road in Green Bay. The child suffered a considerable amount of trauma and his outlook was dismal, at best.

Anytime I'm relayed that kind of information, it kills me just a little. I dread the files that involve kids. There's a lot of heartache in the world—I've seen all sorts of it, but when it involves children it does something else to me. It ignites a passion that insists I work extra hard on the case because that child deserves justice. As a father of (now) three, it's incredibly easy to inject myself fully and compassionately into digging for the truth, and I do. I'm a bit of a juggernaut when I get rolling, and if you're against me, well, I don't recommend that.

From the hospital's standpoint, when a child is severely injured, dying from trauma, or dead, it's considered suspicious, and police are always contacted to get involved. Kids are clumsy, we all know that, but it's pretty damn rare that they're clumsy enough to kill themselves. So it's important, whether it's an accident or not, that we check it out.

The station sent two officers over to St. Vincent Hospital to take an initial report from the child's mother, Teshia and her boyfriend Patrick Donley. They were told that both she and Patrick (who wasn't the boy's biological father) were home when the child, a two-year-old boy named Sawyer, took a tumble down the steps to the basement. Teshia rushed to her son and found him unconscious at the bottom of the staircase. Patrick, thinking Sawyer had simply been knocked out by the fall, took the boy from Teshia and brought him to the bathroom. His intent was to try to wake the boy by placing him in the bathtub and splashing cold water on his face. When that didn't work, they immediately jumped in their car and frantically headed to the ER.

Now, in law enforcement, you're trained to trust no one, always stay in control, and always keep an open mind. We're also trained to question everything and everyone. It was my job to make sure there was no foul play and to verify this tragedy was just that, a terrible, tragic accidental fall.

I prayed I would find evidence that would support the mother's recollection of the incident because the last thing I wanted to do was place suspicion, or worse yet, fault on the mourning mother of this poor, dying child.

First things first, I made my way over to Teshia's house—one side of a single-story duplex—with a couple of officers to do a walkthrough of the house where the fall happened. While I walked around taking still pictures of the place, another officer took a video recording the scene. It had become standard practice to do this because you could get a full idea of the floorplan in relation to the condition of the scene, and more than once the footage had helped us find clues we didn't initially see.

The home was a decent size, not particularly clean, but I didn't see anything unusual about that. Believe it or not, 90 percent of the houses I enter are worse, and the rest are never as clean as the ones you see on TV. So, all in all, it was the typical setting of a single mother with a two-year-old son. There were toys scattered throughout the place, sippy cups, some unwashed dishes…typical.

The wooden stairs that led to the unfinished basement looked similar to most ranch style homes—nothing notable about them, at least. What *was* obvious after I made my way up and down those insignificant stairs a few times was that there was no blood or anything else that I could link to an incident happening on them. That was a bit odd. When things like this happen, there's usually some kind of reportable sign of it.

When there isn't? Well, that usually means one of two things:

1. Whoever told you something happened there was feeding you a line of baloney.

   OR

2. They cleaned it all up—this also breaks down into two schools of thought:

   a. Because they thought they should. I mean, who leaves blood everywhere?

   b. Because they would look guilty if there was evidence—even if they weren't guilty of any crime. Sometimes, it really is just an accident.

Sadly, my unfortunate feeling on the situation was the story was a line of baloney.

First of all, when your child is unconscious from a freak accident, you don't take the time to clean up before rushing to the ER. If you did, it would be assuredly true that you had no care for the welfare of your child, or it wasn't a freak accident at all and you're to blame for the child's state of trauma. Additionally, it was about five hours after the incident had supposedly happened, but it seemed odd that there wasn't a drop of water or any dampness in that bathtub. With two kids of my own, I'd given a lot of baths by that point, and it seemed to me there should have been something obvious to see. Even a quickly discarded towel or a toddler's clothing would have made sense.

Despite my suspicion there was more than meets the eye here, there wasn't a whole lot to go on at that point and no real reason *not* to believe what Teshia and Patrick had reported.

Yet.

It was my turn to talk to Teshia and Patrick.

I made my way over to the hospital and found them incredibly upset and overwhelmed. It wasn't the right time to get into a deep and detailed conversation, so I kept it light, assuring them it was a formality that we look into every child injury case of this nature. I needed them to be comfortable with me because that's really the only way you'll get the finer details in any case. They need to feel like their relationship with you is different—more special than any of the other people you've ever had to question.

The "good cop" is a tried and true method, and like my mom, I swear by it.

It was obvious Teshia was genuinely suffering, and I didn't want to make the situation any worse for her. However, I could sense an uneasy feeling from both them, especially Patrick, who seemed distant and expressionless. At the time, I think I wrote it off as him just being in shock over what had happened.

Even when innocent, people are generally uncomfortable in the presence of law enforcement, and we find their responses are guarded. This loosely translates into a lot of wasted time and resources, which we hate. For obvious reasons, we'd rather people be more transparent. It's generally hard for us to find a balance between fear, respect, and hatred in the eyes of the general population; it teeters for sure, and unfortunately, we're too used to it. As long as we can keep the peace, find the truth, and honor our mission statement[1], we'll continue to find success.

Building rapport can take moments or months, and the effort to successfully do so makes a difference in case progress. Thankfully, it didn't take long before Teshia and Patrick opened up to at least give me the same story the initial officers got. The two of them were behaving consistently with what I'd seen of grieving parents, but something just didn't feel right. Something about the whole situation was still rubbing me the wrong way. I couldn't put my finger on what that was. There was no history of abuse, and no question that Teshia thought the world of Sawyer.

Patrick, on the other hand, had only been dating Teshia for a short time, and although I didn't question the fact that he cared about the boy, I did wonder how deep those feelings went.

I spent the next day talking to Teshia's family and friends, which really didn't go well at all. Teshia was close with her family, and they were very protective of her and Patrick. Most of them were angered that I was prying into the lives of this innocent and suffering young family. Some scowled and swore at me, some told me to get lost and refused to talk, and most of them demanded I leave them alone. I kept trying to tell them we weren't out to get anyone, but had to follow-up with the doctors to make sure there was a legitimate reason for these devastating injuries.

When I did get feedback, I learned that Sawyer was already being told to call Patrick "Dad." This didn't mean much, but it struck me as odd. The other common theme was that Sawyer was a special little child that brought happiness, joy, and laughter to most everyone he met.

On Saturday morning I made my way back to the hospital, this time to check-in on Sawyer and talk to the doctors and nurses who'd been providing his care. Before going into his room, the hospital staff briefed me on their

---

[1] *Village of Ashwaubenon Public Safety Mission Statement: https://ashwaubenon.com/government/departments/public-safety/administration/mission-statement/*

findings. Things they found notable were pinch marks on his scrotum and some minor bruising on his extremities that weren't visible when he had first arrived at the hospital. It was going to be necessary that I have a look and make sure to document the injuries before they disappeared, but it wasn't likely to have any effect on the case overall. I say that no matter how suspicious I am of the case because pinches, bruises, even broken bones are sometimes the result of the ER staff doing absolutely everything necessary to save a life, which is what ended up being the case in this situation. Sawyer got his bruises when they inserted his catheter; regardless, they needed to be documented and recorded. The doctors told me Sawyer had received brain surgery to relieve the cerebral pressure, but despite the drastic measure, didn't expect the boy to survive much longer.

Such heartbreaking news.

I knocked on the door of Sawyer's room in the Pediatric Intensive Care Unit and went in accompanied by a female investigator and a nurse. Many of Sawyer's family members surrounded his bed, although I'm certain he had no idea they were there—the boy's brain was barely active, and he was in a coma.

I had a difficult time maintaining my composure as I looked at him lying there motionless, a seemingly endless series of tubes attached to his tiny little body.

Glancing around the room, I tried to make eye contact and apologize to each of them for the intrusion. The tension was tangible as they scowled, snidely remarked on my presence, and uttered their disgust at my lack of tact and respect. They were justified in how they felt, but it didn't change that I had a job to do. I politely asked them to leave the room for a few minutes while we took some photos and assured them we'd get it done as fast as we could. I did my best to downplay the purpose of my presence there, but they didn't care.

We waited until they had all left the room before we started looking over Sawyer's tiny, limp body. The nurse and I needed to slightly move him and adjust his position to get the photos we needed. His body was warm to the touch and other than the obvious tubes inserted into his trachea, he seemed as if he was merely sleeping. We knew otherwise. With an unfortunate certainty, we knew Sawyer's time on Earth was running short.

I couldn't help but think of my two little boys at home and sulk in the inevitable finality of the death that was dawning on this little guy. I couldn't help myself; I felt the tears start to burn in the corners of my eyes. I squeezed them tightly shut and placed my comparably giant hand on his tiny little chest. I felt compelled to say a prayer.

"God, I know you have to take this little fellow. When you do, hold and protect him on his journey up to you in the heavens." My chest heaved to hold in a sob, forcing me to pause for a moment. "Please God, comfort his family during these difficult days, and for myself, give me the strength and commitment I'll need to find the truth for Sawyer."

I can't explain it, but I felt like my prayer had been heard. Maybe by God, maybe by Sawyer—I'll never know, but the response to my anguish was a feeling of empowerment and spiritual energy.

I opened my eyes and looked down at Sawyer. Right then and there, I vowed to that little man I would find the truth, and if he had anything else to say before he had to go, I was listening.

I composed myself because I didn't have a choice. There was still work that needed to be done. Glancing down on him, it was apparent to me that some of the bruises might not have been consistent with a fall down the stairs, but two-year-olds can be extremely clumsy little creatures. I still didn't have a drop of physical evidence that supported anything but a fall, and other than some petty superficial bruises of different ages, he didn't have any other visible injuries from the fall itself.

I found that so damn weird. The doctors assured me they didn't have any reason to believe it was anything but a fall down the stairs, but I wondered how such a severe head injury could be caused with a lack of any other obvious trauma. To be perfectly logical, even if the boy tumbled down with nothing but his head smacking the stairs, he'd still have more bruising than he did—his whole head would be black and blue. A supposed fall down thirteen steps? One should unequivocally expect visible trauma, but the fact that none was obvious raised my suspicion further.

Sawyer's brain swelling got progressively worse throughout the day, so the decision was made to remove the life support machines. On Saturday, September 6, only three days after he'd been rushed to the hospital, little

Sawyer passed away with his family nearby saying their final good-byes and comforting each other as best they could.

I found it hard to believe that a fall down the stairs could cause such a devastating cerebral edema, but as far as we knew, that was the only explanation we had to go on.

This case wasn't over, but it felt disrespectful to push the family while they coped with this terrible loss. I left them alone for the time being and handled my suspicions professionally. There was enough suspicion surrounding Sawyer's injuries that, upon voicing my opinion as such, the commander of investigations granted my request that an autopsy be performed to confirm the cause of death.

We decided Dr. Huntington in the city of Madison would be our best choice to conduct the autopsy. At the time, he was one of the foremost forensic pathologists in the Midwest and was respected and admired as one of the best in the business. If anyone was going to find the finer details in the autopsy, it would be him. At least, we hoped he would.

On Sunday, September 7, the commander and I took custody of Sawyer's body and traveled two hours southwest to Madison. As I sat as a passenger in the investigator's unmarked, official car, I felt terribly sick to my stomach. I tried to relax and let my mind wander, but there was no shaking my discomfort with our precious cargo. My eyes would occasionally meet with others traveling in the same direction down the highway. With each glance, I was left wondering what sadness and shock those unknowing travelers would feel if they knew the body of a dead two-year-old was in the backseat.

I was distraught with the reality that this poor little angel lay there—not laughing or snoozing in his car seat or pointing at cows in the fields we passed—lifeless as we journeyed to find the truth. A truth that would require him to be put under the microscope like an irrelevant pile of flesh. I knew it was for the right reasons, but it didn't make me feel any better in that moment.

We arrived in Madison, and as respectfully and delicately as possible, we moved Sawyer to the room where the autopsy would be conducted. I've set foot in morgues too many times in my career, and every time I do, an uneasy chill runs up my back. There's something about the smell and vibe in the air that seems to seep right down into my very soul. Cold, damp, and acrid would be a less dramatic description.

Dr. Huntington was an interesting old codger. He met us as we came in and without so much as a hello, got down to business. Although we tried to be as pleasant as we could considering the situation, I'm certain the doctor didn't crack a single smile the entire time we were there. It was almost as if we were inconveniencing him. He must not have felt the same need as the commander and I, who felt we had to make the best of an awful situation. Then again, he was much more accustomed to lifelessness—maybe his coping mechanism was the stern, mechanical façade we were met with.

In all fairness, I suppose there wasn't really much to say. I had expressed my concerns about the severity of the brain injury before we'd even left Green Bay, so when we arrived, he was prepared to dive right into the task at hand.

As he prepped, Dr. Huntington mentioned his professional opinion was that the injuries were likely consistent with the fall. We knew Sawyer had succumbed to subdural and subarachnoid hemorrhaging, and retinal hemorrhaging, but it wasn't until the autopsy started that we realized the true extent of those injuries. He told us he hadn't seen that severity of cerebral edema in a two-year-old in a very long time.

To break it down into layman's terms, a subdural hemorrhage is when blood collects between the brain and the skull. That alone can create enough pressure on the brain to be life-threatening. A subarachnoid hemorrhage is a stroke that's caused by blood filling in those little wrinkles on your brain—also life-threatening all on its own. Lastly, retinal hemorrhaging, in the traumatic form as found on Sawyer, is what happens when the brain is forced back and forth within the skull, impacting and putting extreme pressure on the eyes. All of these issues lead to the word encephalopathy, which is the fancy word they use when they mean brain damage.

Knowing what had caused his death had allowed me the time to do some research on brain injuries in toddlers. I thought it was best to get a head start on understanding the medical lingo before we met with Dr.

Huntington. My findings revealed that subdural, subarachnoid, and retinal hemorrhages were the indicative paradigmatic triad to a non-accidental death in a two-year-old.

The doctor didn't seem all that impressed by my quick-study research and vocalized that my medical opinion had very little merit. He wasn't convinced the injuries were anything more than from a fall down thirteen steps.

I remember feeling as if he didn't want to hear what I said just because I said it. I wasn't a doctor, therefore, my diagnosis was absolutely incorrect. *A blind assumption*, he'd probably thought. *Research indeed*, he'd probably harrumphed. I wondered if he thought I was a young wannabe detective looking for unicorns—well, maybe not unicorns specifically.

Maybe I was looking for something that wasn't there. Regardless of his opinion, I took Dr. Huntington's report with a grain of salt, because to me, the substantial injuries consistent with a non-accidental death were Sawyer's voice from the heavens I was hearing. I had vowed to him I wouldn't rest until the truth be told, and this was surely a sign.

On the trip back to Green Bay, the commander and I discussed the case. He seemed satisfied that although Teshia and Patrick originally lied about some things, it didn't mean either one of them caused Sawyer's death. We also continued to have no physical evidence that would support anything else but an accidental death as a result of a fall.

I was anything but content. I was determined to find the truth.

In the meantime, I would have to remain haunted by the overwhelming feeling that there was more to this case—I'd hit a brick wall.

CHAPTER 6

EVOLUTION OF PERPETRATION. . .

AKA THE TACTICS, THEY ARE A-CHANGIN'

I pondered the details surrounding Sawyer's case for days, and by days, I mean a couple of weeks. The days all bled together. I had made a promise to that little boy, and I fully intended to keep it. I just needed a break in the case. The fact my attempts to make real progress on Marcus's case weren't getting anywhere, either, was making my investigative career nothing short of infuriating.

At least I had a few leads on Marcus's case, so I was able to sidle into a few of those. I'd spent a few evenings at the Ten O'One Club trying to warm up Sasha, but my efforts hadn't fed into the right moment to break the ice on my intentions for being there. I had no doubt I'd get there, but I have to admit, I wasn't feeling like my same old confident self at that point. All I could do was bide my time and wait for things to fall into place on Sawyer's case, while continuing to connect the dots on Marcus's.

Between Skinny and I, we slunk and slithered to acquire information as stealthily as we could, which we found we were shockingly good at. Initially, it was difficult and absolutely exhausting living on a prayer that the people we were talking about Marcus to would keep their yaps shut. But as we talked to more and more people, we quickly found out, over the last few years, Marcus had wronged quite a few women.

Now, I don't know if this is common knowledge, but Skinny and I learned women do a lot of talking to each other. I really mean it—we were shocked. It seemed as though every woman we talked to had her own story to tell as well as the basic details of at least one of her girlfriend's experiences with Marcus. These women, with their intricate, overlapping webs of information, were exactly who I needed to seek out and talk to.

Theresa Martin was one of these women. Seeing as I was still working on warming up Sasha, I figured it wouldn't hurt to broaden the investigation. It also allowed me to keep my mind off of my lack of progress on Sawyer's case.

I found out about Theresa through Skinny, and Skinny had found out about Theresa through one of his closest friends and co-workers, Clara. The two women had lived together a few years earlier while Theresa had been going to college and had remained the best of friends since, so it wasn't surprising Clara knew about Theresa's ordeal.

Although Clara continued to work for Marcus after hearing what Theresa had gone through, she didn't have a feather's weight of respect for him. Clara told me where I'd find Theresa, so I had no trouble tracking her down at her current job.

As soon as I laid eyes on her, it was obvious why Marcus had targeted her. You see, the guy I knew and had hung around with didn't ever set his eyes on a woman who'd be considered common. He went straight for the bombshell; he desired the perfect 10, and he seemed to always get what he wanted, too. Theresa was no exception.

Just as I'd been trying to do with Sasha, I slowly and patiently worked my way up to creating an easy, trustworthy bond with her. It ended up not being all that difficult a goal to reach, as she seemed to take a liking to me much sooner than I'd expected her to. It couldn't have been more than a couple of weeks after my first visit before she was comfortable enough to open up and share her story with me.

I remember the day well. It was on Saturday, September 27, 2003, and she was exuding nervous energy as she sat across from me, bouncing her left leg up and down swiftly on the ball of her foot. There was no doubt she'd been anxious to get the story off her chest—hopefully, this would be the start of the healing process.

Theresa couldn't remember exactly when her story had taken place, but that really didn't matter. It had happened over a year before, and despite not knowing what her experience entailed, I imagined she had other things on her mind besides the date. So, I couldn't blame her when she began her story with: "It was on either Sunday, February 24, 2002 or Sunday, March 3, 2002 when Clara and I ended up at an after-hours bar party with Marcus Somerhalder."

She went on to tell me that everyone there had been drinking, so no one was in any shape to drive home. They waited until around 6 a.m. and at that point, Marcus felt well enough to drive and offered to bring Theresa and Clara home.

They dropped Clara off at home first, but Theresa and Marcus decided they were going to go get something to eat before he brought her home. At least, that's what she'd thought was supposed to happen. Instead, Marcus drove them to two more bars, insisting a few drinks wouldn't hurt. You know, keep the party going.

She remembered that the first bar they stopped at was Beef's Corner Bar in De Pere. They had a couple of drinks and chatted—pretty laid back, apparently. She couldn't recall the name of the second bar, but remembered the place was yellow and not all that far from Beef's. Neither one of us could pinpoint the actual establishment, but it was another point that didn't matter all that much, so I urged her to continue.

While they were at the second, they downed another couple of drinks, and things seemed a little more rushed. At one point, Marcus tried to kiss her, but she put a stop to that right quick and told him nothing was going to happen between them. This was her best friend's boss after all, and Theresa was of the mind that you don't mix business with pleasure.

When they left the second bar, Theresa thought Marcus was finally taking her to get something to eat. Instead, and without even asking, he brought her back to his apartment above My Place in De Pere. As Marcus parked the car, Theresa remembered wanting to protest but realized she was feeling extremely intoxicated. Instead of raising her voice, she got out of the car, followed Marcus up to his apartment, and promptly fell asleep on his couch.

She didn't know how long she had been asleep when Marcus woke her up and told her to sleep in his bed. Her response to him was that she was just fine where she was and reiterated that nothing was going to happen between the two of them. She was feeling too sick to move anyway.

But...

In something like a gentlemanly fashion, Marcus insisted she sleep in his bed, and he would sleep on the couch. She wasn't in any shape to argue, so she humored him, slowly making her way into his bedroom, and in no time, fell fast asleep in his bed.

At this point in her story, Theresa fell quiet. Her expression went blank as her eyes focused straight ahead—seemingly boring through my chest.

"Are you okay, Theresa?" I asked. I considered reaching out to touch her hand, but thought better of it. I didn't want to do anything to alarm her.

She didn't immediately react to my question but took a deep breath and blinked.

I tried one more time to shake her from her stupor. "You know, I could come back another time. I understand this is difficult for you..."

She blinked once more and snapped back to attention. "No, no, Mr. Schermitzler, it's cool. I really need to tell you what this fucking asshole did to me so you can nail him to the wall." And with that, she continued. "I woke up—after I don't know how long—and found Marcus half on top of me. He was kissing me and had his hand down my pants with his fingers in my vagina. I told him to get the hell off of me and went to the bathroom to pee."

She did wonder how he'd got into the room and down her pants without her waking up sooner, but at that point, she was still pretty damn inebriated, and they don't call it "passing out" for nothing. She shuffled her way out of the bathroom, using the walls for stability, and made sure it was perfectly clear to Marcus that she wasn't going to have sex with him.

"If I hadn't been so drunk, I would have high-tailed it out of there right then, but I could hardly see straight, Mr. Schermitzler. I just needed a few more hours, and even with Marcus being all sneaky, touchy-feely, all I could think about was climbing back into that bed."

So, she did. Theresa returned to the bed and fell back to sleep.

It wasn't much later when she awoke once again, this time to Marcus trying to unbutton her jeans.

"I felt so ashamed that I'd gotten myself into this situation. I should have known better."

But I knew she had been manipulated.

We want to think we can be trusting of people we come across in the world, and I've said before that I think it's an important character trait to have. In Theresa's case, maybe she assumed she had nothing to fear because she was with Clara's boss?

I could definitely understand *why* she felt shameful of how things went down, but I knew it wasn't justified. Her reasoning for feeling shame was that Marcus wasn't physically keeping her at his place, and theoretically speaking, she could have left at any time. She had already said she wasn't in any condition to do anything other than sleep, but for whatever reason, she felt that was an excuse and not a legitimate reason.

The victim mentality is a harsh and cruel monster. Little did I know, Theresa was only the first of many like-themed accounts I would hear.

"Theresa, this isn't your fault," I said to her.

She rolled her eyes. Clearly, she'd heard it before and wasn't convinced it was true.

"Anyway, if you can believe it, after I went back to bed the second time, he tried again; then he tried a fourth time after that." She huffed, and I watched as she picked up bouncing her leg nervously once again. "The guy was relentless. The last time I woke up, he was right on top of me, face to face, and *still* trying to get his hand down into my jeans. It was sick."

"So…" I began, "how far did all of this go? Do you think there was finally intercourse involved?" It was a hard question, and my chest felt tight as I asked it. "Oh, and—do you think there's any chance you were drugged?"

"I don't think I was drugged, and I don't think he had sex with me while I slept, but I honestly can't really say for sure. I mean, I made it pretty clear, more than enough times, that I wasn't interested in sleeping with him. He didn't seem to give a shit about what I wanted, though."

They both woke up around 4 p.m. and Marcus drove her back to the apartment she shared with Clara shortly after. On the drive home, she didn't say a word to Marcus about any of it. Beyond feeling embarrassed, she also felt violated.

I can't even imagine the amount of discomfort she must have felt during that ride. I was surprised to hear she'd even accepted a ride from him.

"You know, Mr. Schermitzler, I was perfectly happy never having to tell this story again. I seriously worried I'd be seen as a narc, or that people would say it was my own fault—which I still feel like it is, sometimes—but Skinny and Clara said stuff like this has been happening to other girls." She stared at the fidgeting hands in her lap. "That makes me so goddamned angry."

She was aware of the importance of telling me about her incident, and despite her obvious anxiety, I could sense it was a load off her chest to tell it. I only wish I could have promised it would be the last time. There was a realistic chance I wouldn't be able to keep her off the stand if Marcus's case went to trial.

"They told you the truth, and I can't thank you enough for sharing with me. I know it was hard, and I know you hated every second you had to sit here with me, but we need to hold him accountable for his actions. This will help," I explained.

We chatted a little more before I handed her one of my contact cards, and asked her to let me know if she remembered any other details. I reached across the table to shake her hand, then stood to take my leave.

As I left, I felt better than I had in a while, which sounds weird considering what I'd just heard, but it's true. The last few weeks had been so damn dreadful, and I really needed there to be some kind of break on either Marcus or Sawyer's cases. I admit, I would rather it had been Sawyer's, but at that point, I was going to take what I could get.

I left there utilizing my renewed energy to ponder everything I'd heard. It didn't sound as much like Alisa's case in that Theresa woke up multiple times throughout her ordeal, where Alisa slept through an entire sexual assault. It was also true that Theresa was able to recollect nearly every detail of her assault despite the severity of her intoxication, whereas Alisa remembered nothing.

In Theresa's story, it felt like Marcus had made a special attempt to get her so drunk that she would be rendered helpless to stave off his advances, but it didn't work. So, to conquer Alisa—enter stage right, the new sparkly advancement in consciousness fighting action…drugs. Maybe?

Lastly, I also had to consider there was over a year dividing these events. The planet, and everything on it, is a product of evolution…and I was getting the strong feeling that Marcus's predatory tactics might have evolved as well. I knew nothing for certain, though. Not yet.

In detective work, there are many factors to consider. Every time you feel like you've nailed down something as fact, a new possibility comes to light. A good investigator expects it—welcomes it even. Each new detail, no matter how small, allows my case to become more and more solid.

I didn't have to make any conclusions at this point, so I made my way back to the station to add the newest addition to the victim statement pile. I'd continue to work on softening up Sasha, and once I did, I'd have another story to compare to the three we already had.

Things stayed quiet for a few days, which gave me some time to sift through the cases on my desk, make official notes on my meeting with Theresa, and check if there was any new info on Sawyer's case. Sadly, there was nothing, but fortunately, I wasn't left much time to wallow on the fact.

It was October 3, less than a week since I'd received *my* first official statement against Marcus, when I got a call from Skinny.

"Hey, Scott! How are ya', man?" he asked.

"Good'n you?" I replied.

"Yeah, yeah, I'm good, too. Listen, I got off the phone with Sarah Price a little while ago—do you remember her?" He didn't actually pause so I could respond. He just kept on talking. "Anyway, doesn't matter. She works with me at the Velvet Room and just told me the weirdest goddamned story." He was keeping it together, but I could hear the nervousness in his voice.

"Okay, yeah, let's hear it then, man."

Skinny told me that Sarah had been working the back of the bar a few nights earlier, and by back of the bar, I mean she wasn't out serving from table to table but slinging drinks over the counter. Turns out, she didn't remember the end of her shift or a few hours after it. Someone had told her to get to a hospital and make sure the police heard her story. So, when she called Skinny, he told her she should talk to me. Instead of waiting for her to touch base,

I asked Skinny for her number, hung up with him, and immediately called Sarah.

Thankfully, she agreed to talk to me about the situation, and I told her it would be best if she came down to the station to make an official statement. I also had to let the Green Bay Police Department know what I was doing, because the Velvet Room, and anything unlawful that went on inside of it, was technically their jurisdiction. Thankfully, when I filled them in on the details, I got a hearty "Keep up the good work, kid," which I interpreted as full permission to go ahead with my interview of Sarah.

It worked out for her to come by the next morning. When she arrived, we got our introductions out of the way as I led her to my office. She was a petite woman with a kind face, seemed intelligent and well-spoken, but she looked tired—exhausted, in fact. The shadows around her eyes looked like the product of days of missed sleep, and the eagerness at which she accepted the cup of coffee I offered seemed to back up the theory.

I started off slow, because as I said before, rapport building is so important. We chatted about her job, how long she'd known Skinny and worked for Marcus, stuff that was familiar and ultimately easy to answer.

Sarah sipped at her coffee, and eventually leaned back in the chair and crossed her legs, an excellent indication that she was comfortable. From there, I prompted her to share her story with me.

She had arrived for her shift at the Velvet Room a little before 11:00 p.m. and made a point of telling me she hadn't had a single drop of alcohol before she got there.

"Coming in on the late shift, though," she said, "I had some catching up to do, so I did some quick shots with a couple of regulars and servers. I think I had about six."

Six shots? I raised my eyebrows, not sure if I was shocked or impressed, possibly both. That amount would have had me—a moderately burly grown man—fairly inebriated. I started to feel like maybe this was just a situation where this girl went a little overboard. That is, until she went on to say, "Six shots, I know. It sounds like a lot—it *is* a lot—but I work in a bar, and I drink pretty regular, so I know what alcohol does to me. Six shots is enough to get me tipsy, and a lot of fun to be around, but it sure as hell isn't the formula to get me blackout drunk."

Well, that settled that. She continued.

Sarah had a glass of water at the end of the back bar and insisted she didn't leave her post for more than five minutes the whole night—once to use the bathroom.

Last thing she remembered was at about midnight when she was washing glasses behind the bar, and was told by whom, I don't know, that Marcus walked her out to her vehicle at about 2:15 a.m.

She knows she got home at about 4:30 a.m. because her boyfriend was up, but she has no recollection of how she got there.

"I noticed you pulled up in a car; it's yours?"

"Yeah, and I drove it to work, which I remember, and apparently drove it home, but don't remember that. I also have no damn idea what I was doing from the time I left the bar to the time I got home. That scares the shit out of me." She took a gulp of her coffee. "Not to mention, my boyfriend said I was acting really weird when I got home and just wanted to go to bed." She tipped her head back to finish her coffee and asked if she could have another cup. I was happy to oblige and led her through the halls to the station kitchen.

As we made our way back to my office, Sarah picked up her story, and told me she felt wretched the next morning. "I was dizzy, and that made me feel sick. So sick. I didn't know what the hell was going on with me, so I called Marcus to find out what happened."

I no longer suspected the shadows around Sarah's eyes were the result of a lack of sleep.

I opened the door to my office and we shuffled back to our places. "What did he have to say about it all?" I asked.

"He told me he thought I was drunk because, apparently, I didn't count out my till before I left, and I didn't even take my tips for the night. First of all, Marcus would never let any of us leave without settling our tills, and he's got a strict policy against employees driving home when they're drunk. But…the dude walked me to my car? I dunno man, I don't get it."

She stopped talking, and I didn't want to lose her. It was important that I kept her going so I could get the full story—especially with how interesting it had just gotten.

"Did he have anything else to say? Did you ask him why he let you get in your car if you were drunk?"

"No. I was pretty messed up when I was talking to him, you know?" She plopped her empty coffee cup on the edge of my desk and leaned back into her chair. "He asked me if I felt like I'd had sex, though. I thought that was weird, but I told him I didn't think so. Then again, I still don't know where I was or what I was doing for like two hours... I'm pretty sure I was drugged."

I was feeling pretty sure she had been as well. "Did you tell him that, Sarah—that you thought you'd been drugged?"

"Yeah."

"What did he have to say about that?"

"I told him I was thinking about going to the hospital, and maybe even the police. He told me that if I did, not to tell either of them I had been at the Velvet Room because he didn't need any more hassle. I went to the hospital anyway, and now I'm here. I lost two hours of my life—there's something up about that." She had gone to St. Vincent Hospital where the ER doctor said that it was likely a designer date-rape drug.

Designer date-rape drug, eh?

I was going to have to start schooling myself a little on this. In my line of work, we know a lot about the common drugs, recreational as well as date-rape, but we also know there's always new stuff trending on the underground markets. Chemical kitchens are cheap to set up and run these days.

"I'm glad you're here, and glad you went to the hospital, too. I agree, something's off. Also, what kind of hassle is Marcus referring to?" I asked.

She told me that the night before her incident, a woman had been taken out of the Velvet Room and whisked away by an ambulance. She was apparently violently sick and the rumor was that she'd been drugged. Sarah also let on that she knew Marcus was going through some other legal stuff.

Like her, I was pretty sure she'd been drugged and feeling the same had happened to that girl from the night before. I needed to find out who the girl in the ambulance was.

Even though there wasn't any definitive, tangible evidence that Marcus was guilty, it was getting damn hard to ignore the fact that there was a lot of shit piling up around him. Three possible instances of drugging.

I thanked Sarah for coming by and sharing her experience, walked her out to her car, then padded back to my office to add her story to Marcus's swiftly growing file. As soon as I finished the entry, I dialed Skinny's number.

As it rang, I decided I would make my way over to the Ten O'One Club tonight and put in another go at warming up Sasha.

"Hey, Skinny." He picked up just before it went to message. "I just finished chatting with Sarah. Thanks for that lead. It's starting to look more and more like Marcus is a much different man than I thought he was." Saying it out loud didn't seem to bother me as much as it had previously. I made a mental note of the change in my thought process—I'd get back to it later.

"Yeah, ain't that the truth. Things are getting weird around here, too. The last few days have been the weirdest."

"Do you think Marcus's is panicking because he's guilty?" I threw it out there.

"He doesn't know that I know anything. He doesn't even know that I know about Alisa, and I haven't really noticed him acting any different. It's just weird that two women go down in two nights."

"Yeah," I agreed. "Hey, do you know the name of the girl who got taken away by the ambulance?"

"I think her name is Paige, but I don't know her."

That didn't matter so much. If she rode in an ambulance, there'd be enough information that I'd be able to find her. I told Skinny I was going to check it out, and that I was also going to head down to the Ten O'One Club after work.

I finished chatting with Skinny, tidied up my desk, loosened my tie, and clocked out for the day. I was riding high off of the progress I'd made and wanted to keep the momentum going.

CHAPTER 7

DARK DAZE & FOGGY NIGHTS. . .

AKA THE BEGINNING OF THE SEEMINGLY NEVER-ENDING

I made my way into the Ten O'One Club, looking forward to relaxing with an ice-cold beer. I rarely had the time, opportunity, or even desire to drink anymore, but I knew I was going to enjoy this one.

I was fortunate enough to find Sasha tending the bar, which was an excellent spot to approach her. Despite my best efforts, I hadn't been able to get close enough to Sasha to get any solid knowledge on what kind of person she was, so, at my request, Skinny filled me in on as much information as he had on her.

Based on what he told me, and as I watched her work behind the bar, it was evident, especially with my now keener knowledge of Marcus's taste, that she was exactly the kind of woman he would ramp up the charm for. She fit the same profile I'd seen in Alisa, Theresa, Sarah, and the file photos of Hope. Moving effortlessly from customer to customer, Sasha came across as bold, confident—the kind of lady who wouldn't put up with a lot of shit from guys. She also strongly came across as the type of woman who knew what she wanted and wasn't afraid of working hard to get it.

Skinny said she wasn't promiscuous by any means. In fact, he said she was very selective in who she dated—turned him down a few times, too, I learned. The way she worked behind the bar—she seemed focused, like she wouldn't have time to spend with an overgrown man-child like Marcus.

She seemed the kind of woman who would appreciate an intellectual guy…
though, I didn't know that for sure.

But…

I confess, I wondered what kind of predator Marcus had to be to best
this woman.

I slid onto a barstool, so she'd have no choice but to serve me, and
hopefully, I could get her talking. I got her attention and ordered a drink,
then asked her how she was doing; acting confident and comfortable, like
we were friendlier than we actually were. It works sometimes, trust me. The
"old chums" shtick is a classic gumshoe tactic.

It didn't work.

She'd seen me around the place, she knew who I was; but apparently, I
hadn't made nearly as much of an impression as I'd thought. I already knew
she wasn't fond of my status as a police officer, but that usually only makes
conversations guarded. Sasha didn't seem interested in talking to me at all.

I persevered by tip-toeing around my intention for being there (same as
I'd done every other time I was there) and did my best at making informal
small-talk, hoping an opening would present itself. Thankfully, small-talk is
a thing us investigators have a talent for.

Eventually, she stopped just long enough for me to attempt a
conversation, and I shamelessly spit out what I was there to say.

"Sasha, you know I'm a cop, and I know something happened between
you and Marcus Somerhalder. Would you be willing to talk to me about it?"

She proceeded to lay a heavy scowl on me, and immediately became
standoffish. "Probably not," was all she said as she made her way to the other
side of the bar.

Fine. Okay. That wasn't at all what I wanted to happen. Instead of giving
up, I dialed the conversation back again to more neutral topics, trying to
get her to relax around me. After about twenty minutes of banal chatter, I
could see her letting her guard down. I was a good guy, and I felt like she
was seeing that about me, so I decided to try again.

"You're not alone, you know. There are others who've said they've had
pretty intense run-ins with Marcus as well." I didn't realize how tightly I'd
been clenching the pint of ale in my hand. I eased up and continued gently

picking at Sasha. "I need to know the truth. If I do, I can help you and all the others. There needs to be some justice here. If you're a victim of his like the others I've talked to, I can help you all. It'll be worth it, but I can't do it without you."

Needless to say, Sasha wasn't buying it. I wasn't even sure if she was listening to me anymore. It was obvious she was uncomfortable with the situation, the topic, and me. Who could blame her? I wasn't a friend or even someone she knew; I was a cop, why should she trust me? The vibe she gave off made it clear she had no interest in discussing that part of her life with me. I pretty much knew this was how it would roll; it's how it goes with *many* sexual assault victims. Many of them spend their entire lives telling no one at all.

"That was a long time ago, and I'm over it," was all she said on the matter.

So, she *was* listening to me...

It was clearly an old wound she didn't want reopened, so I dropped the topic once again and went back to small-talk. It was going to be key in building that oh-so-important rapport with her.

I had been at the Ten O'One Club a few times to familiarize myself with her, but the other times I'd gone I hadn't been convinced Marcus was guilty of anything. Now, well, my whole mentality had shifted, and I really wanted to hear what had gone on between them. Skinny was absolutely sure something had because he'd heard it from Clara (Theresa's good friend and former roommate). He knew she wouldn't embellish, and I trusted his instincts on the matter.

Maybe Sasha was hard to crack because she knew I associated with Skinny and Marcus. From her perspective, she probably worried that I wasn't there to look out for her best interest—it was probably a more logical presumption in her mind I was there to protect Marcus from the consequences of his actions. I could just be another player, like him. The thought of being grouped together with scum like him made me shudder. I worried it might actually take an act of God to get this girl to trust me.

Thinking back on it now, there was probably some worry that if I was actually looking for the information I said I was, and she moved forward with telling me her story, she would be painted as a fool—a helpless victim. To some, the only thing worse than being a victim of sexual assault is people *knowing* you're a victim. People often either pity them or think they got what they deserved. Either way, the victim winds up being embarrassed for something that was beyond their control.

As I'd said earlier, she came across as a confident woman—a woman with too much personal pride to let people think of her that way. I had to convince her that I appreciated the sacrifice she would be making in telling me, and that it would be an act of *strength*, one of liberation and justice.

It was obvious that Sasha, like many in her situation, was reluctant to revisit the events she had been trying so hard to forget. There was no doubt she knew what happened to her was wrong and illegal, but beyond that, she'd already dealt with the self-imposed, undeserved shame—fear that no one would believe her and the actions themselves.

I knew I was asking a lot of her to drudge up this part of her past and made sure to let her know that, while I could never fully understand what she went through, I fully understood her concerns about revisiting it. I stressed that her story could be a substantial contribution toward protecting other women from becoming victimized by Marcus. We needed his victims to step up and expose him as the deviant he was so others could be warned.

I talked, and talked, and talked...

I reminded her that she wouldn't be alone in this process, and her terrible experience would be backed up by the bold women who had already come forward with their allegations of his sexual crimes. I was careful not to give Sasha any details of the other victim's accusations because it was crucial she have no knowledge of their experiences. Each woman's story needed to remain completely independent of the other. This was the only way to maintain the integrity of the investigation. First things first, I had to be convinced of Marcus's guilt before I could even think about trying to convince a jury of it. I was pretty much there, but there wasn't tangible proof, so the more info I had, the better.

I had no real idea what her experience with Marcus entailed. If it was anything like the other women's stories, first, there's a chance it would be disturbing to hear, and second, an integral key in patterning his crimes. It would open my investigation to pursue as many charges as possible, and, not only that, if her story was similar to the others, it would strengthen the case and make it more likely they were all victims of the same man. Unfortunately, it would also mean it was more than likely my "friend" was hiding some very dark secrets.

Despite everything I'd said so far, Sasha remained stoic. I kept at her—as is the investigator's way—occasionally engaging her in conversation as she continued to work around the bar. As I watched her, it became clear why bar owners liked Sasha—she was definitely a diamond in the rough. Not only was she pleasing to the eyes, she never stopped working: cleaning, serving patrons, and chatting amicably with them. It was almost calming to watch her.

I had been there for over an hour, nursing a beer, as I watched patrons come and go, before she finally slowed down. I made one final plea. If this didn't work, I'd take the last sip from my pint and jump ship for the night. There would be another chance, unless I pushed too hard tonight, which I was already worried I had. I didn't want to blow my chances altogether, so I made a special effort to come across as earnest, but desperate to hear her story.

"Sasha, please help me understand why so many women are accusing Marcus of such terrible things."

My patient persistence paid off. She finally stopped what she was doing, and for the first time that evening, looked *at* me instead of *through* me. I was relieved I finally had her attention.

"Harper," she called across the bar to a burly gentleman wiping down a table, "can you handle the place for a bit? I'm going to take my break."

Harper nodded.

She untied the age-grayed apron from around her waist and invited me to follow her to the backroom.

Poised and proper, Sasha looked out of place as she sat at a filthy card table riddled with half-eaten bags of chips, opened soda cans, and a stale-smelling, overflowing ashtray. The room was dim, but I could see her just fine as she lit a cigarette, looked at me uncertainly, and said, "I'll tell you what happened, but I don't want to get involved."

I felt like the guy who won the lottery but lost the ticket on the way to claim the prize.

On the one hand, I was extremely pleased I was going to get the information I had come for, and on the other, frustrated she wasn't interested in being involved. The victory I felt when she invited me to the backroom suddenly felt like a fourth-place finish if I couldn't get an official statement out of her. Not that I didn't understand her feelings, but I knew if we were ever going to hold Marcus accountable for what he'd done, I might need her and any other women who had been victimized to testify against him.

I would get over that hurdle if I needed to. First, I had to see if she was going to provide me with anything worthwhile. At any rate, I sat back, and as she took a long drag off her cigarette and crossed her legs, I waited for her to exhale so she could tell me her story.

"So, I don't remember the actual date it happened on, but I remember it was a Tuesday in January, 2001." She took another puff off her cigarette and tapped the ashes into the tray in front of her. "I'd been home all night—one of my rare nights off—and had spent the whole night laying on the couch watching TV. It was glorious."

It was close to 1:00 a.m. when she received a call from Marcus—with whom, she explained, she had been in a casual sexual relationship with since sometime in late 2000. While the two weren't overly committed to each other, they made a point of getting together two to three times a week. Marcus invited her to join him at his apartment above My Place, which was starting to become a huge point of interest for me. Pretty much every woman so far had mentioned it was where they had been with him.

Despite the late hour, she made her way over.

"When I got there, he thought it would be nice to have a couple of drinks before we went upstairs to his apartment. Nothing about the suggestion seemed out of the ordinary because we'd done it before."

"Did you have anything to drink before you left to meet him?" I asked.

"Nope. If I had, I wouldn't have even gotten in my car. As long as I've been in the business, I've known better than to drink and drive."

Good girl, I'd thought.

She had enjoyed a small tapper of beer, and they'd each had two shots of Apple Pucker mixed with Jack Daniels—also known as an Applejack—while they chatted for about an hour.

Throughout that time, Sasha began feeling progressively more nauseous, especially after downing the shots.

"Then, it was like a switch had been flipped." She took one more pull on her cigarette, stabbed it out in the ashtray and folded her hands onto her lap. "I damn near vaulted from that barstool and barely made it to the bathroom in time. I was sick. So sick. I remember not feeling any better afterward, either."

Sasha came back out to let Marcus know she wasn't feeling well, and he suggested they head upstairs to his apartment. Seeing as she was in no shape to drive, she really didn't have any choice, so she agreed—nothing to worry about, she knew Marcus intimately…

"I hardly held it together as we made our way up the stairs. As soon as I got to the top, I pushed past Marcus and ran for the bathroom. I vomited again, and it absolutely drained me. All I could do was lay there on his bathroom floor."

I was pretty sure Theresa hadn't been drugged. I only knew Alisa felt she hadn't drank enough to blackout, but neither had said anything about feeling nauseous or throwing-up. Sarah, on the other hand, felt very sick but not until she woke up hours after Marcus had taken her home.

Sasha got up from her chair and walked the ten feet to the other side of the room. She grabbed a couple bottles of lager from a case against the wall, offering me one.

I shook my head. "I'm fine, thanks."

She returned the extra to the case and came back to the table, cracking the cap off her beer with practiced ease as she sat.

"So, do you think you might have been drugged?" I asked once she'd settled. It was a question I eventually desperately wished I wouldn't have asked.

"Lemme just say this—as I lay there on the floor, feeling like I was dying, that sonofabitch walked into the bathroom, and instead of asking me if I was okay or offering me a goddamned glass of water, he started to undress me." She took a long swig from her beer. "I couldn't have fought him off—I was toast, but I'm certain I told him to leave me the hell alone. In fact, that was the last thing I remembered until the next morning."

"So…you feel like you weren't drunk, but were drugged—is that right?" I hated to press her on it, but I had a strong feeling about what was happening to these women. I needed her to tell me if she felt like she'd been drugged. It would be an important confirmation that I was on the right track with my suspicions.

"You got it, Scott. That's exactly right. It's not a feeling, either; I'm sure of it."

When she woke up the next morning, Sasha found herself naked in Marcus's bed and could hear him in the shower.

"Even sitting up was a challenge," she said. "I felt so sick. I had blurred vision and such a bad headache. It was like there was a fog in my head. I wasn't able to focus on anything, let alone wrap my head around a single thought. All I could do was lay curled up in bed staring straight ahead. I was completely and utterly dazed—it makes me feel nauseous just talking about it."

I said comforting things like, "I can imagine that was a terrible feeling," and, "I'm so sorry you had to go through that," but, I admit, I was distracted by what she had just said.

Her description of how she felt that morning triggered a memory. I had to excuse myself. "Would you mind if I took a quick bathroom break?"

The way Sasha described her experience hit me like a ton of bricks. Talk about déjà vu. Word for word, it was like she was describing one of my own experiences from the year before. From the Applejack shots to the lost time and the foggy brain, I knew exactly how she felt because the same thing had happened to me.

I had never planned on telling this story to anyone—I was going to keep it tucked away so no one would ever know. That's what you do with information and experiences people *cannot* know about you— "skeletons in the closet." This was mine. I had felt a deep sense of shame from the time it happened up until the moment Sasha described her experience. My shame had been overthrown, but I wasn't quite sure what feeling had replaced it…

relief? The event I speak of had been, at that point, one of the most mentally and physically trying times in my whole life, so it was oddly comforting to hear I wasn't alone in what happened to me. Still, the realization was deeply disturbing. Before that conversation, I never would've considered I'd been drugged, but there was no doubt anymore.

It was mid-August, 2002 and we were dawning on that stage of the summer so many of us northern Americans know too well; every second you can possibly steal away is spent outside. You know winter is coming—it's inevitable, so every pint on a patio might be your last; one more camping trip before the lakes cool off; the barbecue is utilized daily because soon it'll be too cold...

I like the fall, don't get me wrong, but it changes people. I swear it does. People get crabby.

Onward...

It had been a beautiful summer. I was still single, Skinny and I were hanging out a little more often, and for the first time in a long time, I was feeling confident enough that I'd started dating again. It was all pretty casual, but it felt good to be back on the market.

Marcus had decided to throw a golf tournament sponsored by the Velvet Room and Washington Street Lounge and had invited me to join in. I was looking forward to a relaxing day of swinging clubs with Skinny and two of his Velvet Room bouncers. Skinny was excited by the team he'd put together. He and I had golfed together many times, so he knew I was an above-average golfer—at least by Green Bay standards. The two bouncers on our team kept their left arms straight and followed through on their swings perfectly. Skinny thought we were a shoe-in for the first-place trophy, but I was just happy to be there.

The weather was beautiful, and much like every other bar-organized golf outing I'd been to—it was filled with prizes, drinks, and lots of laughter. I spent the day hanging out with old friends and making new ones. I even managed to chat up a few women. Needless to say, there were a lot of distractions to throw me off, but I still managed to play a fairly decent game. Now that I think back on it, my whole team played well. We finished twelve under par, which was enough to take third place.

By the time all the teams had finished, I can confidently say just about everyone there was well on their way to being sufficiently hammered. No one goes to this kind of thing without planning on alcohol being a huge part of the fun, and this event was no exception. I know I drank my fair share of beer over that five-hour round of golf, but I didn't feel any worse for wear. I thought it prudent that I stay away from the abundance of shots offered by lovely, scantily clad waitresses in golf carts all throughout the day. I did, however, take up their many offerings of bottled water. I had to make sure I held up my end of the bargain (I'd promised to bring my A-game), and I needed to stay sober so I could drive back to Washington Street Lounge, where Marcus had planned a dinner for all of us golfers.

It seemed like just about everyone from the tournament made it over to the Lounge for the dinner and awards—it was a packed house. People were in high-spirits as they lined up to grab their food from a buffet-style set-up and found seats wherever they could within the bar.

I ended up at the same table as a woman I didn't recognize from any point throughout the day. After spending most of the event with three hulking men swinging comparatively tiny clubs, it was time to branch out socially.

I'm sure I asked her name, and I'm certain she told me, but up until just before I began writing this book, I couldn't remember what her name was. I now know that Carmen and I very much enjoyed each other's company over dinner. She was a young, attractive, twenty-something who'd been recruited by one of the teams as their ringer. A Ringer? Yeah, Carmen was the local golf pro. I don't remember what place she and her team got, but I do remember feeling all that more proud of our third-place finish.

Carmen didn't seem to fit in with the bar crowd we'd normally see in the Washington Street Lounge—she seemed higher class. Nonetheless, she chatted effortlessly with me and the others sitting at the table with us. We both had interesting things to talk about; I was interested in her status as a golf pro, and she thought my job was fascinating as well. I rarely find other people's jobs as interesting as mine, so it was kind of exciting talking with her. That is, until Marcus sauntered over to our table.

This was his event, his day, and I guess I didn't have an issue when he took over the conversation. After all these years, I can't recall what topic had us so distracted from the rest of the room, but I do remember I didn't want the dialogue to end. For whatever reason, when Marcus interjected himself into our cozy little chat, I let him take over. Anytime there was a gorgeous woman around...

The night was young, and it wasn't like I was looking to hook up with this young lady—though she was intriguing. Marcus seemed unabashed about his obvious interest in her, so I excused myself from the table, refreshed my drink, and sought out some other friends to socialize with.

I would occasionally glance in their direction to see if Marcus had put on the moves yet, but by his standards, he was taking it slow. I stayed away anyway. I had no right to cramp his style, and he sure as hell didn't need me as a wingman. I wasn't going to put the moves on her, so I just let Marcus do what Marcus did best—let the player play.

After about an hour, I happened to look over and saw Carmen once again sitting at a table by herself, so I made my way over to rekindle the conversation from earlier.

It bounced back to life as we found ourselves laughing together about just about everything. Also, she said she was impressed by the third-place golf plaque I had just been awarded, but I'm sure she wasn't really.

We were still guffawing at something or other when Marcus brought over two Applejack shots and placed one in front of each of us on the high-top table. It was a gesture I found unusual, especially because he wasn't practicing good shot etiquette by bringing one over for himself so he could join in.

He laughingly said something about not being able to carry three shots and didn't want to bother finding a drink tray—those were only for the waitresses, anyway. "Am I right? Eh, Scotty! Am I right?" He'd laughed.

I didn't agree; I shrugged it off, but neither Carmen nor I turned down the shot. I mean it was free, and who turns down a free shot, right?

"Thanks, man," I said to Marcus before turning to Carmen. "Cheers!" I tossed my head back to down the sweet and sour shot and she followed suit.

This happened at around 7:30 p.m.

Carmen and I chatted a little longer. I remember still tasting the Applejack shot on my lips about the same time I suddenly felt completely drunk.

After that? Absolutely nothing… My memory is completely blank.

My entire existence kick-started at 7:00 a.m. the next morning when my eyes slowly opened to the light of day. I was home; I was face-down on my couch nestled up to a pool of vomit that had overflowed the edge of the couch cushion and onto the floor. I was still dressed in the same clothes I had golfed in, but they were in a serious state of dishevel now. All I could do was lay there motionless as I tried to gather my wits.

As the room spun around me, I was frightened and confused. It must have been twenty minutes before I mustered the energy to lift my pounding head off the couch. It was even longer before I was able to pull my aching body up to a sitting position. When I finally felt confident enough that my current disposition could handle it, I tried to stand up. It was like I had vertigo—like I'd forgotten how to walk, let alone stand on my own two feet. I bumped into furniture as I stumbled to the bathroom, fell to the floor by the toilet, and proceeded to vomit uncontrollably for several minutes.

This had *never* happened to me before. I was a seasoned drinker and knew beyond a shadow of a doubt that this was far removed from my typical physical response to a day of casual drinking. I seriously thought I was going to die. For lack of a better description, I compare how I felt to what I'd imagine it would be like at ground zero of a nuke attack—obliterated.

I was genuinely concerned for my life at that point and decided I needed to call 9-1-1, but every time I picked up the phone to start dialing, I couldn't bring myself to follow through. What was I going to say to my buddies on the rescue squad when they responded? I couldn't fathom my condition being anything other than a self-inflicted hangover, and who would believe anything else? They all knew I was out the day before drinking and playing golf.

Despite feeling like this eclipsed a common hangover, and though I practiced many explanations in my head, "Hey, yeah, this is Scott—I need an ambulance because I got blitzed last night," was the only way this situation would read to them.

I made it back to the still-soiled sofa and continued trying to force my addled brain to find reason in this whole thing. I couldn't.

Instead, a sense of shame set in, coupled with complete despair that I let myself get to the point where I would blackout. There was no significant reason to do so, either. I had been chatting with a beautiful woman, respectfully, that was reason enough to maintain my composure. Despite that, I must have blown right past the finish line because I couldn't remember a damn thing beyond the few shaky laughs that followed the Applejack shot...

Every other time in my life, I've handled alcohol like a champ. I had never before, or since this happened, continued to consume alcohol to a point where I completely lost track of time, memory, or my wits in general—ever.

I laid back helplessly on the sofa, my fingers trying to massage out the nails driven into my temples when suddenly, my anxiety soared—*how in the hell did I get home?*

As shitty as I felt, this thought jolted my gray matter back into action—I needed to know how I arrived home to pass out on my couch. Was my car out there in my driveway? I was sure I didn't want it to be, but was it?

If it wasn't there, where would I find it, and who brought me home? If it was there, how could I have driven it in such a condition when I don't even remember the night?

With new motivation and nauseating effort, I crawled slowly on my hands and knees—stopping twice to retch—to the window overlooking the driveway. I took a moment to calm myself and settle the mess trying to rise from my stomach, then strained to get my eyes open just enough to look out the window.

There it was—my car.

If I hadn't been so dehydrated, I might have started to cry at the sight of it. It was parked in my driveway, but in a place I had never parked it before. I panicked. I felt like such a hypocrite—quite possibly the worst human being alive. An officer of the law since before I was even legal to drink. A man who loved, respected, and never broke the laws he was sworn to uphold, had driven himself home in a state of total and utter inebriation with no recollection of doing so.

With a great amount of effort, I staggered to my feet and slowly made my way outside to investigate.

The doors were unlocked and the keys in the ignition. The seat was also pushed back way farther than usual. If I had driven with it set there, I wouldn't have been able to see over the dash as I stretched in an effort to reach the pedals. Did someone else drive me home? I didn't know.

My heart sunk and I assumed the worst as I walked around each side of the vehicle to carefully inspect it bumper to bumper. I prayed to God I wouldn't find any signs that I—or whoever was driving—had hit something or somebody.

After I made my full circle around the car and found nothing out of sorts, I dropped to my knees and emptied my stomach all over the driveway. There was no holding it back.

Thank God I hadn't dialed 9-1-1. They would have seen my car in the driveway. They would have seen the vomit on my couch, my disheveled clothing... I smelled like death.

I would be fired.

This was *not* me, this was not who I was or how I would ever conduct myself. If I had found any damage, that alone would have changed everything for me. It could have meant I'd struck someone, it could have meant my fellow officers were on their way to arrest me without me ever making that 9-1-1 call.

I thanked God; I counted my blessings, but I still couldn't fathom what could have possessed me to drive that car home.

Even more slowly than I'd made my way out, I shuffled back into the house and crumpled onto the couch. The room was spinning like a merry-go-round, and I had never felt so sick in my entire life.

With great, exhausting effort, I found and placed a large bucket on the floor near my head. I was too dizzy and disoriented to find the bathroom. I tried to sleep between bouts of violent projectile vomiting. I wasn't able to get up till later that evening and didn't feel normal again for at least two days after.

Sometime that evening, I mustered up enough energy to call Skinny. "Hey, man." I sounded pretty rough and I knew it. "Do you know what the hell happened to me last night?"

"No, dude, are you okay? You sound like shit!"

Thanks buddy, thanks. "Yeah, I feel worse than I sound, trust me. You didn't notice anything weird about me last night? Do you know what time I left or how I got home?"

He told me I had indeed been acting strange and appeared to be totally drunk, but he didn't really elaborate on that, and I didn't have the sense at that point to dig any deeper.

"I have no idea what time you left. One second you were there and the next you were gone. You disappeared into thin air, man."

Oh God, I wished I actually had. I bet disappearing into thin air involved way less vomiting.

Skinny had no idea how I got home and had simply assumed I'd caught a ride with someone. I'd had enough of the conversation… I was sickened by my actions. I hung up with Skinny.

I felt even more ashamed, embarrassed, and confused by the fact that even Skinny had no idea what happened to me. I had—it seemed there was no other explanation—driven myself home in a darkened daze.

And, through my conversation with Sasha, had finally come to realize (even though I'd still made some horrible mistakes that night) I had likely been drugged—very probably. There was a good chance it wasn't me drinking to excess despite never having done anything remotely like it before. What I went through and how I had felt paralleled what Sasha described going through.

I thought I'd had a moment of complete weakness—I had made up my mind that I wasn't ever going to tell anyone about how I'd created such a potentially dangerous and uncharacteristic situation.

Hearing Sasha's story lifted a thousand pounds off my chest, but it also opened up my mind to a whole new world of worry, wonder, and something entirely new to this experience…anger.

Pulsing, vile, and vicious anger.

No time to process the feelings right now, I had a fellow victim waiting for me down the hall in the backroom of the Ten O'One Club. I would have to revisit this part of my past after I finished hearing Sasha out. I was there for her and the other victims—I'd have time later to include myself on that list.

I splashed water on my face, dried off, and glanced at myself in the mirror for a moment or two. I was fine. Totally fine. Well, I could feign being fine.

When I returned, I found Sasha had gone back to the case against the wall to grab that second bottle of beer. She was taking a swig as I sat down. "So sorry about the interruption," I said. "Please, when you're ready, carry on."

She picked up her story where she'd left off before my hasty retreat to the restroom. "When my vision finally came into focus, I noticed a blinking red light. It seemed to be coming from a chair across the room. It took me a few minutes, but I mustered the strength to get out of bed. I could hardly walk, and it took everything in me not to throw up. I pushed aside some clothes and found the blinking light was from a video camera. I didn't think twice. I ejected the tape, got dressed as fast as I could in my condition, and got the fuck out of there while that asshole was still in the shower."

Now, a videotape directly translated into one delightfully exciting thing—proof. Oh man, do I ever *love* proof. It's the bread and butter of this racket; without it, every case hits a stone wall.

The timing wasn't right to ask her if the tape was still in her possession, so I made a mental note to bring it up at a more appropriate time. I desperately wanted to get my hands on it and get it registered as evidence, but I was willing to be patient.

I refocused my attention on Sasha as she explained how she left without incident from the back entrance that led through the apartment's garage. She spent the rest of Tuesday ill, like I had been; the videotape entirely disregarded until Wednesday morning.

"When I finally popped that tape into my VCR and started watching, I was horrified. It was horrifying to watch." Her chest heaved with a sob, and I could tell she was pinching back tears.

My own chest was tight with anxiety. I was genuinely afraid of what I was going to hear.

"Do you want to take a break?" I asked. I would have understood if she did, but hoped it wasn't necessary.

"No, no, I'm fine. Thanks." She sniffled and carried on. She described how she watched as he dragged her from the bathroom to his room clothed in nothing but her underwear. "I looked like I was awake, but I had absolutely zero recollection of what I was seeing."

Once Marcus got her to his room, he slipped his forearms under her armpits and lifted her onto the edge of the bed, where she immediately started to teeter forward. "It was so hard watching myself fall face-first to the floor. God it was hard. And you know what that asshole did?" She nearly spit her next words. "He fucking laughed. I laid there, face down on his goddamned floor, and he laughed and told me to get up and get into bed."

She heard herself saying, "No, I'm sick. I want to lay on the floor." She had pleaded with him to leave her there on the floor, but he finally picked her up and placed her on the bed.

She told me she'd watched as she curled into the fetal position, her eyes already closed, and appeared to finally slip into unconsciousness. Marcus climbed into bed to lay beside her and turned on the TV.

In complete disbelief, I listened as she told me how, every few minutes, he'd glance over at her, prod her and ask her if she was awake, but she was totally unresponsive. After about twenty minutes of that, he got up and left the room only to return twenty minutes later, completely naked.

"I couldn't believe what I was seeing. It was shocking but I couldn't peel my eyes from the screen," she said as she stood, grabbed the ashtray, and walked the couple of feet to dump its contents into the trash. Sasha half-tossed it back onto the table, which scattered the remaining ashes onto the already dirty table.

She lit a cigarette and said, "Marcus turned me over onto my stomach and damn near ripped off my underwear. Then he stood over me, spit on his hand and started rubbing his genitals. Oh God, I don't know if I can do this. Shit, this is hard."

She took a long drag and closed her eyes before continuing, like it was easier to pretend I wasn't in the room. "Once he was, you know, aroused, he spread my legs and started having sex with me."

"Oh, Sasha, I'm so sorry," I said. Detectives are trained to be expert listeners and keep our emotions out of cases; however, as she anguished in the story, I couldn't help but unleash some emotion. Bottled up, it would have burst out, so I let more than a few tears slip as she spoke. She wouldn't have noticed anyway, she had yet to make eye contact with me.

I honestly couldn't even imagine how she felt. How could I? It wasn't the first time I'd heard a recount of a rape victim's experience, but nothing about hearing the details could ever truly allow me to relate. My heart ached for her though—truly and thoroughly.

She had continued to watch as Marcus's assault went on for about fifteen minutes. "I saw myself flash into consciousness long enough to demand that he stop. That happened a bunch of times, but he completely disregarded me. Eventually, he rolled me over on to my back and kept at it. In the video, my eyes are closed, but I can hear myself repeat over and over 'No, I don't want to do this,' but that's not even the worst of it, trust me."

I remember thinking as I listened, *how could this get worse?*

Sasha said, her voice cracking, that she watched herself helplessly try to slap him away, but Marcus easily grabbed her arms and held them down.

She struggled, managing to free an arm. She reached over to the nightstand, where her hand fell on his alarm clock. Grabbing it, she tried to hit Marcus, but he snatched it from her, retaliating by striking her in the head with it.

"I trusted him, you know? There wasn't anything serious between us, but we'd been having a lot of fun together. I was perfectly happy being intimate with him—" Sasha leaned forward to rest her elbows on her knees and put her face in her hands. She remained that way for a moment to collect herself, and I waited patiently for her to continue. I would have understood if her emotions overflowed. She had suffered the ultimate betrayal.

She lifted her head, and I could see her eyes swell. "It's my turn for a bathroom break," she said. "I'll be right back." She stood and left the room.

I wandered back out to the front of the bar to grab a glass of water, using the time to process everything she'd told me. I was exhausted, and I could tell she was as well, but if she was willing to continue, I was going to listen.

I felt so stupid for taking this case to make sure my "friend" would be treated fairly. Marcus was nothing like the man I thought he was. I knew he was a player, and while that behavior might be asinine, it isn't criminal. I was starting to realize he clearly had deep-rooted power and control issues that needed to be addressed before more women were hurt.

The thought of having video evidence of the assault was what kept me from totally falling apart through the remainder of Sasha's story. I was extremely curious to find out if he had taped the other women. If they had been in any kind of similar state as Sasha, they more than likely wouldn't have noticed. Either way, it seemed like a slam dunk if I could get my hands on that tape.

Given the fact that Sasha (who was now my best potential witness) had started her whole dialogue by insisting she didn't want to get involved, I knew it was going to be a challenge to change her mind. I also had no choice.

I returned to the backroom and waited. Sasha eventually came back into the room; her eyes were bloodshot and her nose was red. She'd clearly let loose some emotion, and I admired her for doing so, but even more so for coming back strong enough to continue talking with me.

"Are you okay to continue, Sasha?" I asked, hopefully looking as concerned for her well-being as I felt. I'd developed a bit of a poker face over the years—something my wife reminds me of often. "Also, and I hate to sound insensitive, but do you still have the videotape?"

"No. I destroyed it and never talked to that son of a bitch, Marcus, again." She tilted her head back to take a sip of beer, half-slammed the bottle down on the table, then ran a hand through her hair.

Hmmm...

Whether she had truly destroyed the videotape or not, I didn't know, but her body language strongly suggested there was more to this story than what I'd heard so far.

I had been an officer for about ten years by this time and had developed a pretty good sense of when people were lying to me. I was damn near a polygraph, so I was almost certain this feisty young woman wouldn't have just let this rest that easy. Others might have been too afraid to confront their assailant, but I didn't feel like Sasha was one of those people. Under the circumstances, I decided it was best to acknowledge her response as if I believed it, so I brought the conversation around to the other victims I had recently spoken to.

"You know I sympathize with you, I really do. I can definitely understand where you're coming from, but there have been other victims, and they don't have nearly the story that you do... What you have to say could help bring justice to them as well. Wouldn't that be worth it?" I pleaded.

She was looking down at her feet as she nodded her understanding. Then, for the first time, she raised her eyes to meet mine, and said, "I just can't do it. I've moved on. I've worked so hard to forget the pain—I'm trying to trust people again..."

It all made sense to me but there had to be more I could do to get her to understand how badly I needed her to help me, so I could help her and the other women. As much as I knew how devastating it was for her to divulge this information to me, I had to dig deeper into her pain.

"I get it, Sasha. Has anyone else seen the video?"

She averted her gaze and looked back down at her feet, took another deep breath, then said, "Yes."

I knew there had to be more to this story, and I hoped, just maybe, I could get enough information or evidence to prove something.

She lit up another cigarette—I'd lost count of how many she'd had— and explained that she'd showed her mother, JoAnn.

"My mom and I are really close, and as hard as it was for both of us, we thought it was best if she watched it. She was furious and said I should bring it to a lawyer."

"A lawyer? Why a lawyer and not the police?" I asked. I was genuinely puzzled by the choice.

"She thought a lawyer might be able to tell us if there was some civil legal action I could take against Marcus. So that's what I did."

Sasha took the tape to an attorney by the name of Warren Wanezek, and showed him the tape. "He said he'd look into what kind of legal action I could take and call me back."

"And did he?" I only half-heard her response; the knowledge that I could possibly have two other witnesses to what was on that videotape was at least something good. It lessened the impact if she had destroyed the evidence… but that led me to ask my next question.

"Why did you destroy the tape? I don't really understand that. Could you explain your reasoning to me?"

"Yeah, I can." Within that two-week period of waiting for Wanezek to get back to her, Sasha found out she was pregnant with Marcus's baby. "I was devastated, and so angry. God, I was angry!" She clenched her teeth as she said it. "I had to confront him because there was no way I was going to have his baby."

Marcus made a deal with Sasha to pay for an abortion, as well as an additional amount of money, with the understanding that the two would destroy the videotape together. Sasha had already decided not to pursue civil charges—she was too overwhelmed by her financial situation at the time, never mind what she was going through personally.

With a soft, cracking voice she said, "I went ahead with the abortion, and a few days later, Marcus and I met up and destroyed the videotape together with a hammer."

I let out an audible sigh. I probably shouldn't have because it put Sasha on the defensive, and that's not what I wanted.

"He was threatening me, Scott. He was also really damn worried that I'd made a copy of the tape."

"Sorry, Sasha, sometimes the copper in me can't be tucked down, and the destruction of evidence makes me cringe. It's a knee-jerk reaction."

She seemed to understand that reasoning.

"So, did *you* make a copy of the video?"

"No," she said bluntly.

Sasha and Marcus went their separate ways and hadn't spoken since.

I believed every word of what she said and prayed I could convince her to allow me to tell the story. Sasha was a very proud and independent woman and insisted she wouldn't relive this terrible moment in her life ever again, especially in what could be a packed courtroom. She didn't see it the way I did, though—Marcus needed to be held accountable for raping her and the others. I wasn't all that optimistic I'd be able to change her mind, especially right after retelling the horrible and tragically emotional story that left us both seeing through glossy eyes and drained, so I'd leave her alone for today.

"Sasha, thank you for talking to me. I know it was hard."

"It's more than hard, Scott. It's reliving it, and I can't keep doing it."

"You know, if—" I hesitated, "if you never want to speak it out loud again, you could write an official statement for me. It would be immensely helpful, and it might be a way for me to keep you off the stand when this goes to trial. Could you do that for me?" I wasn't so sure I could keep that promise, but my request was absolutely sincere. With her sworn statement in hand, she might never have to talk about this again...

"Yeah, deal." She stood and gestured toward the door.

I nodded my understanding and slid past her to make my way down the hall and back to the front of the bar. Depositing my empty glass on the shiny bar top, I thanked Sasha once more, and made my way out of the club.

CHAPTER 8

I SEE WHAT YOU DID THERE. . .

AKA YOU *REALLY* SHOULDN'T HAVE

Sasha had agreed to write up a statement, so, for the time being, I could nestle everything I'd just heard into my little brain database. She had also shared her mother's information, as well as the lawyer's, so once I had her statement, I'd call on both of them. I'd be able to reprocess from every angle and consider every nuance of her story—a couple of days, she'd said.

Until then, I needed to try and wrap my brain around the fact that I was positive I had also been a victim of Marcus's. A victim...not like Sasha, or Alisa, or Sarah...but still a victim.

The thought instantly angered me. I had been drugged. *I* had been drugged by *Marcus*!

I hopped in my car to make my way home. As I drove, I let all sorts of feelings and realizations seethe through my mind. The feeling of surety that my "friend" had done this to me didn't sit well at all. No human being—especially not one that prided himself on never exposing his body to, or experimenting with, any kind of illicit drug—would be okay with this knowledge. Beyond that, whatever the hell that shit he fed me was, it made me disregard every rule and value I took professional pride in. So, yeah, I was mad as hell.

What if I *had* hit someone when I drove home under its influence—what would have happened to me if I'd done that? Or worse yet, what if

I'd *killed* someone? What would have happened to my family if I'd killed myself? My boys relied on me, and they would need me as they grew...

I was so agitated by the "what-ifs" that my heart started to race, and I broke into a sweat. I had to pull over—I couldn't even see straight anymore.

I put the car in park and just sat there; my hands wrapped so tight around the steering wheel the blood had drained from my fingers. I couldn't fathom how I'd even begin calming down because I couldn't stop one thought from bleeding into the next.

I had run that night through my head thousands of times since its inception, and no matter how hard my synapses were firing, I always concluded it was my fault. Even though, characteristically, it didn't make any goddamned sense, I'd never considered it had been anything other than *my* serious lack of judgement. Just a one-time thing, you know? That one get-out-of-jail-free card—

Or, more dramatically, "Hurry, hurry, hurry! Get your tickets here, folks! For one night only, Investigator Schermitzler completely loses his mind! Don't miss out on this single show extravaganza! A nickel for adults and a penny for the kids. Hurry, hurry, hurry!"

I just wanted to scream. I wanted to pummel Marcus despite knowing it wouldn't do me any good.

I'd spent the last year avoiding alcohol. The occasional relaxing beer was as far as I would go out of fear I might blackout again. I was eventually able to forgive myself just enough to suppress the emotional and mental stress of the event. I was even able to persuade myself to believe it was best to just try and forget the whole thing, since no one had been hurt.

I could relate, in a considerably different way, of course, to what it felt like for Sasha to retell her story after all the work she had put into healing herself.

The foremost question at this juncture was...why the hell had he given me a shot of his secret potion, and what the hell *was* his secret potion? It had damn near killed me!

It was baffling that he'd even risk drugging me; not only did I think he was my friend, but I'm a cop! You've got to have either one hell of a superiority complex, or be a full-on gangster to take the risk of drugging a cop. If he'd do something like that to satisfy his selfish deviant needs and get his fix of dominance, then there was a chance I was dealing with a full-on psychopath.

Was I drugged intentionally or was it accidental? Had he intended it for Carmen? As I'd mentioned before, I wasn't looking to hook up with her, but that doesn't mean my easy chemistry with her didn't intimidate Marcus. He didn't know what my intentions were—although, man to man, he could have asked me. Maybe my intentions didn't matter. I could have been a threat to a very-well thought out plan in which Carmen was to be the key player in a night of semiconscious, forced, sexual debauchery.

The thought made me nauseous. I leaned forward and placed my forehead on the steering wheel to breathe through it.

I hadn't spoken to Carmen since that night, and, at that point, I couldn't remember what her name was, so I wouldn't even know how to find her. Had Marcus got to her as soon as I was out of the way?

For whatever reason, I automatically started to feel like I'd let her down. I should have known that if anything had happened to her it wasn't my fault, but the guilt in that moment was overwhelming. I needed to find her. I added finding the golf pro to my list of priorities in this investigation.

The thing is…I never did put all that much effort into finding her.

Throughout the entire case, and for many, many years afterward, too, I thought often about trying to track her down, but I never did actively look for her. I don't really know why. Maybe it was a fear of finding out the truth. I was sure I'd been drugged, but it wasn't until years later the fact was totally confirmed for me.

I found the golf pro, Carmen, years later, sometime in the spring of 2018. We chatted about the case and this book, and I asked her what happened to her the night of the golf tournament.

Her answer? "Nothing happened to me! My buddy, Bill, on the other hand, thought he was gonna die."

"Oh? How's that?" I asked.

"He called me the next morning and wondered how he got home and said he was so sick he could hardly get outta bed. He wondered what I'd been giving him the night before."

"Holy shit! I had the same thing happen to me that night," I declared. I couldn't believe what I'd just heard. "But why would he think you had anything to do with it?" My attention was extremely piqued.

"Well, I was prepping for a tournament, so I wasn't drinking much that night. Marcus kept bringing me shots, and I didn't want them, so I kept passing them on to Bill."

"Oh, hell. The other girl I was with there had the same experience as Bill. I passed her some of the drinks Marcus made for me, too, and the next day, she thought she was going to die she was so sick."

I had always known there was no way I had overshot my limit and completely lost hours of my life with alcohol. To hear that others had the same experience, well, I'm sorry they did, but damn, was I ever glad to hear it, too. It made all the difference in the world to know the truth. I suffered deeply for a very long time to get to this truth, and I regret not looking for Carmen sooner.

It might not make all that much sense to the average person, but for a very long time, I was incredibly embarrassed at the thought of having to tell my story. To reveal my experience to Sasha, I would have also had to disclose personal details to her, and that scared me. What if she went to my superiors about me driving home?

I was a hypocritical coward. I wanted Alisa, Theresa, Sarah, and Sasha to dig deep and tell their stories so Marcus could be thrown in the clink, but *I* wasn't willing to share my own out loud? This definitely ate at my soul and caused a lot of emotional strife and turmoil in my life for several years— which is a whole different story in itself.

In the end, I was able to draw some comfort from the fact that Carmen didn't report anything before, during, or after Marcus's high-profile case. She probably hadn't suffered at the scumbag's hands on that August evening.

As I sat there in my car, finally able to settle my heart rate, I decided I might not ever know if drugging me was Marcus's true intention. Was I his intended target or just the unfortunate loser of an involuntary game of Russian Roulette? Maybe that unlucky 50/50 pick in shots was what saved that young lady from being Marcus's next victim…

I put the car in drive and made my way home. I was calmer, but I wasn't done with this. Intentional or not, now that I'd figured this little tidbit out, this investigation had just gotten personal.

CHAPTER 9

CLAWING MY WAY THROUGH UTTER SENSELESSNESS. . .

AKA PIN THE TAIL ON THE PSYCHOPATH

I took the better part of the weekend off to spend some time with my boys, and did I ever need it. Things had been pretty tumultuous the last little while, and the happy distraction of unmitigated love—toddler tantrums included—rejuvenated my soul.

It had been some time since I'd had any new info or leads on Sawyer's case, but it never left the back of my mind. I played a little longer with my boys, squeezed them a little tighter, and was happy to read one more story before turning out the lights... Anything could happen to them in their future. The fact that I could outlive either one of them was all too real since Sawyer's "accident," and the thought haunted me.

It was late morning on a Sunday when I waved good-bye to my sons. They usually stayed later, but they had a birthday party or something to attend, so their mom had stopped in early to shuffle them off.

I made my way to the couch with the last cup of coffee from the pot in hand—I knew I wouldn't drink it—it was burnt and bitter, but I had poured it anyway. I was going to sit quietly, maybe read the paper or watch some football...

This repose lasted all of twenty minutes. As predicted, the cup of coffee remained untouched, I hadn't actually read more than the headline on every story in the newspaper, and I had no interest in turning on the TV. So that was that. Without the boys to distract me, my thoughts skulked back to my investigations.

I grabbed the phone and called Skinny to see if he'd thought of any more names or information for me.

"Hey, man, it's Scott. Do you have any fresh info for me?"

"Cut to the chase, why don't ya'?" Skinny laughed. "Yeah, Scott, I'm great. Thanks for asking."

I guess I could have been more subtle.

"I actually did get some info for you, and by info, I mean I talked to Clara again. I don't know how she does it, but she seems to know everyone."

I didn't care how she did it as long as she had names or information I could use. "And what did you find out from her?"

"She mentioned a girl named Lacey. Clara said she was working for Marcus a few months back, but something happened, and she quit. Clara gave me her number—you got a pen?"

Of course, I didn't. I also didn't have any paper.

I scrambled to find what I needed, and as I did so, a thought flashed into my head. "Hey, Skinny, you remember that guy that worked at My Place— uh—what's his name now...?" I lost my train of thought as soon as I saw the pen on the counter next to the fridge. Clearly, I couldn't multitask. "Oh yeah! Peter! You remember him? He worked as the day cook, remember?"

"Yeah, yeah."

"Anyway, seems like all of the women so far have mentioned the apartment above My Place, maybe he's seen something. Do you have his number?"

"Yeah, I think I do. Might as well try." He sounded disinterested. "You ready for the numbers yet?"

After I scratched the numbers onto the edge of my disregarded newspaper, I thanked Skinny and hung up. I'd give both of them a call when I got into the office on Monday.

Fast forward through pretty much that entire week—nothing happened.

I didn't get a hold of Lacey or Peter right away, but I had left messages. I wasn't all that confident my message for Peter would even get through to him as I'd left it with his dad. If he called, great, but it wasn't as important as hearing back from Lacey.

So, with my luck being what it was, I heard from Peter first.

It was Sunday, October 12, 2003, and with nothing better to do, I'd made my way to the station to try and get through some of the other petty cases on my desk. I cracked the manila on the case file of a repeat minor crime offender—a shoplifter—and settled in to read the details. Back then, there weren't cameras in every shop to keep an eye on people's every move, so most of the cases weren't as open and closed as they are nowadays. Thankfully, the universe detected my disinterest in the $250.00 worth of stolen women's delicates—the phone rang, and I snapped up the receiver fast as lightning.

Exchanging pleasantries and reminding him of who I was took no time at all, so we were down to business less than a minute in.

"So, Peter, are you still working for Marcus Somerhalder over at My Place?"

"Nope. That asshole let me go in March. Just outta the blue he told me I had three weeks to find a new job. Didn't matter, I guess; I found a job before the three weeks was up. Thank God, too. I hated working for that guy."

"Oh? Why's that?" Considering Skinny had never had an issue with the guy, and before August, I'd never had any other indication that he wasn't a standup guy and businessman, it was weird how different things looked on the other side of the mountain.

"He treated everyone like crap. He's not the guy everyone thinks he is," he said.

That piqued my interest, but I wasn't able to squeeze more information about that out of him. I didn't get anything useful from Peter. He worked Monday to Friday from 9:00 a.m. until 2:00 p.m., so if there was anyone in Marcus's apartment the night before, Peter usually saw them leaving. Most of the time, it was his current girlfriend, Serenity, but Peter assured me that Marcus was promiscuous with other women. On more than one occasion, it wasn't Serenity who descended the stairs.

He'd only ever been up to Marcus's apartment once for a staff meeting and admitted he'd never noticed any drugs or anything else unusual, and maintained that statement when he told me it was him who cleaned up all of Marcus's after hour parties down in the bar. It was also Peter's job to collect the mail, and while he could say that Marcus seemed to order a lot of stuff online, he couldn't confirm what any of it was—too bad. I would have loved for him to tell me many a sordid tale, or inform me he's ordered cases of a certain drug, video equipment, etc.

Yeah, well, damn. I could have been solving a petty crime. All I could do was thank him for his time and move on.

I still hadn't received Sasha's official statement, and I didn't want to nag her, so I was hoping I'd hear from Lacey soon. I was seeing a pattern emerge, and I wanted to find out if she was going to be another piece in the same puzzle.

I waited two more days to hear from Lacey. Luckily, I was actually at my desk, which was a rare occurrence with as many files as I had on the go, when she called.

"Hi—Investigator Shemimzer?" She muddled my name; I forgave her immediately. "This is Lacey returning your call."

"Lacey, yes, hi." I told her, like the millions before her, how to pronounce my last name, then asked her if it was okay if I record our conversation.

"Yeah, sure. I'm calling you back because I know you wanted to hear about what happened with Marcus. I heard he's going to jail or something?"

"I do want to hear your story, and I'm not sure *yet* if he's going to jail. That'll depend heavily on the kind of information and evidence I get on him."

"Yeah, okay. I don't think my story is that bad, but I've heard a few others, too."

This was already working out better than my conversation with Peter had. If she had a decent story, and if she had names she could share with me, I would be able to ramp up the investigation.

"So, let's start out with a simple question, how do you know Marcus?" With the tape recorder rolling, I sat back in my chair, and Lacey and I had a chat.

Lacey had worked for Marcus at the Velvet Room, and although I'd been there more than a few times over the last few years, I didn't have any recollection of her. She didn't say it, but it was my assumption she didn't remain working there for all that long.

"It was probably about five months ago that it happened. Marcus invited me and another coworker, Serenity, over to My Place after we closed up the Velvet Room. We figured we might as well go."

I wondered if this Serenity was the same one Peter had mentioned as Marcus's girlfriend. Five months prior would have put Lacey's story somewhere in May, which was only two months or so after Peter had been let go from My Place.

"When we got there, he'd already made us drinks and had Frank Sinatra playing over the stereo."

"Do you happen to remember what kind of drink it was? Or if anything about it tasted off?" I wondered, hoping her answer would have been "yes."

"No, I don't remember any of that, but the drink was sweet and sour—something with apple, maybe." Apple was something. Sasha and I shared apple flavor in common with our experiences. "I hadn't really drank much of anything before Serenity and I met up with Marcus, but after a couple of drinks, I felt a definite downshift."

"A downshift," I repeated. "What exactly do you mean by that?"

She told me they both started feeling "weird," so, without any incident, they went home and passed out.

The sad part is, she didn't elaborate on that, and didn't really respond when I asked her to. I don't know if she or Serenity got sick like Sasha and I had, and I assumed, because they went straight to bed, they wouldn't have suffered any kind of blackout effects. I appreciated her story, but I wasn't sure how much of it I'd be able to use.

"So, I know that isn't anything major, but Clara said I should say something anyway."

"You know Clara?"

"Doesn't everyone?" She laughed.

I laughed, too, like I knew, but I didn't.

I knew *of* Clara, but Skinny was the one who was close to her. I was glad Clara knew everyone—I made a mental note to thank her, which I promptly forgot.

To this day, I've never thanked Clara. Until recently, I hadn't realized how big a part she'd played in me finding the names of so many of the women harmed by Marcus. I built an entire case talking to the women whose names she had passed to Skinny, and I didn't even know it.

"Lacey, you said you knew of other women who've had similar run-ins with Marcus. Would you be able to enlighten me a little? If you have names, or knowledge of what they went through, it would be really helpful to the case." I tried to use my wily investigative ways to prompt her to share more information, but she was reluctant to cough up details on the other women. This only made me wonder why she'd brought them up in the first place.

I kept at her, only to hear her say she really didn't want to be involved beyond telling me her story before she proceeded to tell me that Marcus was always coming on to women.

"I can guarantee he's slept with some of his employees," she said, but again, Lacey didn't want to elaborate on that...

Needless to say, the girl was giving me whiplash.

She didn't give me any more information on Serenity, and the only other name I got out of her was an ex-employee named Abby. Lacey said the same thing that happened to her had happened to Abby. She then quit working for Marcus, and last Lacey heard, had moved to Chicago. Beyond that, she hadn't kept in touch and didn't have anything else to tell me.

Well, except...

"When I found out that Marcus had started dating Faith, I thought I should warn her about the kind of guy he was," said Lacey. "I told her not to date him and why."

"Oh? And how did that go?" I was genuinely interested, despite the gossipy undertone of the topic.

"She seemed concerned, but it did no good. She turned around and asked Marcus about it, and he ended up approaching me. He called me a liar and stated that he didn't drug me. He also told me to stay the hell out of his personal life."

I had really wanted this conversation to reveal some sort of substantial information, but all this managed to do was create more questions and confusion for me. My thoughts floated back to the original case involving Hope, the one that had been thrown out on account of it being a "he said, she said" kind of deal.

I suppose Marcus taking the time to approach her was somewhat interesting—it just wasn't useful. I probably would have said the same if I were him...

Damn.

I took what she gave me, typed it out, and slid it into the file with the rest of the information I had collected so far. I was certain I could pin him to the wall with Sasha, Theresa, and Sarah's stories, but for all I'd been hearing, I still didn't have any truly credible proof.

The rest of October moved along at a snail's pace. I didn't have anywhere near enough evidence to get an arrest warrant issued, but I also had an extremely strong feeling there was a lot more to the case than what I had. I continued to do as much subtle digging as I could and was getting tips on Marcus a few times a week.

It seemed word had gotten out that there was an investigation going on, so I was able to connect with many of the women who had their own stories about Marcus. I can't even remember all of their names. Not that they weren't important because every single one of them was, and they deserved to be heard, but they didn't have the kind of information I was able to document. It didn't hurt to talk to as many people as I could, but I still had to be careful and keep things as low-key as I could. It remained a priority that Marcus *not* find out he was the eye of the storm. Although, I often wonder how it was that he didn't find out...

Actually, who cares?

As it goes when you're an investigator, you're not going to solve the case if you don't have a clear outline and line of vision on the whole case. You need to know what happened that forced your services to be required, then you need to build around it. What came before I got involved? What will his next steps be?

The hardest part is trying to get into the person of interest's head. Some-times it's easy to find their motivation because it's a simple response like anger, revenge, or jealousy—you know, the common instigations. Other times, you have to dig deeper into their psyche. Sometimes there isn't a reason other than they're bat-shit crazy. I've felt an astronomical amount of shame and disgust even trying to slip into those troubled heads. It's hard to think like a psychopath—it leaves its mark, I assure you.

It's all part of the job, though. I think we've all got to be a little bonkers in this line of work, or nothing would ever get done.

I'd started to string together a bit of a timeline to try to figure out what the hell Marcus had been doing, when he had been doing it, and who he had been doing it to.

Think back on all those TV shows and movies where the camera pans out on a wall of pictures, files, and notes connected by bits of string, and you'll know what I mean. It's exactly like that. I still had yet to figure out what his motivation was, but the closer I looked, the thicker the line drawn to "psychopath" became.

The timeline I had come up with revealed one major thing—it was full of holes.

I was missing a heck of a lot of the overall story. I had an idea of where it started and ended, but I was missing chapter after chapter in between.

Based on my best calculations, the golf tournament I got drugged at in August of that year was smack-dab in the middle of it all. My version started with Theresa, who I was certain wasn't drugged before she was sexually assaulted, and ended with Alisa, who had most definitely been drugged. At least, I hope it ended with Alisa.

This led me to believe Marcus had begun his predatory sexual escapades by trying to get the girl so drunk she would pass out deeply enough for him to assault her uninterrupted. Unfortunately for him, it didn't work, and Theresa woke up multiple times.

Hope from the original case that was thrown out—to make a woman pass out as thoroughly as she had, he must have started dabbling in drugging his victims. She didn't wake up once and had no memory of her assault. That knowledge created such vast complications in the case.

First of all, at the time, there were more than thirty separate substances that qualified as "date-rape" drugs, and all of them nearly impossible to detect. By the time a victim made it to a hospital to report an assault, even if there were residual physical effects being felt, the drug wouldn't register in blood tests. So, finding which one Marcus was using was going to be a shit-show, and I didn't have the knowledge or means to figure it out on my own.

The idea that he was using substances to subdue his victims also outlined a potentially bigger picture. If he had been drugging people, had he accidentally overdosed anyone? I strongly felt like I had been close—I thought I was going to die! What if he *had* gone too far? What if the deep feeling that there was more to this led me to a trail of bodies? This case was already so heart-wrenching...

The manila file was getting thicker by the day—too much of it with speculative notes and unsubstantiated suspicions—I needed to get some answers.

The entire month of October in 2003 had been one of the most tumultuous months I had ever experienced from a professional standpoint. Even though I had collected all sorts of information on Marcus's case, and closed a few of the ones that had been cluttering my desk, I still felt I was treading water to stay afloat.

At least there had been a minor shift in Sawyer's case. It wasn't enough for me to make any movement on it, but I updated the case file with the new information anyway. I'd take what I could get.

As it goes, an officer interviewed a guy by the name of Chris who told him that on September 3, 2003, he was in the passenger seat of Teshia's car when she got a call from Patrick. Chris didn't go back to the house with Teshia, so he didn't know much, but said Patrick told her Sawyer had fallen down some stairs. She told Patrick to put a Band-Aid on whatever was bleeding and she would be home shortly.

This was interesting news. My version of the story was one where they had all been home at the time of the accident. I had noticed some incon-sistencies between Teshia and Patrick's stories when I had interviewed them and suspected they had colluded to hide the truth of what really happened, but I hadn't found anything to confirm they were lying. Those suspicions were part of the reason why I'd been sitting so uncomfortably on this case for almost two months instead of closing it off and letting it go.

The result of the above information was that Teshia was interviewed again, and the truth finally came out.

She hadn't been home at the time, but immediately turned her car around. When she arrived, she found Patrick in the bathroom with an unconscious Sawyer. He was splashing the toddler's face with cold water in an attempt to wake him, but it wasn't having any effect.

Teshia scooped Sawyer out of Patrick's arms, got in the car, and sped off to the ER.

Upon hearing this, I wondered why she would bother lying about that. The deception didn't make any sense to me. When told, she said it was because she was scared people would think she was a bad mother for leaving her child home with Patrick. Well, I only wished she was in front of me so I could shake her silly.

First of all, at a time like that, why the hell would she care if others saw her as a bad mom more than she cared about her own child's well-being? Secondly, if parents never trusted others with their children, they would never get a night to themselves—that first day of school would never happen. Parents all over the world would be losing their minds because everyone needs a break sometimes.

If Patrick hadn't given any reason otherwise, why wouldn't she trust him with her son?

Teshia still held firm on the certainty that Sawyer had fallen down the steps and was standing behind Patrick's account of the incident. I believed her because it felt like she was telling the truth—as she knew it at least, but it wasn't enough for me. I didn't trust there wasn't more to the story. The one thing I knew without question was that Patrick, Sawyer, and God were the only three to know exactly what happened.

I fully intended to be the fourth.

On October 29, 2003, I learned Patrick had been arrested and placed in the Brown County Jail on an unrelated probation violation.

I decided to take advantage of the situation—maybe I could shake the truth out of him. Being in the clink, he was clearly a troubled guy, but he hadn't come across as a terrible man when I'd first met him. He'd also seemed genuinely grieved when Sawyer succumbed to his injuries—maybe part of that grief was guilt? I owed it to Sawyer to find out.

I arrived at the jailhouse without knowing whether or not he would agree to talk to me. It honestly could have gone either way. If he was innocent, why wouldn't he be cool chatting with me? If he was guilty…well…maybe he was clever enough to maintain his ruse of innocence by *agreeing* to talk with me. It wouldn't have been proof of anything if he had refused to talk, either. Serial criminals were usually pretty astute to the fact that I wasn't on their side, so none of them wanted to talk to me.

Thankfully, innocent or cleverly guilty, I was pleased to find that Patrick agreed to talk to me, *but* not about anything that had to do with Sawyer. At least, not without a lawyer present.

Well, shit.

I had no choice but to respect his rights. I left the jail but did so with the understanding that when he did have a lawyer present, I would have the opportunity to speak with him. I could handle that. It definitely complicated things for me, but I knew my way around lawyers. They can advise their clients all they want, but if the client wants to speak, they're going to.

It was later that same day when I received a call from a woman named Sonja. She was known to both Teshia and Patrick, and because the courts had ordered the couple not to talk to each other while the case was being investigated, Sonja had been acting as a go-between for them.

"Hi Investigator Schlitzer, this is Sonja."

S-c-h-e-r… Never mind.

"Sonja, yes. What's up?"

"Well, Patrick called today and said you'd visited him, but said he didn't talk to you about Sawyer. I think you should put me on Patrick's jail visitor list… I'll be able to get him to talk."

"Okay, well, I appreciate your eagerness to help, but I really don't think it's a good idea. I want you to know, we're planning on moving ahead with charges, though."

"Charges against Patrick?" The news had made her nervous; her voice became shaky.

"Well, if there are charges against Patrick, there will be charges against Teshia. They both lied to investigators about what happened."

"Yeah, yeah, sure. Okay. Thanks." She hung up before I could say good-bye, but it wasn't long before I was back on the phone with her again.

Patrick had called her, and she had shared with him the fact that charges were going to be laid and Teshia was going to go to jail if he didn't talk.

"That made him upset," she said. "He wants you to call him."

"I can't do that," I said. "He's got to be the one that calls me because he requested a lawyer be present if we talk again."

"This is so stupid! He can't get through to the station from the jailhouse!"

"Tell you what, I'll call the jailhouse. They'll ask him if he's looking to talk to me. If he is, I'll head over there. Okay?"

"Yeah, okay, that works."

I hung up and called the Brown County Jailhouse to confirm that Patrick was indeed interested in having a chat. He was. Thank you for rattling his cage, Sonja.

I arrived at the jailhouse a little after 2:00 p.m. and felt strongly that Sawyer was there with me in spirit. I hoped he was, because I was going to try like hell to get the truth.

A hulking guard escorted me to the room where Patrick was waiting, ushered me in, then took his place just outside of the door. The room was bright-white, and starkly furnished with a table and half a dozen chairs. It was perfect. In a setting like this I would see every twitch and twinge he made, which was essential to reading body language—the key to truly successful rapport building.

I grabbed the back of the chair beside his and turned it so I would be facing him while we talked, but I didn't sit right away. I waited for him to stand, which he promptly did, and shook his hand. Now we were equals, and we sat.

"So, I hear you wanted to talk to me?" I asked.

He was staring at the ground as he nodded his confirmation.

"You said earlier that you wouldn't talk without a lawyer, I want you to know that you still have the right to have one present." I thought it best to remind him so there was no confusion. This had to go off without a hitch.

"No, sir, it's cool. I'll talk."

Music to my ears. "I'm going to be recording this conversation, okay?" I stated all the necessary stuff like date, time, who I was and who I was with in the room. I then read him the Miranda Rights[2] and asked him what he wanted to say.

He was clearly tense and uncomfortable, which is never a good way to kick this sort of thing off. So, I started things out slow and led with my easy-going, laugh-it-off kind of lawman act to soften him up and get him comfortable.

Shit happens, right?

Of course it does, buddy, and every guy behind bars is innocent...

Blah, blah, blah.

Truth be told, we should get Oscars for these acts. It's necessary, but so hard, to mask the oozing sarcasm when talking to some of these people.

We talked a bit about life and sports—he was a Packers fan, of course, like everyone around here. When I felt the conversation had been easy and trivial for long enough, I nonchalantly shifted gears and brought up kids, which inevitably led to mentioning Sawyer.

Patrick's demeanor immediately changed, and the tension set back in. I could see him struggling to hold himself together, but the laughs became shakier and more forced, then dissipated altogether. Patrick gave up on the ruse, turned his gaze to the ground and fell completely silent—not so clever after all. This body language showed me he had more to say but didn't know how to say it.

"C'mon Patrick, how 'bout we cut to the chase here. What happened on September third?"

There was a short pause, then he said, "Well, Teshia wasn't there, but I think you already know that part." He was correct. The rest of the story

---

[2] *"You have the right to remain silent. Anything you say can and will be used against you in a court of law. You have the right to an attorney. If you cannot afford an attorney, one will be provided for you. Do you understand the rights I have just read to you? With these rights in mind, do you wish to speak to me?" http://www.mirandawarning.org/whatareyourmirandarights.html*

that followed was, if you can believe it, a fabrication that went something like this:

"Blah, blah, blah, then I found Sawyer at the bottom of the steps…"

Oh, no, no, no, no… I've already heard that version, *buddy*. Let's try again.

I'd conducted thousands of interviews since the inception of my career. I knew every trick in the book, but it still took some skill to ease information out of people. Everyone's different, so you have to figure out what tactic is going to work case by case.

In police work, we aren't allowed to coerce anyone; it's not morally, ethically, or legally correct, *but,* on the other hand, trickery and deceit are absolutely acceptable—go figure.

I knew without a doubt that Patrick cared deeply for Teshia and Sawyer, and I'd heard stories about him treating Sawyer as if he were his own son. Knowing his weak spot meant there was a half-decent chance Patrick would cave if he had any kind of conscience, which I think he did. So, I decided the best way to prod him would be to use Teshia's well-being and Sawyer's soul as tools.

In a soft but direct voice, I said, "You know, forensics is a very strong evidence tool, and Sawyer's injuries just don't make sense to us. It's looking like we're going to be heading to the DA's office with that information." Which was a bold-faced lie. There was no evidence, because Dr. Huntington didn't think his autopsy revealed any, but Patrick didn't have to know that.

I leaned toward him, rested one elbow on my knee and the other on the table, and began talking slowly in low tones. "Not to mention, we now know both you and Teshia lied about what happened the day of the accident. The DA isn't going to like that. When a kid's involved, things like that look pretty damn suspicious, you know?"

I sat back and folded my arms across my chest. "I don't know what to tell you, man. With the inconsistencies and the severity of the injuries… they might try and nail you and Teshia to the wall."

Patrick was chewing his fingernails to the quick as his right leg rapidly bounced up and down with nervous energy. It was easy to tell he was very stressed about what I'd just said. I could see the concern on his face, but he didn't say a word.

I pressed on.

"There are only three people who really know what happened that day: You, Sawyer, and God. You can just bet those two have talked. Are you at all worried about your immortal soul, Patrick?" It was dramatic, but I didn't think it was overly so. "With how the evidence is coming together, I'm pretty sure I'm the fourth man in on it. I think I know what happened as well."

I kept talking and he kept his head down, his eyes fixed on the floor. Occasionally he'd nod his head, as if to agree with me, and a few times I even heard him mutter, "Yessir." I was getting through, which meant I'd found his kryptonite. It was only a matter of time before he'd be spilling his guts.

I continued to downplay the incident as if it had simply been a terrible accident and explained how kids that age just push parents past the limit of sensibility. Sometimes we can't handle it anymore; sometimes we just lose our shit.

"You know, Patrick, there's one thing I know, and you gotta trust me on this—" I leaned forward to try and get him to raise his head and look me in the eye, but no dice. "If I don't get the real story from you now, and they have to dig it out of you while you're on the stand—and trust me, they will—you're going to be in a world of trouble. They'll see that as resistance. They'll say you have no compassion and might even suggest any remorse is purely an act...you don't want that."

Finally, he looked up at me and spoke. "I do feel bad though. I feel awful."

"Based on the lies and the inconsistencies in your stories, what else would they think other than you did it on purpose? They'll try and drag Teshia down, too..."

He was extremely uncomfortable, and I knew I was on the verge of getting him to open up.

"I know you loved Sawyer and you never wanted this to happen, but it did. In honor of him—so you and him can both be at peace—tell me the real story."

Patrick had turned and fixed his stare on the table, his chin rested on his chest, and his fingers interlaced in front of him. He sniffled and I watched a tear slip down his cheek. I was so close… One more time, I said, "It was just an accident—"

"Look, stop, okay?" He interrupted me and lifted his head back up to face me. "I don't know about all this other shit, but I shook him, okay?"

Finally!

"I shook him, then put him down kinda roughly. He landed on his feet, but he didn't stay up."

"What do you mean?" I asked.

"I mean, he fell face first to the floor. He hit so hard."

There it was. The truth. Patrick sulked tearfully—obviously remorseful, but it didn't change the fact that he had brutally killed an innocent and defenseless child.

I believe Patrick admitted to his terrible mistake for the sake of Sawyer and his family, but I think it was for his own benefit, too. I truly don't think Patrick could've lived with this on his conscience for very long, a testament to the fact that despite this horrific act, he wasn't a terrible man.

After getting the confession, I wanted to hear as much as I could. The more I had, the more solid the case would be, and I thought it was important for them to get a clear idea of the kind of person Patrick was.

I tried to comfort him. "I know you didn't mean to hurt him." My empathy wasn't an act, and I think he could tell I was being genuine, so he kept on talking and elaborating on the incident.

"I *really* didn't mean to hurt him, but he was yelling and screaming and throwing a fit. You can't even think when they do that, you know?"

I did know and nodded in agreement.

He had his head in his hands, and I could hear the devastation in his voice. "I couldn't stand it anymore, so I grabbed him by the shoulders and just shook him hard a few times."

"What happened next, Patrick?" I was trying to hide the heaving in my chest, but it was making it difficult to breathe—I felt like I was going to burst. I don't know how I did it, but I maintained my composure—I was there to find the truth for Sawyer and that was bigger than anything I felt.

"I waited about fifteen minutes for him to wake-up, but he didn't. I panicked. I called Teshia, then I brought him to the bathroom. When she got home, we put him in the car and brought him to the hospital."

"Why didn't you call an ambulance?"

"I was just so scared, man. I just kept hoping he'd snap out of it, you know?"

I did not. I would have called an ambulance. "So, does Teshia know this version of the story?"

"No. She never questioned my story, so I never told her what really happened. I'm the only one who knew...like you said: Sawyer, me, and God. Now you."

As much as I wanted to hate Patrick for the devastation he'd caused, I appreciated that he'd come clean, and I made sure to let him know. He knew he'd made a critical mistake but at least he was willing to take responsibility for his actions.

I think back on the times in my life (most of them in my first twenty or so years) when I ran with a lie instead of telling the truth. I remember how it felt, too. I don't think a single one of those lies would have had any major impact on my life if I'd just admitted to them, but I still opted to fib rather than come clean.

I'd work through it in my head fabricating the lie and perfecting how I'd tell it, but it would eat at me and eat at me... I was always so afraid of being caught, though, so I'd eventually fess up. Every confession was either quickly forgiven or turned into another episode of "good cop/bad cop" with Mom and Dad, but I never came out of it worse for wear.

Anyway, *most* of us eventually have to take responsibility for our actions. Whether it be on judgment day—if you believe in that kind of thing—or simply because our strength of character won't let us get away with the lie. We either fess up, forgive ourselves, or pray for divine forgiveness. I suppose tucking it deep down to be forever lost in the body and soul is an option, too, but not one I could personally ever handle. The truth has always set me free, I guess.

I let Patrick know that I was going to get his statement into the district attorney and assured him they wouldn't delay in letting him know how things were going to go down.

When we finished our chat, I stated officially into the recorder that I hadn't coerced Patrick or promised him anything for his statement, then clicked it off. Once again, I stood and extended a hand to shake. Patrick rose slowly, squared his shoulders, and shook my hand. He must have known his confession was going to ensure he spent a significant amount of time behind bars, but he still seemed more relaxed compared to when I'd arrived. Obviously, it hadn't been the thought of going to jail weighing on him.

I rapped on the door to let the guard know I was ready to be let out, and as I made my way out of the jailhouse, I felt such a strong sense of accomplishment. I had kept my promise to Sawyer, and I was certain he was at peace knowing the truth was told.

*　　*　　*

As soon as I arrived back at my desk, I took great pleasure in contacting Dr. Huntington's office about my findings. This might seem a little bit like I was rubbing it in his face, and yeah, it definitely was that, but there was more to it.

The good doctor, despite the findings being right in front of him, completely wrote off the idea that Sawyer's death was anything other than accidental. In doing so, he very nearly closed a case and allowed a killer—no matter if he was an unintentional one—to get away with this heinous crime. Maybe it was what he'd need to hear so he wouldn't be so quick to jump to conclusions the next time he examined a potential child abuse victim. That was my hope, at least.

News about Patrick's confession spread fast with a lot of people not believing it had even happened. Confessions are difficult to attain even in the best of circumstances, and even more so once people are incarcerated. Thankfully, I had the recording and had quickly registered it as evidence—right after calling Dr. Huntington's office, of course.

Sharing the news within the station and Dr. Huntington's office was triumphant but also realizing how hard it was going to be to tell Teshia sobered my celebratory spirit right quick. She cared deeply about Patrick and fully trusted him when he said Sawyer had fallen down the stairs. I worried that hearing the truth, while already mourning such a deep loss, was going to be absolutely devastating for Teshia. I dreaded the conversation, but it had to happen.

Teshia made a beautiful choice in asking her family to be with her when I revealed the truth about how Sawyer had become so badly injured. There were so many different emotions in the room. Some of them were definitely angry and others seemed shocked at the news. Few of them had known Patrick very well, but none of them had suspected he was capable of this sort of thing.

It was so difficult to be there, and I felt so very out of place as they calmed and comforted each other. There was nothing I could say in the way of condolences that would make any impact on what they were feeling, so I sat for a short time in quiet respect, then took my leave.

In time, the family revealed how extremely grateful they were for my efforts and even invited me to his gravesite for some native heritage rituals. I still see the family around Ashwaubenon, and every time I do, I think about Sawyer and what kind of person he would have become. I know everyone who knew him during his short stay on Earth felt blessed by his presence, so the world has inevitably been a little darker since he passed on.

I wish I would have known him in life, but I feel blessed that I was able to bring true closure to his family.

I'm not sure why this universe—or God—allows children to suffer. The universe knows best, I guess, but I'm pretty sure the world would prefer to do without it. Maybe it has to do with the mumbo-jumbo that adversities make us stronger, which I guess I agree with, but I can think of a million ways to toughen up that doesn't involve kids.

CHAPTER 10

OVER AND OVER AGAIN. . .

AKA MY OVER-EXPRESSIVE EYEBROWS

With justice served for Sawyer, I felt like a new man. It was a good thing, too, because I really needed to focus on Marcus's case, and boy oh boy, was I ever ready to get going on it.

I had hoped to broaden my search for victims throughout the month of November because I knew there had to be more women out there who had suffered Marcus's perversion on one level or another. It almost seemed ridiculous that this clown hadn't been caught, processed, and thrown in jail already. Furthermore, I was officially ashamed of the fact that I had *ever* suggested he was a friend of mine.

One particular statement cinched these feelings, and it happened only a few days into November.

I'd heard Katie's name come up as a possible victim no less than half-a-dozen times since mid-October. I finally managed to secure her phone number from Skinny, who got it from Clara, of course, and I wasted no time in dialing it.

She ended up being really easy to get a hold of and was anxious but excited to tell me her story. She was certain she would have some information that would help the case, and I couldn't have been more pleased to hear that.

My interest was definitely piqued, so I was damn excited when Katie kept her word and showed up at the station at 7:15 a.m. the next morning. She was a stunning, petite blonde, and even at such an early hour, had managed to do her hair and flawlessly apply makeup. I'd washed my face and brushed my teeth before I put on my uniform—I think. Katie was another prime example of the high standard of woman Marcus chose to prey on.

She'd mentioned she had a limited time to meet with me, so before we'd even made it to the interview room, I'd broken the ice.

"I'm really glad you're here. I've been collecting data and interviewing as many women as I can so we can officially charge Marcus. I know it'll be difficult, but I'm not here to judge you; I'm just here to listen."

"Yeah." She was following close on my heels as we made our way through the halls of the station, so the sigh she let out was clearly audible. "I've never been in a police station before, and I feel badly that I didn't come sooner."

"Why's that?" Better late than never…

"Well, I feel guilty because maybe my story would have prevented other victims, you know?"

Yeah, I knew, but it didn't take away from the fact that she was here now. Her feelings of guilt weren't uncommon; in these situations, victims tend to suffer a lot of it. It's extremely difficult to convince them it's okay that they had to sort through their own experiences before they can help anyone else. We always want victims to report incidents right away, but we understand it isn't a realistic expectation. It's hard as hell to wrap your head around healing your mind because *sometimes* you don't even realize it needs healing.

A lot of victims blame themselves. No matter how traumatic the experience, they don't see themselves as victims. Instead, they internalize what happened in order to find ways in which they could have prevented the situation—the "I should have known better" stigma. There's no way for them to *truly* heal if they maintain that mindset.

When you break a leg, you go to the hospital, they throw some plaster on it, and your body takes care of the rest. There's no denying the damn thing is broken because you can't walk on it, and if you can, well, you've got one hell of a pain threshold. In the end, the bone heals and you move on from the experience.

No one *ever* says, "Well, I brought this broken leg on myself. It's my fault it happened, so I'll set it and plaster it myself and hope for the best," because that would be ridiculous. Victims of sexual assault do, though, and it's all too often a terrible by-product of the PTSD caused by their experiences. Some of them can sort through it and come to terms with the fact that it wasn't their fault; some of those achieve that by seeking help, but the rest don't even recognize they're suffering.

I felt Katie fell into the latter category. I would need to hear her story before I could say it with any real confidence.

After a few twists and turns through the halls of the station, we'd arrived at our destination. I opened the door and said, "No need to feel guilty, Katie. You're here now and that's really the most important thing. Please, have a seat." I gestured for her to enter the room, and before I followed her in, asked if she wanted anything to drink.

"I'm fine for now, thanks."

I closed the door behind us and took a seat across the table from her. The room we used for interviews (when our desks weren't at all presentable) was small and cozy with padded walls that effectively absorbed any and all extra sound. Although the room was stark, it was comfortable.

"I'm going to record this conversation. Please, begin when you're ready," I said, the room making my voice sound soothing.

"Okay, so I met Marcus sometime in the middle of August, 2002, and in the stupidest way, too."

I made note of the fact that August 2002 was when Hope, the first girl to make a formal complaint against Marcus, said her assault happened.

"I honestly don't even remember who I was trying to call, but I dialed the wrong number, and it was Marcus who picked up."

Instead of simply hanging up the phone, they started chatting and eventually decided they wanted to meet each other. Katie didn't know how old Marcus was and admitted she didn't care. She kept talking because he sounded cute and he'd promised that she and her friends, despite not being old enough to drink, could come out to the bars and drink alcohol with him and his friends. I'm sure it was an attractive offer—she took him up on it that very next weekend.

"Because it was the first time we were meeting, I asked a few of my girlfriends to come along. They were excited to have drinks in a bar, but I was more excited to meet Marcus." Katie let out a deep sigh, and I could hear the repeated "snap" as she fiddled with a button on her purse. I could see she was quickly losing confidence.

"Go on, Katie, please. Remember, I'm here to listen, not judge." She gave me a bit of a smile, so I knew she was okay to continue. "If there comes a point when you need a break, just say the word."

She nodded and thanked me, then continued. "Nothing really happened that night. We went to a bar called Ned Kelly's, then a little later he took us to the Velvet Room. When I found out Marcus was the owner of the place, I asked him if he'd give my friend Grace and me a job."

"And what did he say to that?" If he was trying to get into her pants, I doubt he'd have said no.

"He kinda laughed it off, but we didn't care; we were having a lot of fun. Marcus bought us drinks until we were thoroughly wasted, but all of us got home without any problem."

A few days later, Marcus called Katie up and asked if she and Grace wanted to join him again for drinks. When she hesitated, he told her he could get them both jobs at his bar, but they had to come out with him first. Grace couldn't go, but Katie decided she was comfortable enough hanging out with Marcus one on one, so she went alone to meet him at his bar, My Place.

"When I got there, he was already sitting at the bar. He had a drink made for me and invited me to join him."

"Do you remember what the drink was?" I asked.

"No, we started talking right away, so I didn't pay much attention to what was in my glass."

Understandable, I suppose. A little unfortunate for me, though. I would have loved for her to say it was an Applejack shot.

They had that single drink, then made their way across the street to another bar, where they played a drinking game that involved dice. Not being a seasoned drinker, she was quickly becoming tipsy. It was at that point Marcus invited her to his apartment above My Place. She didn't want the night to end, so she agreed.

By the time they got upstairs, Katie was really feeling the drinks and fully admitted she was further along than tipsy. Feeling a bit like the room was spinning, she plopped herself down on Marcus's bed. Next thing she knew, he was completely naked and roughly trying to pull off her skirt.

"At that point, I was feeling *really* drunk, so I don't remember if he got undressed in the bedroom, or what, but I knew I wasn't interested in sleeping with him. Not yet, anyway. He kept trying to get my skirt off, and he wasn't being subtle about it." Katie's voice got louder as she said, "I was trying to hold my skirt on, and he wasn't taking the hint, so I kind of flipped-out and yelled, 'No! You're not going to do that!' then rolled off the bed away from him."

Katie removed her purse from her lap to place it on the floor, and I was thankful. I wasn't sure how much longer I could have listened to her snap and unsnap that button. Unfortunately, she placed a hand on the table and began clicking her nails on the top. A small price to pay for the information, I supposed, and none of her nervous ticks overshadowed my compassion for her or her bravery for telling her story. Still, the clicking faintly reminded me of Chinese water torture. Nah, it wasn't that bad.

Despite her insistence that she was going to leave, Marcus tried desperately to get her to stay. While I'm glad she didn't, I really wish she wouldn't have told me she'd driven home while inebriated.

"I had to go."

I tried to keep my brow from furrowing as she attempted to justify her decision to get behind the wheel. "I have no doubt he would have got that skirt off and had sex with me. If I was any drunker, I can guarantee he would have got what he wanted, too, because I was barely able to fight him off as it was."

I'd failed at controlling my brow and know I was giving her a stern look. I don't think I could have wiped it off my face even if I wanted to; there's *always* a better way to get home.

She made it home safe that night and decided she would never be alone with Marcus again.

If it had been me, I would have gone a step further and never seen him again. A few days later, she and Grace agreed to meet up with Marcus at My Place for drinks. It pretty much went the same way as it had the first time around—he fed the women drinks all night, and being underage, they took full advantage of the opportunity.

At about 3:00 a.m., the trio moved their little party upstairs, where they continued drinking and doing shots on his balcony.

"It wasn't long after we got upstairs that Grace went inside and passed out on Marcus's couch. I didn't stay out there much longer, either, because I was really, really drunk, and I could hardly stand up anymore. I remember stumbling over to the couch, so I could lay down beside Grace."

Marcus had other plans for Katie, though. He pulled her off the couch and into his room, where he proceeded to have sex with her. She couldn't remember most of it, but Katie was certain she'd told him she didn't want to sleep with him.

"I was scared of him and didn't know what to do. I sure as hell couldn't drive myself home like last time. I was way past that. Even if I could have, Grace was passed out so hard there was no way I would've been able to get her off the couch, down the stairs, and into the car."

Katie stood up and stretched her arms above her head. We hadn't been in the room all that long, but it wouldn't surprise me if its modest size had made her feel claustrophobic. It was kind of sensory depriving, too, now that I think of it.

She remained standing but picked the story back up. "By the time Marcus had got to me, I was just about dead weight. I was kind of awake, but there was no fight in me, and he damn near had to drag me to the bedroom to do what he did to me."

Now, a comment like that was especially important to note in *this* case. She had said they were drinking heavily all night, so there was as much chance that she was too inebriated to walk as there was that she was drugged to the point she couldn't walk. With no solid proof, it was only hearsay either way, but I still felt I needed to ask, "You said Marcus made all of the drinks—do you feel at all like you were more drunk than you should have been? I mean, compared to the amount you drank, did you, even for a moment, suspect you might have been drugged?"

"I don't know. I honestly can't say if I was drugged. I had never been so drunk that I'd blacked-out before—that scared the shit out of me. I also don't think I drank enough to cause a black-out, but I can't even be sure of that."

I could hear the agitation in her voice.

"Marcus had said he wouldn't be able to get us jobs until sometime in December, but by the second week of September, both Grace and I were working at the Velvet Room. This complicated things for me because inappropriate things continued to happen with Marcus, and I was genuinely afraid to do or say anything that might compromise the job. I was making so much money, and I honestly *thought* I had control of the situation," she said as she sat sideways in the seat, facing the door, and crossed her ankles.

Katie avoided spending any time alone with Marcus, but there were still times at work and outside of it where they were together socially as part of a bigger group. In one of those situations, against her better judgment, her friend Olivia talked her into calling Marcus so they could go out drinking.

Marcus was perfectly happy to oblige because that was his thing, you know? He was always in if the plan was to get beautiful women wasted. It was his jam, if you will.

Katie, Olivia, Marcus, and a few of his fellow bar owner friends met at a Green Bay pub called Bugsy's. The drinks flowed freely all night and the women took advantage of it.

"I admit, I drank a fair amount, but I also tried not to have too much. I needed to keep my head on straight when Marcus was around, but it was also really fun to sit around with all of those bar owners."

"So, you might have flown past your limit? Your head might not have stayed as clear as you'd wanted?" I asked, and it was a fair question. Whether or not she drank so much that she would qualify as "wasted" wasn't the point of my asking, either. I had to ask because I personally knew the difference between drinking a lot then passing-out and drinking some and blacking-out from being drugged.

"I had more than I'd planned on having, but I know for a fact that I wasn't any more than tipsy when Marcus suggested we leave Bugsy's to move on to the next bar." Katie uncrossed her ankles, sighed deeply, then shrugged off her sweater and swung it over the back of her chair. Knowing what I do about body language, her actions were indicative of a need to take a break.

"Would you like a cup of coffee or anything? Do you want to take a few minutes to stretch your legs?"

"No, no, thanks. I'm just so uncomfortable talking about all of this. I'm fine, really." She took a deep breath and settled back into her chair, placing both hands on top of the purse, which she'd brought back to her lap.

I'd guessed wrong. "Okay, no problem. Let me know if there's anything I can do to help make this easier for you." I could appreciate her discomfort, just as I had with the other women I'd talked to and was glad she was willing to press on. As long as she knew I was listening and trusted I had her comfort in mind, I would get a more detailed story from her.

"Sure, thanks," she said, and continued. "Anyway, when we left Bugsy's, I got into a car with Marcus, and Olivia got in with a friend of Marcus's named Ryan. Like I said, we were all supposed to head to another bar to continue the good time, but that's not what happened."

Instead, Marcus drove her to My Place, and Ryan and Olivia arrived right after. The four of them went up to the apartment where they proceeded to have a couple more drinks.

"I was done after that," she said, staring down at her hands, "and could hardly keep my eyes open. I planned to stay in the living room with Olivia and Ryan because I figured it would be safer. Both of them seemed to fall asleep fast, and it was as if Marcus had known—down to the second—the exact moment they would be out of commission because he swooped into the living room and *insisted* I'd be more comfortable sleeping in his bed."

Katie remembered very little of what happened from there on out. She absolutely recalls stating that she was fine where she was and that she couldn't walk. "He had to drag me to the bedroom. I don't know if that was because I couldn't walk, or if I was that adamant against going with him, but I know he got me to the bedroom, got my clothing off, and had sex with me."

"Do you have a clear recollection of the sexual encounter?" I asked.

"No. Not any clear recollections, at least. I know he took my clothes off because I was naked the next morning, and I know I had sex because, well, I'm sure he didn't use a condom—he never did. I also remember flashes of it as it happened, but I don't know how long it lasted. It's like I had amnesia."

Katie was on the verge of letting loose her emotions. I could see the tears start to gather on her bottom eyelids before finally spilling onto her cheeks.

Without interrupting, I slid the box of tissues resting on the far corner of the table toward her.

She snatched a couple and dabbed at her face, careful of her makeup, then stood, turned the knob on the door, and mumbled she'd be right back.

I paused the recorder and decided to stretch my legs as well, which I did by exiting the room and wandering the hall as I processed what I'd heard so far.

As I paced up and down the hall, I pondered on the fact that, more than all the others, Katie seemed to feel very shameful about her encounters with Marcus. This was something I could understand, as it really seemed as if she kept putting herself into situations where he could get to her.

She'd said she didn't want to do anything that would compromise her job at the Velvet Room, but how could a job be more important than a person's physical and mental well-being? I had a difficult time wrapping my head around it because, of course, I wasn't in her head and didn't know what sort of life she'd led before meeting him. For all I knew, maybe she felt she had to put up with crap like this. Maybe she'd been objectified so many times it had become commonplace to simply accept that she would be treated this way by men? I couldn't say, but it made me shake in anger as I thought about it.

The other thing I considered as I paced was the fact that I couldn't ascertain if Katie (and possibly Olivia) had been drugged. Katie said they'd both felt amnesic affects, but with enough alcohol in their systems, it's very possible that was the culprit.

I didn't wander far from the interview room, but by the time I got back to its doorway, Katie was making her way down the hall toward me. She thanked me for the break as I closed the door behind us, and we sat back down.

"Ready to continue?" I asked, hoping she would be. One corner of her mouth curled into a flicker of a smile and she nodded, so I eased back into the conversation. "The next morning, when you and Olivia left Marcus's place, how were you two feeling?" I felt guilty for wanting her to tell me that she and Olivia had been utterly out of commission like I had been. Like I'd said, I wouldn't wish what I'd gone through on anyone, but I had to confirm whether or not I had another likely case of drugging on my hands.

Her answer sounded more like the women were hungover, but I still wasn't totally convinced that was the case. Katie had said she felt tipsy when the four of them got back to the infamous apartment above My Place, but a couple of drinks later, both women felt they couldn't fight off their sexual assailants? I didn't have the foresight to ask Katie what drinks they'd been given at the apartment, but it still didn't add up for me. Maybe Marcus had known they were already half-cut, so he'd only given them a small dose of his "rape potion." Maybe it was enough to push them over the edge, but not enough to make them deathly ill like Sasha and I had been.

Damn stupid speculation. I love just about everything about my job with one of the exceptions being damn stupid speculations. It's a necessary and hugely important part of most every investigation, but with my active imagination and talent for overthinking (a benefit in this line of work, for sure), sometimes I get sick to the teeth of having to figure things out. Sometimes, I simply want the investigative stars to align—every answer suddenly and logically sorted into the case's manila folder, then lovingly placed on my desk. Believe it or not, it does happen, but only on simple cut and dry cases, like a guy robbing a gas station where they actually *have* working cameras. Ta-da! Solved.

This was *not* one of those cases, and it was killing me.

With as many women as I'd talked to and stories I'd heard, the casefile on Marcus had grown exponentially, but I still needed to find something tangible to arrest him. On that line of thought, I quickly shot another question out to Katie. "Do you happen to remember seeing a video camera or any recording devices in Marcus's room?"

"No, but it was still fairly dark in there when we left that morning. Then again, I didn't see anything like that when I went back to his place the day after, either." Katie cringed as she placed two fingers on her temple and began rubbing in a circle. I couldn't tell if she was expecting me to sigh and look down my nose at her, or if she was getting a headache.

I had told her I wasn't there to judge her, but…whatever. I didn't sigh or do anything else—all I could do was try and hide my annoyance.

Okay, that's a lie. Like the furrowed brow from earlier, I couldn't help myself. My eyebrows nearly launched themselves into my hairline as I said, "You went *back* to Marcus's apartment?"

"Yeah. I'd forgotten my cell phone." She continued to slowly rub her temple and looked up at me. "I had promised myself I wouldn't even step over the threshold, but when I got there, he invited me to come in and watch TV, and I said 'yes.' I don't know what the hell I was thinking. It was as if he was controlling me; like I couldn't have said 'no' even if I'd wanted to. Or maybe I thought I'd be safe because I was sober? I don't know. Either way, it didn't end well."

"What do you mean?" My eyebrows descended into worry.

"He didn't even have to say anything. He just slid my underwear off and started having sex with me. I let him because I didn't want to lose my job."

Again with that comment—it made me livid. No one should feel like they need to satiate a sexual predator to keep their job! It was utterly asinine, but if she hadn't felt so strongly about it…

"What made you feel like you had to go through that to keep your job, Katie?" I *had* to know.

"Because if I didn't let him, he would fire me and tell all of his stupid, asshole bar owner friends about it, and I wouldn't get another bartending job." She was definitely ramped up now. "I needed money for college. I couldn't risk not having a steady job."

I know what kind of world I live in. I feel such sorrow knowing that some women feel they have no choice but to accept things like this need to happen so they can get ahead in the world. I'm a feminist—we should all have equal opportunity; our gender be damned.

I'm now the proud father of a beautiful little girl, but back then, I hate to admit the first thought that entered my mind was, *thank God I don't have any daughters.* I thought I'd certainly have had a heart attack by forty from the perpetual paternal anxiety. My heart was breaking for this lovely woman in front of me, and I hardly knew her.

"That last time, on the couch, I didn't struggle or tell him to stop, but I still didn't want it. I just felt I didn't have any choice."

I let my shoulders drop a little as I couldn't help feeling defeated on her behalf. It wasn't the right thing to feel though, and I knew it. It didn't bother me that I felt such compassion—of that I'm proud—but what she actually needed at that point was empowerment. I felt even more determined to stand up for her, Marcus's other victims, and women everywhere.

"Where does this story go, Katie? What happened after that last time with Marcus?"

"I tried to stay away from him as much as I could, which wasn't easy because I took as many shifts as I was offered, *and* he wasn't shy about putting his hands all over us girls at work. He'd slap and grab our asses, and tell us to take off our tops and work in our bras to get better tips and make the clientele happy. It was disgusting, but it was better than being in a room alone with him."

Katie grabbed for more tissues on the table, but she didn't seem to be crying anymore. Instead, she dabbed at her nose, then kept on talking. "When I started dating my boyfriend last November, Marcus got particularly venomous. He was spitting rude and degrading comments at me every chance he got. I finally had enough and walked out of that fucking place in January of this year."

"I'm so happy to hear you've moved on."

"Yeah, I am too, in most ways," she said.

"Why in only some ways?" I was surprised to hear her say it and was interested as to what reason she could possibly have to not be absolutely overjoyed at never having to walk through those doors again.

"Grace still works there." That cleared things up. "I'm…scared she's being sexually abused, too, and he refuses to use condoms. *Refuses*," she said. "What if he passes on an STD? What if he gets a victim pregnant? Just thinking about it makes me feel sick; I can't let him do what he did to me to Grace, or any other girl for that matter."

Based on what I'd heard from the other women, I'd already figured Marcus wasn't particularly worried about anyone's sexual well-being but refusing to wear a condom didn't make sense. Leaving semen as evidence when you're a serial rapist is monumentally stupid.

"Well, I can't do much about her decision to continue working there—that's up to her, but I can promise that I'm doing everything I possibly can to get Marcus off the streets."

She thanked me and apologized for not coming forward sooner. "I really don't want anyone to know that I put myself in such a stupid situation, but I really don't want Grace, or any other woman, to suffer at his hands. He's cunning and manipulative—that's a scary combination when paired with a blatant disrespect for women."

Was she ever right...

CHAPTER 11

VICTIMS, PROFESSIONALS, AND LANDLADIES. . .

AKA OH MY

I wrapped things up with Katie so she could hustle off to wherever it was she had to be next. She didn't say it, but I'm certain she'd stayed at the station longer than intended. I appreciated her willingness to help because not all the women who had come forward were interested in making their verbal statements official. It was frustrating, but if it came down to needing any one of their stories I could be very persuasive.

Before Katie left, she'd given me Grace's phone number. Katie had already encouraged Grace to come into the station to talk, but she wasn't convinced her friend would carry through. Hopefully, I'd be able to convince her. I gave her a quick call before heading out to lunch, and when it went straight to voicemail, I let her know who I was and left it at that.

Throughout the nearly three months I had been working on this case, I'd spent many hours on and off of the clock, in restaurants, bars, and pubs all over Green Bay trying to find stories, answers, and explanations about Marcus and his accusers. If I had thought things were busy then, November had most certainly catapulted me into the eye of the hurricane. The manila folder meant to encase everything I'd dug up on Marcus remained constantly open in organized chaos on my desk. It was too portly to close by that point anyway, and since I'd passed along many of my lesser cases to other investigators, there was nothing to interfere with the sprawling notes. Closing it would have quickly become redundant as the steady flow of direct calls from potential victims and notices from other public safety avenues continued to come in. Clearly, word had gotten out that the long arm of the law had a firm grip on Marcus Somerhalder's coattails.

I was at the point in the case where I was ready to take the next steps. I had done my research, I'd heard the stories, and it was time to engage the next level of justice—the arrest.

Before an arrest could even be made, I needed a heck of a lot more than what I had. Without tangible proof, like what you'd consider a murder weapon—or a videotape like the one Sasha and Marcus destroyed—there was no way I was going to ever get this nightmare of a case closed.

Enter: the unfortunate truth. If Sasha had only made a copy of that videotape… I don't blame her though; she had no idea how much bigger than her this case would become. I had finally received an official statement from Sasha. I also had the good fortune of getting in contact with her mom and the lawyer she had contacted, both of which had seen the video. It wasn't perfect, but it was two more people who could substantiate Sasha's claims.

Still, I needed more than what I had.

I wasn't going to be able to find proof unless I was allowed to go digging through Marcus's life, so the next logical course of action was to get access to it. I needed a search warrant, and in order to get one, first I needed to give the case some teeth. My best possible bet was to inject the case with the professional opinion of someone who had deep knowledge of the criminal mind—more specifically, the sexual predator's mind.

A few days after I'd interviewed Katie, I got in contact with a man named Robert, who had been working for years as a probation and parole agent for the Wisconsin Department of Corrections. More specifically, Robert was part of the Sexual Offender Intensive Supervision Team, so I figured, if there was anyone who could legitimize a search warrant application for a sexual deviant like Marcus, it would be him.

Robert had worked with hundreds of sexual predators over the years and had unofficially become the local expert and an invaluable resource on the topic. I couldn't wait to hear what he had to say about Marcus.

He wasn't able to meet in person, which was somewhat inconvenient, but only because I had to explain and summarize each victim's case over the phone instead of handing him my manila folder. Then again, I think I would have suffered the kind of anxiety that would've killed me if I'd had to let it out of my sight. Seriously, I'd never before been so protective of a collection of papers.

Needless to say, Robert was intrigued by the case. I could hear him scratching down notes as I brought him up to speed on the key players. He also wanted to know the timeline on Marcus's alleged offenses, and I admit, I didn't whisper a word about my drugging being in the middle of that timeline. That information was still only mine to know, and I wasn't convinced it would have any impact on the case anyway. None the wiser, Robert took what I gave him, and was able to paint a pretty clear picture for me.

"Sounds to me like you've got yourself a marauding predator," he said matter-of-factly.

I had an idea of what he meant but knew I'd be better off asking him to clarify as I scribbled my own notes into the file.

As he explained it, a marauding predator, in regard to Marcus's case info, meant he didn't access the same victim every time. Even though he revisited some of his victims—Katie, for one—he wasn't afraid to seek out new women to play his games with. An even more enlightening, albeit melodramatic, description of a marauding predator would be a serial killer. Let's name a few: Jack the Ripper, The Zodiac Killer, Ted Bundy. Catch my drift?

"I've dealt with guys like this before, and I can guarantee, based on your timeline, his predatory techniques are evolving. A year ago, he was experimenting with alcohol to submit his victims and he's now moved on to drugging them."

"Well, unfortunately, I can't prove he's been drugging these women, but that's where you come in." I paused and waited for his response, which didn't come in the form I'd wanted. I had hoped he would make quick work of it and tell me I could count on his support, so I could file the search warrant with the judge sooner than later, but Robert had more to say.

"He'll continue to evolve, you know. He'll get tired of the game he's playing. It won't excite him for long."

"What would be the natural progression to what we're talking about here?" I asked, but I was pretty sure I knew the answer—Jack the Ripper, The Zodiac Killer, Ted Bundy—and while his answer was something like that, he threw in a curveball I hadn't expected to hear.

"Well, it's by no means a guarantee that it would get this far, but, characteristically, there is a chance it could go as far as serial necrophilia," he said with deadpan bluntness.

I have no idea what my reply was. As if the floppy disk for that brain-file had been wiped, I have no recollection of how I responded to "serial necrophilia."

So, he *could* go as far as killing someone to get off?

I'd seen and heard a lot of crazy shit at that point in my career, and since then, I've heard things even weirder, but the initial level of shock I'd felt in that moment was substantial.

Approximately three months earlier, as a matter of fact, I had an acquaintance who owned bars, occasionally bought me drinks, and who I *knew* was a serial womanizer. In an about-face shift, he'd become a marauding predator who baited, drugged, and raped women, and who could eventually evolve into a man that baited and *killed* women to have sex with their lifeless bodies.

What I didn't know back then was that this psychosis had an official title: somnophilia3, AKA sleeping beauty/princess syndrome, but to this day, there isn't all that much known about it. Essentially, Marcus was aroused specifically by the idea that the person he was raping was in no shape to resist him.

Finally, Robert went on to tell me the exact information I would need to move ahead with the case, and I couldn't have been more thankful.

---

[3] *Somnophilia (from Latin "somnus" = sleep and Greek φιλία, "-philia" = love), also known as sleeping princess syndrome and sleeping beauty syndrome, is a paraphilia in which an individual becomes sexually aroused by someone who is unconscious. https://en.wikipedia.org/wiki/Somnophilia*

"You know," he said, then cleared his throat right into the phone—that I clearly remember. "You said he had videotaped intercourse with one of his conquests, did you not?"

I confirmed that it had been Sasha and reminded him the tape had been destroyed.

"It doesn't matter that you don't have that one because there's an extremely good chance that if he's done it once, he's done it twice, and so on." Interesting... "It's well known in my circles that this type of offender will most likely maintain *collections* to relive his moments, refine his skills, and inspire and encourage bolder fantasies."

He continued on to say that if Marcus was adept with a computer, he probably had collections of pornography saved and possibly hidden on his hard drive. "In lieu of, or in addition to videos, he might even have journals describing his feelings and thoughts about his fantasies."

"This is incredible information, Robert." I meant it, too. I couldn't wait to get off the phone with him, but before I did, I asked, "Would you do me a favor and throw this information together into a formal statement for me?"

He agreed to oblige, so I gave him the case number, thanked him profusely, and slammed the phone down into the cradle. I might have even followed it up with a fist pump and a "Hell, yeah!"

I left the office that afternoon without any doubt in my mind that I was going to have a search warrant in hand in no time.

I returned to work the next day too excited to do anything other than begin putting the information required for the warrant together, and as I did so, decided to do some subtle pre-emptive digging into Marcus's life. He had long since moved from his digs atop My Place in De Pere to an apartment in Ashwaubenon—my town. I don't know why, but I loved that he was officially in my jurisdiction. I was going to bring him down on my native soil, and it gave me goosebumps just thinking about it.

I called ahead to Marcus's landlord, Laurie, who had helped us before in other investigations—mostly drug related, and she seemed keen to help out again. This was delightful news because the reason for me calling was to inquire what his "trash habits" were, and what the easiest way to get access to his garbage would be.

"Oh, you mean that Somerhalder asshole?"

I did indeed. "Yes, ma'am," I replied. "Also, if you have any idea about his comings and goings, the information would be much appreciated."

"Yeah, of course. Should be easy enough to do."

Laurie didn't hold anything back—whatever they were paying this woman to manage the apartments wasn't enough. I wondered if she'd been a spy in her former life. She knew *everything* about *everybody* that lived in the complex, and I was fortunate enough to hear about nearly half of them before I was able to refocus her.

As it turned out, Marcus seemed to be a constant blip on her radar, so she knew a lot about what his usual daily habits were. Laurie wasn't at all shy about the fact that she didn't like Marcus all that much, and I figured it was probably because of that reason she kept such a close eye on him. It was a theory, anyway, but I craved a more definitive explanation.

"I wonder, Laurie, have you had a run-in with Mr. Somerhalder? Or have you seen anything to garner such a strong dislike for him?"

She explained that all tenants knew they were expected to throw their bags of garbage directly into the communal dumpsters. Apparently, to the full and bitter animosity of Laurie, it was above Marcus to complete this task and he commonly pitched his refuse bags out his patio door. She told me how he'd leave them piled there until she got so fed up with the mess, she'd be forced to collect and bring them to the dumpster herself.

"That princely little prick ignores me every time I tell him it's *his* damn job, *not* mine." She spat her words like they were the cause of a terribly bad taste in her mouth. I'm sure she felt justified in her disgust for him, and I wondered how her opinion would change if she knew why we were requesting access to his garbage.

Besides this vexing issue with Marcus, Laurie had never noticed anything unusual about him or what he was throwing out. "Of course, I never sifted through his garbage like you guys are planning to do." Lucky for her, too.

The job of a police investigator is rarely glamorous, but there are very few tasks more degrading than sifting through and analyzing someone's trash. If it wasn't such a damn good way to recover evidence, and hopefully in this situation, help build a case for a search warrant, I'm certain we would have banished the practice a long time ago.

Maybe I'm letting the cat out of the bag on this, but more often than not, it's a very lucrative process. People just don't think anyone, especially crisp-suited officers, are going to bother crawling through their leftover beef stroganoff to get to the pinch bags and blunt roaches. It's easier for them to assume, once the bag is tossed, it's gone forever—destined for the local dump without knowledge of, or repercussion for, the seedy secrets within. For the most part they'd be right, but if we've got our eyes on you, into the stroganoff we go. So, if you're doing something the pedantic legal forces in your neighborhood wouldn't approve of, be careful what you chuck in your bins.

I thanked Laurie for her time and let her know I would be in contact again when I had the warrant in hand.

Despite our best efforts, we didn't find anything evidential in Marcus's trash, so I had no choice but to hope Robert would be quick about getting his report to me. The days passed slowly as I waited for him to send along his official statement, so I spent my time organizing, analyzing, and familiarizing myself with every piece of data within the file.

At the time, I was basing my conclusions on ten years of professional experience and was fairly confident I'd already seen pretty much everything this job could throw at me. Of course, and I'm sure you can guess, I was terribly wrong. In the almost twenty years since this case, I've learned there's no roof on criminal creativity. Every time I think they've thought of it all, I'm surprised once again.

It's been said many times, by many people, and it's a statement that will forever hold truth—*the difference between genius and stupidity is that genius has its limits.* You would not believe some of the shit I've seen, but those hearty tales will have to wait.

With ten years' experience under my belt, I had frequently witnessed many levels of the wildly exciting and desperately low effects of intoxication on many different types of people. While I'm certain cops all over the world can say they've seen it all, I strongly believe my declaration of seeing more than any of them have is true due to one fact—home Packer games.

There is absolutely no place like Lambeau Stadium to watch an NFL game—no competition. Furthermore, Packer fans are like no other fans in the world; they're a happy, amicable, cordial, and welcoming scramble of people, win or lose, and they drink a *lot* of alcohol on game day. Packer games and booze are synonymous with each other, no doubt about it, and any fan you ask will be happy as all heaven to admit it. So, when I say I've literally dealt with tens of thousands of drunks in one way or another, I'm not exaggerating one tiny bit.

This brings me to my next point, and the whole reason for bringing this all up—each person is different in their tolerance to alcohol, but typically, unless imbibed in *extremely* high amounts, doesn't ever result in someone completely forgetting they've had sex. This was especially true as I read through the copious pages of data I'd amassed on Marcus. Many of his victims stated they suffered serious discomfort in the genital area after nights they couldn't remember; meaning, had they been conscious, the sex would have been painful.

Also, every single one of the women I initially talked to were experienced drinkers, knew their limitations, and were acutely aware of how alcohol typically affected them. It should also be noted that not a single one of them believed the deficits in their memories were caused by them pushing past their levels of tolerance for alcohol.

My hopes were set very high that if I could search every inch of his house and his businesses, I would no doubt find the secret potion of his Modus Operandi.

It was on November 28, 2003, as I sat at my desk cataloging page after page of the case, nearly ready to abandon the monotony to take my lunch, my task was interrupted by the ringing of my phone. It had been an uncharacteristically quiet day, so I dropped the paper in hand and snatched up the receiver before the first ring had finished. "Investigator Schermitzler here."

"Hi Investigator. My name is Grace, you called me a couple weeks back?"

I'd called her a few times in the last two weeks, but I wasn't going to correct her.

"I'm sorry I didn't get a hold of you sooner, but I'm still not even sure if I want to be involved in your investigation."

"Uh, yeah, it's okay, really. I'm glad you called me back, and I can perfectly understand how you're feeling right now." I sat up a little straighter in my chair as I prepped to repeat the same thing I'd said to nearly every woman involved in this case over the last few months. It always started with, "Look, it would be incredible if you could tell me your story. I know how hard it is to drudge up an experience you really want to bury, but I need your help so we can make sure Marcus can't hurt anyone else."

It still shocks me when I think back on how hard it was, through the many, many conversations I had with all those different women, to get the information I needed from them. Especially when I compared it to the unnecessary need to convince Laurie, the landlady, to throw Marcus under the bus based solely on her anger over piles of garbage. With what Marcus had done to them, you'd assume his victims would have been compelled without coaxing to see him pinned under our polished boots. It's strange to explain this, but not a single one of the key witnesses told me their story out of anger. I suppose it doesn't matter; in the end, I got the information I needed from all of them. They felt strongly that no woman should ever go through what they had, and I couldn't have agreed more. At least, we all shared that in common.

"Yeah, yeah, I know," she replied to my plea. "Look, I'm not even sure that what I have to say is going to be of any use to you, because when my story happened, Marcus and I were kind of seeing each other. Well, I think. I'm not sure. It was a weird situation." She exhaled loudly into the phone before continuing. "Anyway, my point is, I'm not entirely sure you'd qualify it as rape."

"Well, how about you fill me in on the details, then we can discuss what they might mean to the investigation."

"Okay, yeah. So, I've been working for Marcus for a while now; he gave my friend, Katie and I jobs at the Velvet Room sometime near the end of 2002. I'm terrible with dates, so I don't remember when exactly."

"Katie doesn't work there anymore though, I hear."

"Yeah," she confirmed, "she quit at the beginning of this year. I miss having her there, but whatever. She hates Marcus and doesn't think I should be there, either."

I agreed fully and completely with that statement.

"Most people have already jumped ship from the Velvet Room, and I'm pretty sure I'm going to be following close behind."

That was interesting news. I knew there was a bit of chatter about the fact that there was an investigation into Marcus, but it wasn't at all public knowledge. I hadn't heard anything from him indicating he had any clue about what was going on. Although, I admit I had been making sure to steer clear of him. Skinny was still working at the club, and had been keeping tabs on Marcus for me, but he hadn't noticed any major changes from the guy.

"Anyway, I knew Marcus was seeing that Faith chick, but when she wasn't working, Marcus and I did a lot of flirting. It was sometime in August, I think, when he called me up to meet him after hours at his apartment."

"Was he still living in the apartment above My Place in De Pere?" I knew he wouldn't have been by then, but I wanted confirmation—which she gave me—that he'd brought women to the apartment in Ashwaubenon. Grace went on to tell me about her experience with Marcus, which sadly, included quite a few things I'd heard before.

She'd went over to his apartment where he fixed her a drink. Grace admitted she'd already been drinking, but knew she wasn't anywhere near drunk. After that first drink, her entire memory went blank until she woke up to Marcus having sex with her.

"In fact, there are a whole bunch of hours that I can't remember from that night," she said with a tremble in her voice. "I didn't see him all that much after that night—only when I was at work, really."

"Do you feel like you were drugged that night?" I had confidently deduced that she had been, but I was curious if she thought the same.

Maybe she wasn't as seasoned a drinker? She was barely twenty, but despite the legal drinking age of twenty-one in Wisconsin, most kids already knew their limits long before they were old enough to get into the bars. This was doubly true for any one of them who got a job in a place that served alcohol. There are a bunch of states in this glorious country where it's legal to serve alcohol at the age of nineteen, but not legal to drink it. It's apparently a system that works, but I can't help but wonder how strictly it's enforced.

I can't even think of a time when I've gone into a bar, pub, or the like, and wondered if the server slinging my pint was underage and drinking.

"I can guarantee I was drugged that night." The confidence had come back into her voice. "And from what I've heard, Marcus has doped up just about everyone."

"What makes you say that? Do you have any proof? If so, I would love to get my hands on it." I tried not to sound too eager.

"No proof, but I know for a fact Katie's sure she was drugged."

Damnit! They'd talked. Of course they had. They were friends.

"I just know that I've never in my life drank so much that I slept through sex, and besides that, where did the rest of those hours go? I don't even remember getting undressed, or kissing him, or even going pee! How could I just wake up long enough to know I was having sex and not know anything else?"

Grace was almost hysterical by this point. She wasn't yelling into the phone, but she was clearly distressed. I felt awful for her.

I did my best to sooth her. "Grace, Grace, it'll be okay. With your help, and the help of so many other women, we'll be able to make sure he pays for this. Nailing him to the wall is my one and only focus, okay?"

"Yeah, sure, Investigator. I'm okay now." She sounded less upset, at least.

"Is there anything else you want me to know?" I asked gently.

"Yeah, there is, actually."

As it was with Sasha, Grace became pregnant. When she confronted Marcus about it, he agreed to pay for an abortion.

"I'm so sorry to hear this, Grace. You're not the first woman he's done this to. By the way," I added, "I definitely qualify this as rape."

I inquired as to whether or not she would like to talk to someone from Victim Services. She declined, which I wish she wouldn't have, but every woman before her had done the same, so I wasn't surprised. "Would you be willing to come into the station to make an official statement?"

She agreed, and told me she would come in on December 2, but sadly, for whatever reason, she never did make her way down.

Two days later, Robert's educated and professionally opinionated statement arrived. I was certain Marcus was hiding something and I was going to comb every nook and dusty cranny of the Velvet Room, the Washington Street Lounge, and his Ashwaubenon apartment to find it.

I had most everything ready for this moment, so it took no time to finish preparing the affidavit and search warrant. I made my way to the circuit courts in Brown County so I could get a judge to review, and hopefully, sign my document without question.

The building that houses Green Bay's finest judges is, like my father, stoic and distinguished. Its glorious architecture saw it built three stories tall and laid brick by brick with gray and brown stone. I couldn't help but gush with pride as I walked with purpose up its front steps and into the marble-floored foyer.

I had walked through those doors hundreds of times to get warrants signed, but this time seemed so much different to me. The papers gripped firmly in my hands meant more than any that had come before because the consequences of my failure felt astronomically greater. I needed the importance of this affidavit to be recognized and the warrant issued without a hitch because I needed to see the second of the two most profound cases of my whole life brought to justice. Their suffering, their stories, their right to feel safe were the backbone of this case, and I was going to make sure, like I had with Sawyer, these women got the closure they deserved.

I confidently handed the judge the affidavit, thinking there was no way he would deny me permission to enter and search Marcus's residence and bars, but the second it left my fingertips, that confidence deflated ever so slightly. The longer the judge perused my report, the more I questioned my work: did I have enough to support this warrant request? Would it be dismissed as unsubstantiated, biased finger pointing?

The judge would occasionally lift his head from the paperwork to stare down his nose at me, which didn't help my confidence, but I didn't get the impression he was doing so in anger. It seemed more like thoughtful contemplation; he'd hold the look for a second or two, then look back down to the paperwork. The way he looked at me, it was as if he could see into my mind and was double-checking my judgment, honesty, and the accuracy of the information. Or, maybe I was mumbling and didn't realize it, and he was trying to get me to stop because I was breaking his concentration.

I sat quietly (I think) in my own world, anxiously awaiting his certain (probable?) approval, but after about fifteen minutes of watching the judge meticulously review my work—quickly diverting my anxious stare away from him every time he looked up—I *really* started to question my affidavit and warrant procedures. I was damn near certain all of the information was correct but was my format, procedure, and even spelling good enough for him to sign away Marcus's constitutional rights? The minutes seemed like hours as I crossed and uncrossed my legs, picked at my cuticles, and chewed my lip, when finally, the judge responded.

He was astonished at what he had read and how much information I was able to obtain from the victim witnesses. This comment fully reinstated the confidence I'd had when I walked into the building.

He had a few questions in reference to the credibility of my potential victims and how the information was acquired, but those were easy to answer. I had audio backup for most of them, and I hadn't had to coerce anyone to talk. I was quick and concise with all of my answers, as if I had meticulously prepared for any and all questions the judge could possibly have about the affidavit.

Like I said earlier, we should get Oscars for the work we do... I'd had things fairly well organized to build this affidavit, but I'd rushed the process of throwing it together to get it into his office. I was so sure the information within would speak for itself and I wouldn't have to open my mouth other than to thank the good judge for his signature.

It worked that way, for the most part. His questioning couldn't have taken more than five minutes before he signed my affidavit and warrant application.

Judges are to remain always impartial—they see nothing but the facts—but his judge's demeanor spoke for itself. I could tell he wanted nothing more than for me to find justice for these women, especially if what I was reporting to him under oath was true. He was anxious to see my post warrant report.

I shook the judge's hand, grabbed all the paperwork, and he sent me on my way. I had to restrain myself from breaking into a run once I made it back into the main hall. I wasted no time in getting to my cruiser; my mind racing with excitement as I made my way back to the station. There was still so much to do and think about to coordinate such a substantial warrant search.

I absolutely knew, without a doubt in my mind, I would find evidence of what kind of monster Marcus was. What I wasn't prepared for, even though I really should have been, was how fully crazy the investigation was going to become next.

CHAPTER 12

WARRANT EXECUTION DAY. . .

AKA WELL THEN, WHAT DO WE HAVE HERE?

You know how in police procedural movies and TV shows, the SWAT team blows out the hinges on a door, then storms into the room to catch the perpetrator unawares? Well, shit actually goes down like that sometimes, and it's even as exciting as it is on film. What isn't usually mentioned (because logistics are boring) is the sheer amount of organization an operation like that requires. Sadly, in this case, there wasn't any need to break down doors, but we did need to conduct three searches simultaneously. It was necessary to plan it that way so Marcus didn't have a chance to ditch the goods or destroy any evidence.

There was obviously no way I could carry this out on my own, so I requested the assistance of some fellow investigators and officers, and together, we took a couple of days to formulate our plan.

I was going to need three teams and decided four members per team would be the most effective number. That way, we could break up and get things done with quick efficiency and avoid tripping over one another.

I was lead on the team that would go to Marcus's Ashwaubenon apartment, and the two other teams, both answerable to Investigator Lawler, would move in on the Washington Street Lounge and the Velvet Room, respectively.

There was no need for SWAT-like gear. Each officer carried their standard gear and firearm; investigators didn't have to suit up, we wore khakis and a polo shirt—so much smoother. The only specialized equipment we required for the day were video and still-shot cameras. Sounds cumbersome to carry both, I know, but this was before the wonderful age when you could make phone calls from the two combined devices. Technology has definitely helped us cut some corners, which is incredible because documentation, despite so much tech advancement nowadays, remains so vital to every case we work. We need to be able to see absolutely everything, but we're often too focused on certain aspects of an investigation to immediately connect the dots on other things that might be important to the case.

It was early morning on December 5, 2003 when, as my team geared up, I called ahead to Laurie, the property manager, to let her know I had the warrant in hand and we'd be arriving in an hour or so.

She sounded quite pleased that we were ready to go and let me know Marcus was usually gone by that time…or hadn't arrived home yet, she couldn't be sure. I thought that was a bit odd considering how late he always seemed to be up. I really didn't pin him as an early riser, but there or not, it didn't really matter—we were prepared for either circumstance.

I took some time to quickly brief the teams before we made our way out of the station. Based on what I'd talked to Robert about, I had a pretty good idea of the sorts of things we would likely find if he was indeed the predator he was being accused of being. I had put together a checklist of possible items and things to keep an eye out for. My hopes were high that we would be able to find his secret potion, but I admit, I had no idea what exactly it'd look like.

We knew for a fact that Marcus had videotaped at least one victim, so equipment that would allow him to do that and the physical videos themselves, were at the top of the list. Besides that, we were looking for any and all liquids—if there was a stupefying agent anywhere in there, we needed to find it. Of course, we couldn't be certain what else could be considered evidence, so we would have to look closely at the most mundane things and bag everything we wanted to know more about.

We broke into teams and made our way to our respective locations. When my team, consisting of Investigator Tim David, and Officers Jody Crocker and Mike Haines, pulled into the complex lot, Laurie met us with an enormous grin plastered on her face. We showed her the search warrant; she then handed me the key to Marcus's apartment and escorted us to his unit and garage area.

"I saw him leave about an hour ago, maybe more. It was right after I talked to you, Investigator," she said.

No matter... Like I said, we were ready for anything. I'll admit though, it took a weight off my shoulders. I had been slightly worried he would be there when we arrived, and while I knew I would have to face him eventually, I was relieved it wouldn't be just yet.

I notified the two units tasked with searching his businesses that Marcus was not at his apartment, so they would be ready to handle his possible presence at their locations.

With that, it was time. My blood was coursing with adrenaline and excitement as we approached the door. Officer Haines and I would be the first to enter, so we drew our guns, and took a moment to mentally prep.

Despite all of the positive energy surrounding this moment, it was quite bittersweet for me because this was merely a transition. There were three possibilities in this case:

1. I was going to come up with nothing—bitterly having to admit I had been outsmarted by Marcus. Why would I think this? Because even though I knew he was guilty, maybe he'd caught wind that we were planning on laying the smack down that morning and ferried all the evidence away when he'd left.

2. I would find so much evidence that I'd need to work another three months on this case. Maybe this warrant was just a new, bigger manila folder in the making. This would be fine so long as the end result was Marcus crying on a jailhouse floor.

3. Lastly—the most unlikely and angering possibility—all those women had been lying and Marcus was... Nope. I can't even finish this point. Marcus's innocence flashed into my head for a millisecond as we stood outside his apartment door, and I refused to give it more time than that.

I desperately hoped *and* feared it was option two because if he'd found out we were on our way to him, he would have had time to ditch any evidence. I had considered it might've even been the reason why he'd left so early in the morning. If the first possibility was a reality, it would be damn near impossible to prove the kind of predator Marcus was.

Skipping the part where I'd cross my fingers for luck, I reached out to knock three times on Marcus's door and announced our lawful presence. When there was no response from inside, I slipped the key into the lock, turned the knob, and cautiously took a peek into the apartment.

The immediate coast was clear, so, leading with my pistol, I entered with Officer Haines close behind, eyes peeled for any movement. We did a quick sweep of the place to make sure there was no one inside before Investigator David and Officer Crocker joined us. We'd expected to find an empty apartment, but it wouldn't have been the first time we'd run into a surprise occupant. I felt even more at ease as we waited for Investigator David to quickly but thoroughly take photographs and video of the scene—the apartment.

It seemed like a typical bachelor pad: takeout containers scattered all over an old coffee table, dishes in the sink, empty liquor bottles and beer cans on the kitchen counter. It was clear this was merely a stopping point for eating, sleeping, and drinking without any consideration for entertaining guests; well, not recently, at least. Beyond that, nothing stood out that would immediately indicate this could be the residence of one of the most notorious serial date rapists.

I had uncovered enough shocking and perverted information from the women I'd spoken to and suspected it would only be a matter of minutes before I'd discover evidence of Marcus's sick crimes.

Once the film and photographic records were finished, I holstered my gun, stretched a pair of latex gloves over my hands, and finally began searching the residence for evidence.

I started in the kitchen, then moved on to a small utility closet, neither of which turned up any significant evidence, but the search was young.

Investigator David and I chatted back and forth about this and that, as we peeked into, poked at, and prodded everything we came across, while the officers searched closets, etc. We'd already snagged some photographs we'd found on his fridge and in his living room, but as I slowly made my way toward Marcus's bedroom, I had the strongest feeling I was going to find what I was really looking for in there.

Before I could get to the bedroom, I needed to search through the linen closet. I cracked the door open. Upon first glance, nothing within appeared to be suspicious; there were towels haphazardly folded, some washcloths, a few rolls of toilet paper, and four neatly lined-up bottles of the same shampoo. Marcus kept his hair short, so I couldn't see the need for a stockpile of shampoo.

For whatever reason, I snatched one of the bottles from the shelf and carefully, away from my face, unscrewed the cap. I took a look inside, then depressed the sides a bit so I could get a whiff of whatever was in there. I knew one thing for certain: it sure as hell wasn't shampoo. There was no obvious smell. I wasn't going to get any closer to it, so I recapped it. I checked the remaining three bottles in the same way—none of them appeared to be shampoo, so I threw them into an evidence bag. I'd let the crime lab figure out what the liquid evidence was.

I finished my search of the linen closet and made my way to the end of the hall. I looked into Marcus's room, and sitting right there in the middle of it, looking out of place but in plain sight, was a large trunk secured shut with a heavy-duty combination lock. Being that I almost expected to see something just like it, I wasn't at all surprised. That didn't lessen my excitement. Still, what could be so important it would require a mammoth-sized trunk with such an impressive lock?

"Crocker!" I yelled as I took a few long strides into the room. I knelt down and gave a quick tug on the lock, then said, "Go grab your bolt cutters out of the squad car for me, will ya?"

"On it," he replied. He couldn't see me, didn't ask why I needed them. He simply complied. He must have sensed my urgency; hell of an officer.

While I waited for him to return, Officer Haines joined me, and we continued to poke around in Marcus's room. Nothing turned up more suspicious than that trunk, but we did find a bottle of hand lotion and a roll of duct tape under the bed.

Rolls of duct tape found under beds, as we've realized in our line of work, are usually there for the purpose of binding people. When we find duct tape in your toolkit or garage, or in that junk drawer in your kitchen, we aren't likely to nab it if there's no reasonable need to view it as evidence. Under the bed, though, I can pretty much guarantee it isn't being used to patch a hole in a tent or a duct, for that matter. In a suspected rape case, duct tape is, without question, an item we snag, bag, and tag.

Officer Crocker and his bolt cutters made short work of the lock, and when he lifted back the lid, he let loose a "Well then, what do we have here?" before stepping back so I could see inside.

The trunk was stashed full of VHS tapes, stacked neatly, but not in any obvious order. Some of the tapes were purchased movies, and the rest appeared to be recordable tapes—some had a sort of code written on the labels and others were left blank.

Conveniently, Marcus had a dusty TV and VCR on his dresser, and I was going to put it to use. With no need to be picky, I snatched one of the videotapes from the top of the pile and slid it into the machine. I grabbed the remote control resting beside the VCR, clicked the TV on, and stepped back to have a look.

There was very little doubt as to what we'd find on the tape, but it really didn't make it any easier when the static settled into a dark, grainy, but visible image of Marcus having sex with an unidentified woman. It was sickening. I can guarantee none of us will ever forget what we saw and felt as we observed the initial few seconds of what became the first of many hours of video footage.

I didn't even bother stopping the tape; I jammed my finger onto the eject button, put the tape back in the trunk, and seized the whole damn trunk as evidence.

There's no way of truly describing how absolutely paradoxical my feelings were as I stood there watching the officers labor to load that trunk of sin and horror into the back of the squad car. I shuffled back and forth between anger and elation, then disgust and an extreme sense of accomplishment. Every emotional shift left me more and more sure of one thing—just for right now—emotions be damned. *This is gonna be a slam dunk*, I thought to myself.

I now had evidence of what appeared to be a woman being videotaped while in the midst of having intercourse with Marcus. Had she consented to be videotaped? I would find that out. Had she consented to have sex with Marcus, or was this rape? I would find that out, too. I knew, not factually, but without a lick of doubt, this wasn't going to be the only videotape with similar content on it. With my best guess at that point being over fifty additional tapes, I would definitely find evidence to present to Marcus. Knowing there couldn't possibly be anything else he could do other than confess to all of the sexual assaults trumped every other feeling I had—and there had been a lot—in the last ten minutes.

It seemed so simple. Once this evidence got into the hands of a judge there would be only one path left on the planet for that scumbag Marcus Somerhalder to walk down. How could he, or anyone for that matter, contest this irrefutable evidence of his own making? Marcus was going to jail, and I planned to fully revel in that knowledge…

My thoughts of grandeur plunged quickly into melancholy when I realized just what that trunk actually represented.

It meant a strong—no, more like inevitable—likelihood that there were going to be more victims, and with them, more emotional destruction. My heart sank and my feeling of pride disintegrated as it dawned on me, as the lead on this case, I would be tasked with the disgusting job of watching, analyzing, and logging the contents of each and every recovered videotape. It was going to be my job to watch as Marcus turned his prey into victims, and that didn't sit well with me at all.

I was pretty sure I could predict how each of those women would feel when they found out they were on one of those tapes. I knew they would be horrified at the fact that we knew they were on those tapes because we would have had to watch them to find out. I had no doubt I was going to dread going to work each morning until this task was done. Lastly, I hated that I would be contributing to any feelings of helplessness and victimization they might have felt since their encounter with Marcus.

My thoughts were interrupted when Investigator Lawler's voice crackled over my radio, "686 to 684, Marcus Somerhalder's vehicle is parked at the Velvet Room. How should we proceed? Over."

"Copy that 686." With evidence in our possession, I confidently said, "Take Somerhalder into custody and get him back to the station."

Officer Haines and I made our way back into the apartment to do one more quick sweep of the premises, while Investigator David and Officer Crocker went back to the station with their deviant cargo.

We had just returned the key to Laurie when we got word that Marcus was in custody and they had arrested the Velvet Room's cook, Bart, as well. I didn't have any idea why they'd taken the cook into custody because his name had never come up during my investigation, but this case had been full of surprises so far, so one more wouldn't have shocked me one bit.

It took no time for us to get back to the station, excellent because all I wanted to do was sink my teeth into Marcus. I definitely had my eye on the prize.

Thankfully, debrief was extremely quick and easy because there wasn't a lot to talk about. Bart was in for charges unrelated to my case, and the other teams hadn't brought back more than a few photographs as evidence to process. I might have worried about that fact if not for that massive trunk sitting in the evidence cage and the questionable dark bottles of shampoo soon to be on their way to the state crime lab.

I excused myself from the room, and with anxious excitement and my massive manila folder tucked under my arm, I made my way to the interview room where Marcus was being detained.

*   *   *

As the team leader on the investigation, it was my task to get the truth out of Marcus. At the moment, I was feeling pretty confident in my ability to do so. Well, that's not necessarily true. I knew I wouldn't have any trouble getting him to talk, I just wasn't sure I was going to get the whole truth, and nothing but the truth out of him.

Being that this was only the initial interview, and I hadn't seen any more of the videos yet, I relaxed, knowing I had time. No need to rush or push too hard... I had all the time in the world.

I turned the last corner that led me to the interview rooms, and there, through the glass, I saw him. He was sitting back in the chair with his legs crossed in front of him. He sat there in his expensive jeans and a black designer hoodie, bold as brass, with a smug look that screamed, "There's some kind of mistake; I shouldn't be here."

I opened the door and smiled at him, but only because I couldn't help myself. It's such a satisfying feeling to have the upper hand. When he looked up and saw me, I swear I saw a wave of relief fall across his face. His shoulders relaxed slightly, almost as if he'd let his guard down a little.

"Sherm!" he said. "Boy am I happy to see you, buddy."

With that, the smile slipped from my face to settle into one of a more stern professionalism; I was *not* his buddy, but it would definitely work to my advantage if he thought I was.

I looked Marcus right in the eye, and trying to sound friendly, said, "Wish I could say the same, man. Things are looking a bit hairy. How about we have a chat. Let's see if we can't figure all this out. Okay?"

"All right," he replied, looking up at me as I towered over him.

"First things first, and I hate to do this to you, *buddy*." I don't think he detected the dollop of sarcasm I applied to the term of endearment. "But, I've got to do this." I proceeded to let him know that he was being charged with multiple counts of sexual assault, then read him his rights. "Do you understand?" I asked when I finished.

"Yeah, I get it," he stated. "I know my rights." He set his jaw firm.

Goody. I didn't say it out loud, but wish I had. What I actually said was, "I'm hoping we'll be able to sort through this fast." I took a seat across from him as the accompanying officer removed the cuffs from Marcus's wrists. I inserted a cassette into the tape recorder and pressed play.

"Yeah, all right, I've got nothing to hide, man."

I already wanted to slap him. "Look, Marcus, I'm gonna be frank with you—you're being accused of multiple counts of sexual assault. When I caught wind of the initial investigation in August, I took on the case to make sure you were treated fairly. That's what friends do for each other, right?" I kept a close eye on him as I spoke, but so far, he'd remained composed. It was early yet. I hoped he'd quickly resolve himself to the fact that he'd been caught and tell me what I needed to know to make short work of this.

"I know people make mistakes, so I want to hear your side of all of this, because as it stands right now, things really aren't looking so good for you."

I didn't wait for a nod, grunt, or for him to speak, I simply kept on talking. "We've got quite a few women accusing you of raping them. I did my best to find out whether or not the accusations were true, and when it came down to it—"

"Like who?" He interrupted me, looking a little like he was going to cry. "I know that Alisa chick is after me, but no matter what she says, the sex we had was consensual. I've only ever had consensual sex."

I gave him the names of a couple more women who had come forward and agreed to be a part of the case. Marcus didn't deny having sexual contact with them. This was a good start with one exception—when I told him we strongly suspected he'd drugged many of the women, he insisted that wasn't the case.

"I didn't give any drugs to any of those women." He was looking up, but not at me, and shifted in his chair as if he was uncomfortable.

That was a damn lie, but it didn't matter because I figured I'd have no trouble proving it when it came down to it. "Well, that may be the case, but we have reason to believe there was more than alcohol at play because many of the alleged victims claim they don't remember large portions of time while in your company. Those are fairly strong allegations, especially when you consider all of them are certain you had intercourse with them while they weren't conscious enough to fend you off."

"I never had sex with any of them while they were unconscious, and I didn't drug anyone—those fucking women are lying," he stated confidently, but I could see through it.

He wasn't appearing as cool and collected as when I'd first sat down, but understand, he wasn't coming across as agitated, either—just firmly matter-of-fact. I wanted to push a little harder, so I thought it might be the right time to try and reason with him.

"Look, for the sake of everyone involved, why not just come clean? You've been caught fair and square, and with the evidence we've found, you'd be doing yourself a real favor if you spilled your guts. I mean, what reason would these women have to lie, Marcus?"

He leaned back in his chair and rested his arms on the table. He still hadn't looked at me. "I dunno man, but all of them wanted to crawl into bed with me, I swear to God."

Oopsie. Better not swear to the big guy, *buddy*.

"Okay, then." I followed suit and leaned back in my own chair, then folded my arms across my chest. "If you've only ever had consensual sex with all of these women, how would you explain the video tape of you and Sasha?"

There was the slightest shift in his demeanor—I could feel it more than I saw it. I was certain he was embittered by the thought of me seeing that tape, let alone having it as evidence. Seeing as he had destroyed the tape with Sasha, who had assured him she hadn't made a copy, I was hoping I'd squeezed just hard enough to get Marcus to pop.

He started to tear up, but I didn't know how to read the emotional response. With the insistence that he didn't rape anyone, it certainly *wasn't* remorse.

He didn't whisper a word about the videotape. Marcus shifted to hunch forward in his chair, bringing his nose close enough to his hands to give it a scratch. "Sasha was obviously on something that night. We had a couple of drinks and some shots and listened to some music."

"Which was before you needed to drag her from your bathroom to your bed, take her clothes off, poke at her to see if she was awake, masturbate in front of the video camera..." I took a deep breath and calmly continued, "...have sex with her while she was apparently unconscious, then hit her over the head with an alarm clock when she tried to fight you off?"

"Well, I don't know about any of—"

"Or," I interrupted him. "Why you needed to give her money to hush her up and pay for the abortion?"

"Look, that was a long time ago, Sherm. I don't remember a lot of it, but that's just how Sasha was; she was a freak." He stated she liked to have sex all the time and talked about getting videotaped—she thought it was kinky and the idea turned her on.

"So, did she give you permission to have sexual intercourse and tape her while she was unconscious?" I inquired.

Marcus sure as hell didn't tell me she gave him permission. In fact, he didn't give me any answer at all for almost a minute. He shifted in his seat again and simply stared up to the left-hand corner of the room. I followed his gaze—not even a cobweb to be seen.

When he finally spoke, his stance regarding Sasha was that she had unusual sexual behaviors so Marcus just assumed she was okay with being videotaped. I'm not sure how he made the connection between kinky meaning videotaping was A-OK, but my synapses didn't fire in a, "I'll look for any excuse to justify my actions" way.

When it came down to it, Marcus didn't give solid answers to *any* of the questions I asked, but repeatedly said, "I don't know what to say."

I knew what he should say…

"How about the truth, Marcus? It's all I'm interested in hearing." I had reminded him several times throughout the interview that charges were inevitable, so it would help everyone if he would only be honest about his actions.

Despite saying that, I knew by then I wasn't going to get the real stories out of this guy. I swear to God, something I'm comfortable doing, Marcus still believed he was going to be able to prove himself innocent. Why else wouldn't he fess up? I also considered, but only briefly, that the guy might be bananas enough to actually believe he hadn't done anything wrong. Maybe his views on sexual encounters really were that askew.

Maybe he thought I was bluffing on the evidence, which I kind of was at that point; I'd only seen ten seconds of that one video, but he didn't know that.

Even with the feeling that my effort to get the truth out of Marcus was futile, I pressed on. Maybe he'd slip up.

"Do you remember spending some time with a woman named Theresa?" I asked. "She says you tried to kiss her and made several attempts to get into her pants. She officially states you ignored her declarations that, although she said it many times, nothing was going to happen between the two of you." I went on to explain a little more of her story. "Is this true?"

Marcus didn't answer immediately; he sat there as if deep in thought. I leaned forward to look down into the tape recorder; we'd only gone through about a quarter of the tape, so I had time to wait.

"Yeah, Theresa, I remember her. I hung out with her sometime in January 2002, I think," he finally said.

"Yeah, you did. Can you tell me about it?"

He remembered going out drinking to a couple bars in De Pere with her but didn't remember trying to kiss her or her telling him that nothing was going to happen.

"She had said she was worried about anything happening because her roommate, Clara, works for me at the Velvet Room. I think you know her, too, Sherm."

I knew of her; Skinny knew her better. Moot point in that moment.

"Anyway, we went to Beef's in De Pere, but I don't remember going to any other bars. I thought she was hot for me, but I don't remember anything happening when we got back to my house. I sure as hell don't remember trying to get on top of her or anything else." He insisted he was really drunk but couldn't recall if she was drunk, too.

I didn't believe that for a second; I think Marcus Somerhalder remembered every little detail of every *single* thing he put those women through. From what I'd learned from the women and noticed myself while at the bar after the golf tournament, Marcus wasn't a heavy drinker; none of his victims ever described him as being wasted or even inebriated. Then again, none of them, or even myself, could say with any confidence that we had enough wits about us to notice his state.

Considering what Robert had told me about the kind of psychosis markers Marcus was displaying, he would have likely kept track—hence the videotapes. I'm betting he knew every detail he ever recorded, right down to the seconds they happened.

I wanted to take a break but decided it would be better to just press on. It was getting harder by the second to keep my shit together, but it was my job to stay cool. I pushed down the frustration, and continued to be as buddy, buddy as I could.

I decided to bring up Alisa next, and he promptly rolled his eyes and shifted his sitting position again at the mention of her name.

"I definitely had sex with her, but she wanted it." Marcus told a tale of a night out drinking at the bar with Faith (his current girlfriend at the time), Alisa, and Piper. They ended up back at his place in Ashwaubenon—the apartment we'd searched two hours earlier. "We were all having a great time drinking and chatting, and even though Faith was there, Alisa wasn't holding back on the flirting." He cleared his throat. "Hey, can I get a glass of water or something?"

Yeah, sure, buddy, *I'll get the firehose.* I stood and took the three steps to the door. I cracked it open and asked the officer outside to nab us a couple of bottles of water. I clicked the door shut and sat back down. "Please, continue," I said.

"Sure. So, Faith went to bed first and Piper followed soon after; once she did, Alisa and I had sex."

The officer knocked on the door, cracked it, and passed two bottles of water through. I nabbed them from the disembodied hand, cracked one and handed it to Marcus. I twisted the cap off of my own bottle, then took a swig as I sat back down in my seat.

"Look, the most I'm guilty of with Alisa is that I cheated on Faith with her. She's lying through her teeth if she says I raped her. It's probably a cover-up so she has an explanation for her boyfriend." He finished talking and leaned forward to get a drink, squeezing the bottle to get the water into his mouth. I wanted to shove the whole thing down his throat...

Instead, I took a deep breath. It's my job to keep my cool.

"So, you deny any illegal sexual contact with Alisa?" I tried to confirm.

"I didn't rape her, okay?" he said with conviction.

Still, I couldn't get a read on him. He had leaned forward, his face inches from the table top and was rubbing a hand in circles from the base of his neck to his brown hair. Maybe it was an effort to make me feel sympathy for him, but it wasn't working.

"You got it, boss," I said.

"Are we done here, Sherm? You know this is all a scam, right?"

"Marcus, this is absolutely the farthest thing from a scam." For a second or two, I considered he might be from another planet. I was baffled by the fact he was still trying to maintain his innocence. I wondered if it was because he thought he was that good at lying... Nah, he couldn't possibly have thought that. I have seen pretty intense stages of denial though...

I digress; I moved on to my last line of questioning. I asked him about Katie. "What do you remember about how things went down with her?"

"I met her and her friend Grace and some other girl at Ned Kelly's. You know, that pub downtown?"

I nodded my confirmation. I did indeed know the place.

"Anyway, we had a few drinks there, the girls got giggly, and we moved the party over to the Velvet Room."

"Did you know those women were all too young to be in Ned Kelly's?"

"No. They never said anything about their ages. I just assumed they were old enough or they would have told me otherwise. You know?"

What a ridiculous thing to say as a bar owner. He would have known better than me that no one is ever going to admit they're underage if someone is offering them alcohol. If he didn't know, I didn't feel like I was the guy to inform him.

"They didn't have any trouble getting into Ned Kelly's, so I didn't bother to check their I.D.s when we got to the Velvet Room."

"All right. Moving on; what else happened that night?"

"Nothing that night. All those chicks went home, but I ended up seeing Katie a few times after that." He went on to say that if she was accusing him of rape, it was total bullshit. "The girl was infatuated with me, and we slept together for like three months."

So, in other words, he basically denied any wrongdoing in reference to Katie.

"Those fucking girls, Katie and Grace, are lying to you. That's a felony, isn't it, lying to the police?"

"Don't worry about them, Marcus; I think it's best that you only worry about yourself right now. Even if those two are embellishing, the allegations against you are bigger than them." Not to mention, I hadn't said Grace was accusing him of anything. She was, but he didn't know that yet.

Marcus claimed a lot of women disliked him because of what he has.

"What do you mean by that?" I asked.

"When you own a couple of bars, people tend to see you as the most interesting man in the room."

It was a statement I could relate to. As a safety officer, I often experienced the same sort of attention. What I didn't do is exploit that attention by drugging and raping everyone who thinks I'm cool.

"You know, a lot of those women in that file of yours are just crying wolf. I slept with most of those women after the dates they say I sexually assaulted them. Sasha and her mom still come into the Velvet Room for drinks all the time."

"Marcus, whether that's true or not, Sasha and the rest of those women are victims. Their statements are real and they're hurting. I suggest, one more time, that you tell the truth," I implored.

"And nothing but the truth, Sherm?"

I'd had enough. I got up from my seat. "That's right, Marcus, and nothing but the truth. We'll talk again soon. For now, I've got a lot of paperwork to take care of." I turned off the tape recorder, popped the tape out, clapped Marcus on the shoulder like old chums do, then left the room.

As I made my way down the hall toward my office, I couldn't help but feel a little dejected. He didn't speak a lick of honesty but did manage to shift his position twenty times, shed a crocodile tear or two, and log a full hour of staring at the upper-left corner of the room.

It had already been a long day, but not getting anything along the lines of a confession, I thought it might be a good idea to contact Faith, Marcus's current girlfriend. If she wasn't absolutely breathing fire at the fact that we'd arrested her boyfriend, maybe she'd be willing to have a sit-down with me. Maybe she'd seen things and would be willing to share details. I had nothing to lose.

First, I needed a moment of silence.

CHAPTER 13

THAT'S WHAT HE IS. . .

AKA GODDAMNED NARCISSISTIC SOCIOPATH

I sat down at my desk, closed my eyes and rocked back and forth in my office chair, trying to clear my mind. I continued in this fashion for, I don't know how long, when my solace was interrupted by a knock at my door. My eyes shot open to find Investigator Tim David looming on the threshold of my office. "How's it going, Scott? Get anything out of Somerhalder?"

I forced a smile and said, "I now have no doubt the man is a raging sociopath."

"Oh?" He chuckled. "I thought we already knew that about him. Anyway, I stopped by to let you know I got all of today's evidence logged and secured. It's ready to go whenever you are."

"Thanks, Tim." Was all I could muster.

He nodded, then stepped out of my doorway to continue down the hall.

Investigator David was right. We had already deduced Marcus was a sociopath, but that interview solidly nailed down the psychosis for me. No one but a sociopath could do what Marcus had done and maintain the notion that they were entirely innocent. With a healthy mind, it was difficult for me—knowing without question what the truth of the situation was—to allow Marcus to keep his stocks in the "no, dude, I'm totally sane" market. I had to do it, though. Like I had done when I needed the truth out of Patrick to bring closure to Sawyer and his family, I sunk to Marcus's level. Being relatable to the worst kind of people is exhausting but necessary work.

I took a couple more minutes to relax, then cracked open the case file to locate Faith's phone number. It almost seemed weird that I didn't know all that much about Marcus's current girlfriend, but honestly, I wasn't all that concerned about someone who chose to be around him just yet. There were more than enough victims to worry about, but now I needed to know what things were like closer to home.

I dialed her number, and like it was a lullaby, nearly got lost in the steady tone as it rang. When she answered, I snapped back to attention.

"Hello?" she said, sounding like she was out of breath.

"This is Investigator Schermitzler from Ashwaubenon PD. Am I speaking with Faith? Did I catch you at a bad time?"

"Oh shit, no, no, not a bad time, and yeah, this is Faith. You're calling about Marcus, right? I know he got arrested, and I've been trying to figure out what the hell is going on."

"Well, I'm the guy who can fill you in, but I think it would be best if you came down to the station. Would you be willing to be interviewed in reference to this situation? There's a chance you have information that could help." I didn't define who it might help because it was a safe bet she was on Marcus's team.

Faith agreed to come by later that afternoon. With that to look forward to, I relaxed back into my chair and closed my eyes. I needed to give my brain some time to shuffle through, process, and organize everything that had happened so far in the day.

I was definitely upset about how the interview with Marcus had gone, but as I thought about it, I really didn't find the situation all that perturbing. If anything, Marcus's stance on the accusations would only complicate the inevitable jail time—might even increase it—but that wasn't my problem. The district attorney would be in charge of worrying about that. Since lawyers aren't all that prone to suffering their own feelings during a case, let alone other's, they would probably find a way to use Marcus's obvious sociopathy to their advantage.

I know I would.

I spent the rest of that afternoon documenting and writing reports, making sure things were in order, so I'd be ready when it was time to take the next steps.

Faith arrived at the station at around 4:30 p.m. that afternoon, accompanied by her parents whom she brought along for support. I was happy to see such a tight-knit family because it would help her cope through what I was sure was going to be some quite traumatic revelations.

There was more space and comfort to be found in my office, so I popped out of the room to nab an extra chair. We got settled, and Faith introduced me to her parents, Pete and Darla.

It was hard to deny just how similar Faith was to the rest of the women Marcus had targeted. She was a tall, delicate, beautiful blonde with an infectious smile. As we informally chit-chatted, she came across as intelligent and had a delightful gleam about her despite the obvious anxiety regarding her presence in my office.

"Thanks so much for coming down here today, Faith, and I'm very glad your parents have joined you." They nodded and I continued on to say, "I'm almost certain you aren't aware of much of what I'm going to tell you today. I'm also certain you're not going to like what I have to tell you, so I think having them here will be very beneficial." I looked to each parent with a half-smile and a slight nod.

"Before I get into that, there are a few details I'd like to get from you."

I could tell she was bursting with curiosity, but before I could open the proverbial can of worms, I had a few questions for her. I was shocked to find out that Faith was only nineteen years old—too young to hear the kind of information I had to share with her. It made her parents' presence there all that much more understandable, too. I also learned she had been dating Marcus for approximately nine months; they maintained their own places, but often stayed over at each other's apartments.

"Do you have any idea why Marcus is in police custody?" I asked.

She shook her head, and I could sense she was already on the verge of crying. She obviously knew Marcus was in trouble for something, but I was genuinely surprised she didn't offer up even a guess as to what got him into trouble. Faith really had no idea just how serious the situation was.

"Okay, well, I'm not going to sugar coat it for you because I don't think it'll help you, and I don't think I could even if I wanted to." I cleared my throat and continued, "Some of this stuff is going to be shocking and pain-ful to hear, so I just want you to be prepared for anything."

"Okay, Investigator, I understand," she said softly.

So, without wasting any more time, I began explaining the history of Marcus and sharing (without revealing any identities) some of the witness statements and evidence we had against him. There was no question that she was stunned and surprised, but she didn't cry; she did begin pondering her relationship with Marcus, though. Still, I could definitely tell Faith very much cared for Marcus, and initially, was prepared to protect her man.

She had been with Marcus for long enough to know that something had definitely been stressing him out lately. "I'm not sure why I'm here. Is there something I should personally be worried about? Is there anything I'm going to be charged with?" she said with a waver in her voice.

Clearly, she was uncertain as to why she was involved, but nothing about her or her demeanor came off as suspicious. I had no reason to believe she was involved in anything that Marcus had done.

"Look, Faith, I didn't bring you here because I think you're in cahoots with Marcus, I brought you in here because you're closer to him than anyone. There are a lot of women out there that are hurting really, really badly right now, and as much as you and I might want to *deny* they've suffered at the hands of Marcus—all signs pretty much point to him."

It wouldn't have been fair to add that the signs were made of shockingly bright, flashing neon, so I held back.

Faith sat quietly in thought for a moment, then said, "It's happened a bunch of times to me, you know."

"What do you mean?" I inquired.

"There have been a whole bunch of times when I couldn't remember what happened in an evening."

Now, that was a revelation.

"Did it only seem to happen when you were with Marcus?" I asked, getting excited, and then immediately felt guilty for it. It was a conundrum of feelings, really. Although I would *never* make light of her suffering, hav-ing his own girlfriend speak out against him would resonate with the judge and jury.

"*With* him? Yeah, you *could* say that. To be perfectly honest, there were times, the most recent being Thanksgiving night, when I'd go to bed at my house and wake up naked at his apartment several hours later."

"Excuse me?" I was shocked. He'd transported her from her own apartment to his without her having any recollection?

"Seriously, it happened more than once," she said.

I looked to her parents, both had a look of appall on their faces, the same as I'd have if it was professional to show it. Clearly, they hadn't been made aware of things like this. Although, they hadn't seemed all that shocked when I had mentioned the other cases. Then again, I'm sure hearing about it happening to other women is completely different than hearing it happened to their little girl. These days, I can relate.

"Also," she went on, "it was a while back, but I found a videotape of myself. Marcus had recorded us having s—sex." She stuttered. "But, in the video, I clearly wasn't conscious while it was happening." She chuckled a bit, but it was in discomfort. "Boy, that's hard to say out loud."

Darla took her daughter's hand and softly tsked as the tears started to gather in the corners of her eyes. She leaned forward to snap a tissue out of the box on my desk, dabbed at her eyes, and seemed to toughen up after that. I appreciated her strength; Faith needed that more than she needed her mother's pity. Her dad remained stone-cold, his jaw set firm. I can only imagine what he was holding back.

"I don't mean to sound insensitive, but do you still have access to the videotape?" I asked.

"No," she said as she looked down to the ground. "I was pissed when I found it, so I confronted Marcus about it. He got violently mad at me; said it happened over a month ago, and I gave him permission to do it, but I was too drunk that night to remember I did. That was bullshit. 'It was like five feet away from you, Faith. How could you not see it? I propped it up on my couch,' is what he told me. He was so furious I'd even suggest he would do something like that without me saying it was okay that he smashed the tape and shook me up a bit."

"He hurt you?" I asked.

She nodded.

"Marcus had a way of turning each and every issue and disagreement upside down on me. Even if something was clearly his fault, in the end, he was so good at passing the blame, he'd have me convinced I was the reason he did what he did. The argument would end on that note, too—me believing I was the one that had done something wrong."

"I hate to say it, Faith, but without the anger you're describing, that's exactly how Marcus justified the cases I presented him with this morning. He insisted it was their fault—they wanted it and they asked for it. That's a major character trait of two kinds of psychoses. Do you know what they might be?"

"I can just bet that one of them is a goddamned sociopath," Pete piped up.

"Correct, sir. The other is a narcissist. Marcus is blameless—thinks he can do no wrong and the problem is always someone else's."

"Sounds exactly right to me," said Faith. "Every time I questioned him about a blackout his response was that I had gotten too drunk, or I was just crazy and making stuff up. I was starting to believe him. You know," she said, then shifted her position to face toward her parents. "I didn't tell you guys, but I've been having a really rough time the last few months."

"What do you mean, sweetie?" Darla asked, panicked.

Pete looked like he was going to be the first official case of spontaneous human combustion—his face was red as a ripe tomato.

"I've been to the hospital half a dozen times—you know how I keep asking you for money?—it was for hospital fees. I've been having stomach issues; bouts of uncontrollable vomiting. There have also been times where I've lost hours and hours of memory. I had no idea where the time went, what I did during it, or how I got from one place to the next..."

Essentially, Marcus had brainwashed Faith into believing she was losing her mind, and the simple fact was that she was a very confused drunk. She loved him and trusted him, so why wouldn't she have believed him when he said it? As far as she was concerned, it must have been a true fault of hers—she was the one who kept blacking out, and she had no reason to suspect the asshole was drugging her.

She admitted that he wasn't as good at being accountable for his actions as he was at passing blame, but she still wasn't convinced her boyfriend was the terrible man I was suggesting he was.

We chatted a bit about Alisa's allegations against Marcus, and she admitted that she knew he had cheated on her with Alisa.

"I was sleeping in Marcus's bed when this supposedly happened," she said. "And I have a hard time believing I wouldn't wake up if a girl was truly being raped in the next room."

Marcus must have put in some time manipulating her mind for me to have gotten that answer out of her. To her, the false logical response he'd fabricated for the incident was enough to assure his innocence. Marcus had also told her that Alisa couldn't resist the opportunity to have sex with him, and he was too drunk to know any better. I presume Marcus had whittled away at Faith's self-confidence and pride to a point where she felt Marcus could do no wrong. Or maybe, it was just safer to believe him?

"Do you really believe that, Faith? You think that because Marcus says she couldn't resist him, the allegations of rape are simply washed away?"

She looked a little stunned by my statement.

"You need to realize that all of the women who've made statements regarding unwanted sexual encounters with Marcus have no knowledge of each other, and still, many of their stories are quite alike...that's no coincidence." I stopped talking when I saw the look on her face—she looked so defeated, and I felt awful about it.

Faith said nothing. She simply stared straight ahead, chest rising and falling deeply as a steady stream of tears descended upon her cheeks. I could see how tightly she was squeezing her mother's hand for support, and I understood. Not only was Faith losing the man she loved and trusted, she was realizing what the allegations against him meant.

He's a sexual predator.

He's an abuser.

He's a champion manipulator.

He's a sociopath.

She had no idea that his psychoses would progressively see him become more and more volatile. Without saying it in so many words, I had just informed her that their relationship was just another good time for Marcus and had meant very little to him.

"Wait," she said as she snapped out of her trance-like state and looked up at me. "So, I'm not crazy, I'm not a terrible, mindless drunk, and I like, don't have a tumor in my brain making me lose my memory?"

"Probably not," I confirmed. "I think the problem is that you've been drugged many, many times."

"I'm one of his victims," she said quietly. Faith then turned to her mom, "You're not going to like some of the stuff I need to tell Investigator Schermitzler."

Darla nodded her understanding.

Faith then looked to me. "Marcus has been very verbally abusive and violent since I confronted him about the incident with Alisa," she said. "Not to mention, he's forced me to have sex with him a bunch of times. He doesn't give a shit if I want it or not—he just *takes* it from me. It happened this morning."

There it was.

"That sonofabitch," Pete piped up, then looked at me with fierce intensity. "It's a damn good thing you've got that asshole in custody."

I nodded to Pete and was quick to ask her to elaborate.

"Marcus and I got back to my place this morning at about 4:30. We'd been out at the Velvet Room drinking after hours. When we got back to my place, Marcus found out I'd received a phone call from another man, and an argument broke out between us. He lost his mind, and there didn't seem to be anything I could say to calm him down." She looked down at the ground and took a deep breath before she continued. "He was screaming all sorts of horrible things at the top of his lungs—names, threats, insults—it wasn't long before he started pushing me around. He finally slammed me up against a wall, then left the apartment.

"I decided to shower before I went to bed, but when I got out of the bathroom, my phone was ringing. It was Marcus—one after another, he'd called thirteen times since I got in the shower. I picked the last call up just before it went to message. He still sounded angry; said he was coming back over and I'd better be 'fucking naked' when he got there."

She paused for a moment to dab at her nose with a tissue, and I looked over at her parents. Pete was still red in the face, no doubt trying his damnedest not to speak his mind on the matter. Darla, on the other hand, wasn't holding her emotions back, and was wiping her eyes and nose, unable to contain her tears as she murmured and cooed maternally.

Just after 8:00 a.m., he arrived back at her downtown Green Bay apartment and banged on the door until she opened it.

"I didn't even have the door opened all the way and he was back to calling me vulgar, disgusting names. I don't want to repeat them in front of my parents." She looked to me for understanding, then to her mom, who gave her a meek smile and encouraged her on. "Marcus was angry because I wasn't naked like he'd *ordered* me to be. So, he grabbed me by the shoulders and started shuffling me backward toward my bedroom. He pushed me backward onto the bed, then yanked my panties down to my knees and proceeded to—to..."

"Sexually assault you," I offered.

"Yeah," she said it almost as a sigh.

Faith let go of her mom's hand and stood up, pretending to look at the pictures on my office wall. "I was kicking at him and begging him to get off me and to leave, but he just kept at it. He covered my head with my comforter, but that didn't stop me. I finally got in a kick to his head and another to his chest. All that managed to do was piss him off enough that he grabbed my legs and pinned them to my chest using his shoulders, and got even rougher as he—he—"

"Oh my God, Faith," Darla sobbed. "Are you okay, baby?" She stood and embraced her daughter from behind.

Faith turned to bury her face into her mom's shoulder and let loose her tears as her father stood to join them.

To give them a moment, I excused myself from the room.

I didn't stray away from my office; I closed the door behind me and leaned a shoulder against the wall in the hallway. I felt somewhat guilty for not feeling more emotionally invested in what was going on in there, but I also didn't think it would make a difference if I was. Faith had her parents to lean on, and that had more impact than anything I could offer at that point. It had been a long, emotional, and exhausting day for me, and I'm certain I was becoming numb from the over-exposure. I also didn't want any of these women to feel like I pitied them; my strength would always be more beneficial to them. I wanted to be seen more as an advocate of justice and empowerment.

I could tell they weren't ready for me to enter the room; I could still hear the gentle sobbing and parental cooing. It warmed my heart at the same rate that it broke it. I wished there was never any need for this sort of comforting. I dwelled a moment on it, then my mind began to wander…

I couldn't figure out how Marcus did what he did to Faith for so long—they were together for nine months! Beyond that, how the hell did he get away with doing what he did to the other women, either? He was incredibly good at overlording these women. He would play with and manipulate their logical minds as if he had the ability to hypnotize them. If there really were people out there with superpowers—good or evil—his would be captivating, then conquering a woman's spirit. He was a haunting villain that had no qualms about taking advantage of his victim's most innocent and charming character traits, like kindness, youthful naïvety, and trustworthiness.

His victims were always younger, less experienced when it came to life and relationships in general. And, for whatever reason, women who were already inebriated and/or employed by him seemed to be his favorite targets to exploit.

I can only speculate as to why he went after the women he did: each and every one of them was beautiful, highly intelligent, well-spoken, and motivated; maybe dominating them was the ultimate conquest. All the men wanted them, but Marcus got to have them—no—*take* them.

Each one seemed to be the type of women who had it all, including men vying for their attention and affections, and with that, their experience with those men surely included them being treated respectfully. They probably never suspected any of their potential suitors to be a narcissistic sociopath. Getting their attention was only the first (and most innocent) of the many victories Marcus sought over his victims.

There was no safe ground if Marcus wanted you—he was going to get you whether you were interested in him or not. The thing I didn't understand, because I'm not a sociopath, is why he would want to drug and rape the women who *did* want to be with him?

He had completely manipulated Faith into becoming another pawn in his evil game, but why? She was a caring and willing participant.

So, this psychosis—this somnophilia—was the reason? He could only become sexually aroused if these women were faux dead? Despite the somnophilia, Marcus was still, without question, a narcissistic sociopath. He would have to be in order to justify, as he had earlier in the interview, blaming the women for him being in hot water.

Poor Faith. It was so heart-wrenching to realize how treacherously she had been played by this asshole. Although I'd already suggested what kind of man he was, she would soon have to come to terms with the brutal reality that her boyfriend was an unapologetic serial rapist. She didn't deserve this, and I couldn't imagine how deep this knife would cut her—or how she would deal with such deep betrayal.

I heard the hinges of my office door creak and turned to see Pete's head peep out. "Uh, Investigator Scherflitter?" he said, innocently slaughtering my name. I was used to it. "I think we should leave, but Faith says she isn't quite done talking to you."

"You bet." I turned on my shoulder and made my way back into the room to sit behind my desk.

"Look, I don't have much more to say today. I want to go home, but I wanted you to know, what I went through this morning hurt a lot, and I'm positive I've got bruises. So..." She looked at me, her eyes were red-rimmed and I could see she was on the verge of crying again. "What happens next?"

Excellent question.

"We've gotta stop him, Faith. Would you allow myself and a female colleague of mine, Investigator Lawler, to come by your place tomorrow? We'd love to look around for evidence. Also, I think it would be helpful to the case if you would allow her to take pictures of any bruising. Would this be acceptable?"

"Yeah, that can happen tomorrow."

"Okay, great. It would also be incredible if you could give a formal statement to Investigator Lawler tomorrow as well." I didn't want to push her, but if she was willing, I didn't want to miss out on any opportunity to make Marcus look worse in the eyes of the court.

"Sure," she said.

We all stood, and I offered to walk them out to their car.

As we made our way through the station, we finalized details regarding what would happen the following day. "Thanks so much for coming down here today." I spoke to all of them. "I promise to do everything in my power to protect you from ever getting hurt by this man again."

They thanked me, we exchanged handshakes, and off they went.

I made my way back to my office to grab my jacket and head home. It had been a damn productive day, and I knew I was going to sleep for the first time in a long time like the dead that night.

The next morning, Saturday, December 6, I was up long before the sun, which isn't a hard thing to achieve in Wisconsin in December. I woke feeling invigorated and ready for the day, which *is* hard to achieve in Wisconsin in December, but I couldn't contain the excitement I felt in following-up with Faith. Her statement would be a vital piece to the case we presented to the Brown County district attorney, and I couldn't wait to have it in hand.

Investigator Lawler and I made our way to Faith's apartment at around 9:30 a.m., armed once again with video and still-shot cameras. She welcomed us in and I introduced Lawler to Faith and her parents, who had arrived to support her.

Faith gave us permission to look around, and we chatted with her as we moved through her small space.

"He really only keeps a toothbrush here," she said, and she was right. We took pictures and video and looked around for anything of evidentiary value that Marcus may have left behind but didn't find anything that would be relevant or useful to the case.

"Have you seen any weird containers of liquid or pills or powders you don't recognize lying around?" I asked.

She hadn't, but she did say that she'd had a container of liquid multivitamins on her night table for the longest time, and one day, it was all of the sudden gone. She had no idea where it went but admitted Marcus stayed at her place alone sometimes. We hadn't come across anything like it in our search of Marcus's establishments, so it was pretty much a useless detail, but I noted it anyway just in case.

"I'll keep an eye out for anything suspicious," she said.

I was so pleased at how cooperative she was being. I hoped it was because she finally knew she was safe.

"That would be great," I said. "I know things were a bit emotional yesterday. Is there anything else you'd like me to know, Faith?"

"Well, I'm wondering if I should go to a hospital. There are some things I think I need answered."

"What sorts of things?" I asked, but she really didn't have to answer if she didn't want to.

"Well, for starters, I'm about two weeks late for my period. Not to mention, I've had a few urinary tract infections recently—I even ended up in the hospital for one of them. I got tested for STDs shortly before I met Marcus, so I know I was clean going in."

"I think your best bet would be to get tested for STDs again. It might take some time to find out if you're pregnant, but will you please let us know the results? We'd also ask the same for the STD testing," I asked. "Maybe, if you're willing, it might be easier if we could have access to your medical records?"

I explained that if Marcus was passing some terrible things around to her and the other victims, they all deserved to know. Not to mention, if she'd been in the hospital a bunch of times claiming memory loss, that would be on record, too.

Faith nodded. "That's a scary thought. I'll head into the hospital on Monday to get tested and sign the form to release my medical records."

I thanked her and we continued to chat idly and off topic for a few minutes before I suggested Lawler take photographs of the bruising.

"Do you want me to come in there with you?" Darla asked.

"No, Mom, I'll be fine," she said as she and Investigator Lawler made their way to Faith's bedroom.

Once they closed the door, I had a chance to talk with Faith's parents privately. Despite their obvious feelings of horror and disgust with the situation, they remained pleasant. It was clear they thought the world of their daughter, and I was keenly aware of how difficult it was for them to remain so calm and supportive for Faith.

I can guarantee, if I had just learned this happened to my daughter, I may not have been able to control my anger. They should have won an award for their exemplary ability to manage their extreme emotions and tremendous anger toward Marcus.

Lawler and Faith returned within ten minutes. Faith, looking a little red in the face, but Lawler was gently consoling her.

I advised her on how to contact Victim Services if she needed to talk through how she felt about everything she'd learned over the last couple of days. I followed up with, "Faith, if you remember anything, or if you have questions, please know you can call us at the station anytime."

She gave me a weak smile and thanked me, the weight of the last couple of days had clearly taken its toll on the poor girl.

On the way out I added, "If you come across anything suspicious, whatever it might be, assume we're interested in knowing about it and give me a call. Okay?" I handed her my business card.

She managed a quick okay in response.

With that, we closed the door on Faith and her parents, hoping they would work together to help her carry on through everything that had, and still was, going on.

Although she followed through on everything she said she would, we didn't get any new information from her. Fortunately, Faith was negative for any STDs and she wasn't pregnant with Marcus's child. That didn't change the fact that Faith was added to the list as yet another victim of first-degree sexual assault.

I slid her file into the mammoth-sized manila folder and promised myself I'd use every word within it against Marcus Somerhalder.

CHAPTER 14

PANDORA'S TRUNK. . .

AKA LITTLE BOX OF BIG HORRORS

I took the rest of the weekend off to enjoy some much needed time with my boys and unwind from the previous 48 hours.

First thing in the morning on Sunday, December 7, 2003, I stood at the entry way of the evidence locker, arms folded across my chest, just staring at Marcus's trunk of horrors. I was so anxious about cracking it open and beginning the daunting task of reviewing the videos, but it had to be done. I had already briefed my lieutenant and secured his services as one of the video reviewers, but I knew I would need more people.

I took the ten steps to reach the trunk, wrapped my hands around the handles, and heaved it over to the heavy metal table in the middle of the room. With the lock no longer on the trunk, I had no excuse left, so I cracked open the lid.

Looking down at the contents, my heart rate instantly picked up.

I reached in to grab the first stack and placed them on the table. By the time I put the last stack on the table, my total count came to seventy-two videocassettes. I heaved a deep sigh, picked up my pen, and cracked open the new manila folder (created for the video review process) to scratch my first note: *72 videos contained within trunk.*

With that, I placed them all back into the trunk, intimidated by the large number of videotapes, and left the evidence locker. It was time to officially build a team and find out just how big this case was going to be.

I partially hoped the video we watched in Marcus's bedroom was the only tape that contained violent sexual acts. As much as I wanted to make sure Marcus got his just rewards, I would rather find there weren't any more victims than who I'd already found. I wanted to believe the video in the trunk labeled *M*A*S*H* was the movie and actually contained Hawkeye spewing witty one-liners and Corporal Klinger in knickers and lipstick, but I was doubtful that would be the case.

Despite my every effort to keep a healthy mind throughout this case, I knew if I found many more victims within the video files it would take its toll. Alas, I had no choice; there was nothing more to do than mentally prep myself for whatever demon might rear its ugly face when we began viewing the evidence.

I only wanted a few key officers to be involved with documenting the tapes, so beyond my lieutenant, I commissioned two other officers I knew to be passionate, diligent, and respectful in every aspect of their work. I had to keep the women's privacy forefront in my mind while remembering that anyone who had to watch the tapes would likely be emotionally affected. I did my best to give them an idea of what they were in for, which was easier said than done. What made it such a hard task was knowing I could only guess at what we might see. While I was confident in their ability to professionally handle pretty much anything, I hated that any of us had to witness what was on the tapes. I was worried about my officers' well-being—I didn't even know why yet. One thing I could do was assure them that no matter what evidence we found in that trunk, at least we'd have each other to rely on for support.

Beyond our own mental and emotional needs, it was of the utmost importance that we *not* make these women victims again. It was an order that findings would remain discreet and confidential throughout the processing of this critical evidence.

Once the review team was in place, we set up a makeshift viewing area in the chief's conference room and limited access to only the three officers working with me and the commander of investigations.

With no reason to put it off, we dug into our work.

As we organized the VHS tapes for viewing, we came across quite a few of them that Marcus must have, in his haste to get the recorder on, just grabbed because they were the nearest videotape. Otherwise, we couldn't fashion a reason why he would bother stashing videotapes with movie titles in the trunk. Despite how the tapes were labeled, every single one of them had to be viewed from start to finish. We needed to assume the title had nothing to do with the content, and also had to consider that maybe after the movie was over, there might be footage we needed to see.

So with that in mind, we slid the first video into the VCR. When it was done, we watched the next video, and the next after that, and followed that up by watching another…

Over the next three days, every videotape recovered was quickly reviewed by my team and I, and the still vague contents were logged. There were seventy-two evidential tapes in total that would need to be picked apart. Needless to say, Marcus had been a very busy predator. The only positive thing I could say about the experience was that $M*A*S*H$ the movie remained innocently intact.

When clear enough images of faces were visible, I was called into the conference room to see if I could ID the females. In that initial viewing of the videos, I saw images and footage of a few of the courageous women who had already spoken with me, including Sasha, Faith, and Grace.

We were also able to positively identify the three different locations Marcus had used to satiate his perversions. Many of the videos were filmed in his apartment above My Place in De Pere. We also found some that would have been made while he lived in the apartment we had searched in Ashwaubenon, where the trunk was found. The last location was an apartment in a tidy red brick building on Decker Avenue in Green Bay. It was a lovely, older area of the city, unbefitting of the atrocities that happened within it. We decided it would be best to re-categorize the videos based on the locations where they were filmed.

From there, it absolutely proved to be a whole mess of work.

I had no doubt Marcus knew what was on each and every one of those tapes. I'll bet the asshole even had some sort of system of categorization, but to the rest of us, it just looked like a whole mess of VHS tapes.

Never mind what he knew, even if he'd kept detailed lists of what could be found on each tape, we still had to watch every single one. With a comprehensive account of what we found, we might be able to avoid any-one else ever having to see what was on these tapes. Like I said, it was of the highest priority those women never felt victimized by Marcus Somerhalder, or anyone else for that matter, *ever* again. If we had to view them in court, so be it, but I was going to do all I could to prevent that from happening.

With such an amazing and supportive staff in the Ashwaubenon station, it wasn't long before other officers began offering to help us watch and log data from the tapes. As much as I would've loved to have taken them up on the offer, I thought it best to decline. I was certain it would be better to protect them from the sickening consequences my team and I were already experiencing. Although we hadn't yet taken a close enough look to know what finer details would be revealed, we'd seen more than enough to know we'd be viewing horrid criminal acts.

With the initial viewing and logging complete, it was time to really dig deep. The three officers and I alternated working in pairs. We had three videos in our possession at a time, and with those videos *never* to be out of our sight, we would lock ourselves into the makeshift viewing area. Armed with a pen, paper, and the remote to the TV/VCR, we would sit for hours carefully dissecting and examining frame by frame for potential identifiable scars, birthmarks, tattoos, clothing/jewelry clues, etc.—anything to help us figure out who these women were. Oftentimes, this meant pausing, rewinding, and re-watching the video, making the process painfully cumbersome.

These videos were *not* naked people doing what naked people do; this was not porn, and there was no pleasure to be seen on their faces. Most of the victims were heavy lidded, non-responsive ragdolls on a bed or a couch. One victim was assaulted on the floor. We watched, and as we did so, we hated the feelings of shame and humiliation we felt on their behalf because those feelings were wrong; sickening—but, we're only human for God's sake.

Video after video we watched more and more perverted sexual exploitations of these young ladies. We saw, in each and every moment we watched, utter degradation. There was no way a single one of those women would have allowed Marcus to do what he did to them.

I know I've touched on this a few times, but there was a destruction of trust and the complete lack of respect displayed in these videos—the total disregard for their half-conscious pleas to Marcus to stop. Even in the varying debilitated states many of his victims were in, they said or showed that they were not consenting to his actions. Sadly, none of them were of sound enough mind to put a stop to what was happening. We watched, and we were witness to the brutal rapes of helpless, impaired, and often unknowing victims.

Unlike with the scariest parts of every horror flick I've ever seen, I couldn't look away—it wasn't even an option. It was my job to see it all and know it all, and I hated every second of it.

None of these women had any idea they were being recorded, at least, we suspected they didn't know. Not a single one of them ever looked at the camera with any recognition of its existence whatsoever. I think you get the idea of how terrible it all was, but honestly, there were so many other things that came about as we made our way through the evidence. This was just the beginning.

Watching, cataloging, and searching for the most minute details was one thing; seeking out and informing victims was a whole other thing altogether.

From living in the area, hanging out at his establishments, and knowing Marcus, I was able to identify some of the victims we saw in the videos as women I had talked to in the past three months. But, as we moved from video to video, I knew less of the victims and my notes grew to include a substantial number of women who were only distinguishable by their list of details—those scars, tattoos, birthmarks, and so on were so important. It was rare that we could tell what color the eyes were, but hair color was usually visible. The problem with hair color was that it was easily changed, so it wasn't always a reliable detail.

Pairing identifying markers we collected from the videos with the photographs we'd seized from Marcus's apartment and bars allowed us to positively ID a few more women. These were women that I was familiar with, but I hadn't contacted any of them or known they were possible victims prior to the search warrant.

Once we were 100 percent certain of who a girl was in a video, I would call her. Instead of filling her in on the news right away, I would ask a few questions to make sure I was talking to the right person. I would start out slow with questions like "Do you know Marcus Somerhalder?"

As we continued to chat, if they confirmed certain past dating information, I would ask them if they ever gave Marcus permission to film them while they were having sexual relations.

When they said no—because they all said no—I would explain the circumstances and why I thought it might be them in the video. Some of the women didn't even know they'd had sexual relations with Marcus. Needless to say, they all took the news differently and it was never in a good way.

For most of them, it was cut and dry; once they knew what was going on, we would work quickly to get them down to the station so they could view the tape and confirm it was them.

There were some women who reacted quite differently. They would deny ever having a relationship with Marcus and refuse to cooperate or even come in and watch the video. I couldn't blame them for that. After all, if you weren't aware that something awful had happened to you, why would you want to find out? Ignorance is bliss, I hear.

There were others still who would agree to come in, view the tape, then deny it being them—even when I knew without a shadow of a doubt it was definitely them we were watching. For whatever reasons, it was easier for them to deny the existence of the video footage than admit anything had happened. I wondered what those women's stories were. Maybe they hadn't had a bad experience with Marcus? Maybe they'd enjoyed their time with him? I suppose some of them could have been cheating on spouses or boyfriends and wanted to make sure the proof of it never came out, never mind what their experience with Marcus was.

No matter the answer, it wasn't my place to question them on their decision to remain silent, and I sure as hell wasn't going to force them. In the end, it didn't matter. There were enough identifiable women who were willing and able to work with us, and that's what was most important.

Once we were left with hours upon hours of video filled with unidentified victims, we didn't have any choice but to present the case to the public.

So, with the alleged serial rapist, Marcus Somerhalder, in custody, and the initial review of evidence completed, it was time to show this case's ugly face to the public. On December 28, 2003 media outlets that fed information all over Green Bay and its surrounding towns, villages, and hamlets revealed

Marcus's very illegal doings. Within seconds of the first story breaking, our phones started ringing, and it was going to be a long time before they let up.

We'd learned from some of the women that the only sexual encounters they'd had with Marcus had been in 1999, which meant, with it being nearly 2004 at the time, five years later had seen many of these women move on with their lives: getting married, with boyfriends, or moved away. I thought it was incredibly courageous when a husband or boyfriend would come along to offer comfort and support to their lovely woman. There was a lot of heartache, so I was glad these women didn't have to see what they did all alone.

I was too busy during that time to sit back and ponder on it, but now, with more time and perspective, it really is unbelievable that he got away with videotaping women for five years before he was finally caught. Without any thinking required, it was clear at the time that Marcus was a stealthy deviant because even the women who had consented to have sex with him hadn't agreed to being videotaped.

As the calls came in, we did our very best to get as much information as we could from them. All of them were nervous throughout the phone calls, and many of them had stories of what went on while they were with Marcus. We tried to keep the information coming in as organized as possible, but sometimes, the sheer amount of it was overwhelming. It was also difficult to decipher how many of these calls were valid complaints. To sift through those telling the truth and those who were simply attention seekers, it was important that every possible victim come to the station to make an official statement. With what they had to say in hand, I would easily be able to determine if they had actually suffered at the hands of Marcus or not because by then, we knew exactly, point for point, what he had been doing to his victims.

I couldn't believe the turnout we got. Including the original victims, we ended up with a total of thirty-three official complaints, and that wasn't anywhere near the final total.

Each of these brave and amazing women wrote up official statements for us. It wasn't surprising to see how closely their experiences paralleled from what we'd already heard from women like Sasha, Hope, and Katie. Over half of those women claimed they were, or thought they might be, victims of Marcus in some capacity or another. The rest of them made statements, but more or less wanted to know if they were in any of the videos we'd confiscated.

Several of the women who gave written statements indicated they sometimes "blacked-out" or had unusual memory loss when they were around Marcus; more than a handful of them added that they suddenly got ill and suffered acute bouts of uncontrollable vomiting. Most of them assumed it was because they had too much to drink, and that assumption led to the popular declaration that it was something they had done that provoked the sexual assault.

That last comment is easily the most common declaration I hear from victims of sexual assault, and they genuinely feel justified when they say it. I can't tell you how many times I've heard admissions like, "Well, I was pretty flirty that night," or "I was wearing this low-cut shirt and a really short skirt."

Good God, no. No!

Those are not assault provoking things. There is nothing out there that should provoke rape! Everyone, and I mean *everyone*, should be allowed to express themselves and feel safe. They should never feel like they have to change how they dress or how they act to prevent someone from attacking them. Rape is the heinous act of a sick mind and nothing a woman does should be considered as provocative to that end.

We deal with provocation day in and day out. Even if it isn't the base of the problem like drugs and alcohol would be considered, it's always the end-all to the be-all, if you know what I'm saying. "He kissed my girlfriend," or "She cut me off in traffic," are idiotic but common justifications for repercussions like dealing out a knuckle sandwich or slamming on the breaks so the jerk tailgating you rams into your bumper, but they're just excuses.

It's the same when it comes to sexual assault. Excuses come from every side, though—the victim, the accused, and worst of all, the people who play into rape culture by blaming the victim.

Women only think their skirts are too short or they're showing too much cleavage because they've heard complete assholes, both male and female say, "Well, in that kind of outfit, she was askin' for it."

Utter bullshit.

Our bodies are our own business. If I'm looking dapper—bowtie, cummerbund, and all, and my lapel is askew, you let me know—I'll fix it or I'll *ask* you to. You don't get to touch me without me *letting* you touch me. The same rules stand for every other situation that relates to touching someone else.

To help with this, I've put together a three-step guide to being a respectable human and keeping your hands to yourself.

1. If her skirt is too short, or her shirt's cut too low, or his ass looks ripe to squeeze—look but don't touch. Yah got it?

2. If anyone says, "No, don't touch me,"—don't touch them, or immediately stop touching them. Yah got it?

3. Just for this example, let's pretend the words "drink soda" and "have sex" are interchangeable. If someone tells you they don't want to "drink soda" with you, but you think they're just playing the "I'll say the opposite of what I really mean" game and force them to "drink soda" with you, you're probably going to encounter a badass cop, like me, dealing with you justly. Forcing someone to "drink soda" is rape. Yah got it?

The sad thing is how deeply engrained into our minds the excuses for rape culture are. Victims need support, understanding, and empowerment so they can heal and rise above feeling victimized. If we continue to excuse and justify the idea that anyone *deserves* to be a victim, then we're advocating and permitting the creation of more and more victims.

Until, that is, you're the victim yourself. Then what?

You might finally understand what I mean, but it'll be too late.

If we as a society don't eradicate rape culture and empower victims by then, you'll remain a victim, suffering shame and fear you shouldn't be feeling, too afraid to shrug off the self-blame and heal.

We've created and nourished the bystander audience; a society allowed to chatter from the shadows in hushed tones as they point their fingers down at victims *and* abusers alike. I'm haunted by the fact that, without the dramatics, this is nearly seen as accepted standard practice. We really need to pull our heads out of the sand on this topic, especially when this topic comes around to encompass abusers who use stupefying drugs to debilitate victims.

Especially when our list stating the names of women who *knew* they had sex with Marcus, but couldn't remember it, swelled so quickly. All of them insisting without hesitation or doubt it had happened because of the way they felt in the morning—tired, sore, and tender in their vaginal area. Some stated they were in the midst of or finishing their period; when they came to in the morning, they had bled all over Marcus's sheets.

It was also interesting to hear that many of them, when asked what they drank when they were with him, said he served them Applejack shots—on the house, of course. I'd long suspected it was his delivery drink, but these confirmations solidified it as fact in my mind. There's a lot of flavor in those shots and they're down the gullet in a second, so it was the perfect drink to hide his nasty little potion in.

Lastly, many of those very same women who talked about the "on the house" Applejack shots also said they remembered the part of their evening where they were in Marcus's bar, My Place, but woke up the next morning in his upstairs apartment naked, in his bed, with no recollection of how they got there.

It was the same sort of experience Faith had mentioned having, although she was dragged from her downtown apartment in Green Bay to Marcus's apartment in Ashwaubenon—that was easily a twenty-minute drive. I hoped the crime lab would crack open those shampoo bottles from Marcus's apartment soon and provide me with the exact drug I was dealing with. I'm an extremely diligent investigator, but I worried it might be damn near impossible to prove what Marcus had been dosing these women with. Despite the visual evidence of women with glazed, half-lidded, and closed eyes being tossed about on a bed, we didn't have a lick of physical evidence that proved there was more than alcohol at play.

If those shampoo bottles didn't contain a stupefying agent, I was going to have to track down what the hell Marcus had been using on these women. I'd do it, but I knew it would take time.

Another similarity between the pre- and post-warrant victims was that none of them could remember if a condom was used. I'd heard from several of the victims that Marcus didn't like wearing condoms. Hearing as many as I had say they had fluids leaking out of them in the morning, and a couple of women informing us that shortly after having sexual relations with Somerhalder they contracted chlamydia or herpes, it was clear this was a truth.

I thought again about how Faith had come up clean—not to make light of any of this, but the girl should have taken up gambling after beating those odds.

With so many women anxious to know if their images had been found in Marcus's trunk, and seeing as we couldn't allow anyone to simply sit down and watch the video evidence, we came up with a better plan. When the women came down to the station to make their statements, we'd also ask them for permission to take Polaroids, so we could document defining features like birthmarks, tattoos, and stuff like that. We'd already done the very same thing throughout the video review, so we would easily be able to compare the new victim photos against the notes we'd already made. There wasn't a single one of them who refused to have pictures taken.

From there, we built each of them a file, which included the distinguishing feature pictures and their statement, then we'd return to our video notes to see if they matched any of the "Polaroid notes" we'd taken. The system was incredibly efficient, and we were able to identify several of the women from the videos.

When we were positive we could ID one of the victims from the files, we'd call them back into the station and ask them to view and confirm if it was them in the video. I dreaded having to tell each and every one of them. Their first articulation was usually one of surprise, as if she was that one woman he would *never* do that to, which was then followed directly by anger toward Marcus.

Every time I prepped a woman to show her a video I was confident she was in, the behavior was the same; she would go back and forth between feeling strong and empowered to being horrified by the fact that my officers and I had seen her so verily exposed. The women who had consented to having sex with Marcus knew we would be seeing their most intimate moments.

Still, the women who had no idea how awfully vulgar their videos were, only that they had been videoed being sexually assaulted, sometimes began these sessions in such horrible states of panic that they had to leave the station. They always returned to try again—brave, more ready, and resigned to the fact they wouldn't like what they saw.

As with the pre-warrant women, some admitted it was them in the videos but were adamant in their refusal to be a part of the case. They had all sorts of reasons, and every single one of those reasons broke my heart. So much of it revolved around what I'd said before—about victims blaming themselves, but most of them felt shame. They were desperately worried about what their spouse/boyfriend would think of them.

Some women were very afraid of what Marcus would do to them if he ever found out they'd agreed to be a part of the defense against him.

The rest? Well, the rest were afraid of having to tell their parents. To avoid what they perceived as humiliation, many women chose to have their cases dismissed, even though they could've easily been proven.

But the biggest issue I ran into, time and time again, was the fear of people not believing them when they testified.

I tried and tried to assuage those fears, but they were so engrained in their minds. The fear of not being *believed* was why many of them, even without any doubt in knowing they'd been assaulted, didn't go to the police in the first place.

They had been duped, violated, abused—you could even loosely say some of them had been abducted as they were transported from one place to another while out of sorts. Yet, that wasn't enough to get them into the police stations and hospitals because their fears trumped the experience...and so many women feeling the same way saw me suffering hopelessness. There were moments when I felt such anger at society and the justice system I proudly served—how could we ever allow things to get so bad that it was easier to be submissive than it was to stick up for yourself?

Everyone has known someone who's been victimized in one way or another. A person whose car gets hit by someone who then drives off without taking responsibility has insurance to get their car fixed. Yet a woman, bruised, sick, and disoriented doesn't feel justified in going to a hospital and reporting it? What have we done?

The longer this video review process went on, the harder it became to hear about them waking up mid-assault with Marcus's fingers on them, becoming debilitatingly sick, waking up sore and bruised, waking up not knowing where they were... It still makes me choke up when I think back on this point in the case.

I gave each of them the option to view their respective videos alone. Most of them appreciated the offer, especially the ones who'd brought supportive loved ones. The last thing many of these women needed was me, or anyone else, to be sitting right next to them while they watched themselves in such compromising positions. Still, a few of them wanted me or a female officer to accompany them into the room. Those who went in alone tended to stay in the room long past the time the video was done playing. I'm certain it was time used to process what they'd seen. I comforted many tearful women as they exited the viewing room, many of them admitting they felt betrayed and humiliated. I had done my best to prepare them for what they were about to see, but in many cases, there was nothing I could say to make things better after they left that room full of pain.

Once they'd calmed down enough to dry their tears, I'd tiptoe around their emotions to help them convert their trauma into a fiery inferno of confidence and the right to legal retribution. I wanted them to help me seek justice against Marcus's actions and betrayals. I implored them to see that it was my objective to build an extremely strong case and there was power in numbers. With so many of Marcus's victims standing together to prove what a monster he was through their sworn statements, it would be a declaration of strength and comradery. And, in doing so, annihilate those feelings of humiliation—wash their hands of the self-inflicted feelings of guilt because those were never theirs to suffer... Those feelings should have totally and always belonged to Marcus.

"With so many statements," I explained to them, "no victim will need to face testifying in a packed court room."

Promising they wouldn't have to speak about their experiences in a courtroom was extremely comforting to the women. It was an effective tactic in getting some of them to agree to let me use their statements, and yet, in many cases, it was still a hard sell. The truth of it was, I wasn't so naïve to think I could guarantee that I could keep them, or the videos they were in, out of the courtroom. I think many of them realized that and decided to call me on my bluff. It was much easier for these attractive, bright, successful, and popular women to sweep the whole experience under the rug so they didn't compromise their futures. Not that they would have, but I know they felt they were safer by refusing to help and denying the crime.

Thankfully, many of these courageous women understood the importance of stopping Marcus and preventing this cycle of sexual deviance from continuing. Maybe some of them realized they would never be able to conquer the hurt of knowing they were one of his victims if they did nothing about the fact.

I was empathetic toward everything these women were going through, but I simply had to be a bigger presence than a shoulder to cry on, a "there, there," and a pat on the back. Every single one of them needed that, but what they needed more was reinforcement that their involvement in bringing Marcus down was of critical importance.

It was emotionally exhausting. There were mornings where I spent an extra ten minutes in bed just trying to will myself to sit up, and it was a small victory when I did. I'd have to battle again to get myself out of the shower. Then once again, sitting in my car, a ten-minute pep talk just to get the key into the goddamned ignition...

I did it, though. I did it because you can't talk to that many suffering people about how they need to rise above and fight back if you can't even get your ass out of bed to fight alongside them. Right?

Right.

Still, I can't deny this case messed with my psychological well-being and confused the hell out of me. This was especially true once the case went public.

To recap, some of the women were physically hurt by Marcus's actions and perverted needs, but all of them were psychologically hurt. Even the ones who had willingly climbed into bed with this creep had a hard time because they ended up experiencing a version of what we call "survivor's guilt." They were glad they hadn't suffered like the drugged women had, and they felt awful about it. Add to the fact that all of them were there because we'd found them in Marcus's macabre video collection—you can't deny it would have been a difficult thing to flex your mind around day in and day out.

Once everyone knew about the case, they also knew about me, and I absolutely hated the recognition. Not nearly as much as I hated how it altered my whole personality, though.

I was still a fairly young man being in my thirties; I was recently divorced, sexually active, and dating. I had a girlfriend at the time, and while this case had made me quite popular with the opposite sex, I was in absolutely no mental state to appreciate any of the attention. I would never call myself a player, but I was a viable dating option for a lot of women; an avenger of sorts, although not in a Marvel sense. It made no difference because I had a hard time seeing any interested women as sexy, or attractive, or anything other than just human.

I had always been very sexually active, but as I was dealing with this case, I just couldn't find any interest. I certainly wasn't getting any delight or arousal out of watching the tapes. Honestly, it turned me off of sex for a while. It was so difficult to go to work and watch what I did for several hours a day, then want any sort of intimacy later. I was mentally and psychologically exhausted. In other words, as a coping mechanism to what I had been enduring, I shut down almost every intimate emotional response. I think it would have wrecked sex for me forever had I not learned to deal with the issue; I wish I could have applied that same sort of blocker to every emotion I endured throughout that time.

I never talked with anyone about the sexual facet of my issues, but even without mention of that, people on the outside had no ability to understand what it was like under the umbrella of this case. Not that I could blame them, they didn't know any better, but some of the stuff they said to me was so blatantly insensitive I was ashamed for them when they said it.

It always started out innocent enough. "Hey! You're that guy working on the Marcus Somerhalder case," they'd say, sometimes offering a hand to shake. "We used to go to that asshole's bars after our rec league games!"

"You and loads of others," I'd reply.

"It's pretty awesome that your job is watching porn all day now, am I right?" They'd laugh and clap me on the back.

Some of them almost came across as jealous, nigh on envious, that I was getting paid to watch those unbelievably vulgar videos. I couldn't go anywhere or do anything around the Green Bay area without someone making a comment about the case or making some repugnant remark about what these women were doing on the tapes. I was sickened by the lack of compassion displayed by these people.

Not only that, but it was difficult to not take their comments personally. How *dare* they suggest I was any kind of man who would take pleasure in this! The thought made me nauseous and every time it did, the thought of what those amazing, hurting women must have been feeling would come rushing to the forefront of my mind. If I was suffering that badly, what they felt must have been tenfold.

Still, there were others; people who didn't envy what I was doing but still completely misinterpreted what it was I was doing. My girlfriend at the time, for example, would question me on why I had to go to work and watch "porn" all day.

How did *she* not get it? A woman who, under the right circumstances, could have very well been in any of those women's shoes. She was bright, beautiful, charismatic—Marcus's type! Thankfully, she never met Marcus, but really? Never once in her life had a beautiful woman like her been victimized? And by that, I don't mean rape, but she'd never suffered unwanted touching? Had she never experienced being treated like an object to be possessed instead of a human being to be respected?

Maybe I'd just seen too much of it in my line of work. I suppose I assumed most women had experienced sexual assault or at least harassment in one form or another, whether they were able to laugh it off or not. Either way, from a feminist standpoint, I couldn't understand why she wasn't more sympathetic.

I never responded well to her inquiries because I couldn't fathom how she justified ignoring the obvious truth that this went so far beyond the realm of these being naked images of women. I couldn't understand it at the time and didn't even know how to talk about it with her—it was just so narrow-minded.

I didn't respond well to much of anything at that time because I con-stantly felt like I was having an out of body experience—I didn't feel anything like the man I had worked so hard to become. It seemed like no one in my world related to what was going on within it. There was such a lack of empathy and sympathy, and it was baffling to me.

People felt badly for the women I was working so hard for, and rightly so, but I was never factored into that equation—even when I reacted in ways that showed I should have been.

"Heck, I wish I had your life, man! Porn all day, every day. You're one lucky sonofabitch!" I'd hear.

My heart would sink as my anger rose. "You gotta be kidding me! I'm watching women get raped!"

"Whoa, whoa, man. Calm down."

Calm down? How about I Hulk rage, eh buddy? I thought, but never said that or did.

I'd relax, but only because I had to. It was a façade though; what appeared as "calming down" was simply me tucking back the rage, confusion, and other emotions I had no outlet to shed. Would they have said the same thing if they'd put themselves in my shoes? Probably not.

When I think back on all of it, the one and only positive side effect of the attention I got was how hard fiercely loathing that attention forced me to work. I wanted out of the video rooms, I wanted the images out of my head, I wanted my sex life back, my mental health back, I want that goddamned manila file sealed shut and whisked off my desk…

But, there was nothing I wanted more than to see Marcus rot in a jail cell for the rest of his life. I hated the man.

I was filled with consternation that Marcus, someone I had respected and considered as a friend at one time, had put me in this giant, overwhelming, and wholly unbelievable situation. It was clear at that point Marcus was sick and needed help, but it didn't stop me from wanting to repeatedly ping his head against the bars of his cell. I resisted only because I had to—he would have to answer for the devastation he caused, and I would, through every legal avenue and loophole I knew, ensure that happened.

CHAPTER 15

CASE #04CF841...

AKA STATE OF WISCONSIN VS. MARCUS B. SOMERHALDER

Now, this is where the story gets complicated, because despite the obvious guilt of serial rapist, Marcus B. Somerhalder, the case was riding on a whole bunch of variables that spread throughout an incredibly intricate timeline. For example, as the video review raged on, Marcus was already attending what would become multifarious courtroom appearances.

Multifarious? Yes. What the hell does that mean? Let me explain briefly what I promise to expand on later. According to Merriam-Webster, it means *having many varied parts.* Here's a list of synonyms to make it perfectly clear: diverse, many, numerous, various *and* varied, diversified, multiple, multitudinous, multiplex, manifold, multifaceted, different, heterogeneous, miscellaneous, and assorted.

It seemed, although it wasn't really the situation at all, that I was in front of a judge every damn day from the time that asshole was taken into custody to the time they finally closed the case. Why? Because beyond the many names I needed to add to the courts' list of victims, Marcus had his own agenda that included a seemingly never-ending list of issues, objections, misunderstandings, pleas, appeals, requests... He only had time on his hands, so he spent that time dreaming up new ways to get his ass out of jail, or at least, suffer the situation less. Beyond that, it seemed as if everything I did to put the man in cuffs was going to be questioned as well. It was wholly ridiculous, and I didn't have time for it.

This wasn't all that was going on for me—the sorting of the intricate timeline was only one of the proverbial guns to my head, forcing me into near-constant focus.

Besides the many court dates, the continuation of the video review, the case going public, interviewing the influx of potential victims, avoiding street fights with case-ignorant chumps suggesting I was watching porn all day, more celebrity status as the lead on the case than I wanted, and leaving it all behind to be a father, son, brother, and boyfriend, and trying to keep my damn head on straight through it all to figure out what the hell Marcus had been slipping into his victims' drinks.

I couldn't be certain, in fact, I had no bloody idea at all if he'd been using the same substance from the time he began drugging to the time he was caught. There was as much chance he had a long-standing subscription to the stupefying drug of the month club and had the chance to change up his weapon of choice often.

All I knew for certain was that between myself and many of Marcus's victims, there were far too many of us who felt there was no question they had been drugged by him. No matter how obvious it seemed to everyone, I knew I couldn't rely solely on the videos as proof that the women had been drugged. And, lastly, seeing as I hadn't heard back from the crime lab regarding what the hell was inside of those dark shampoo bottles, I (grudgingly) couldn't assume it was anything other than shampoo.

I remembered keenly how I'd felt after my run-in with his magic little potion, and I'd heard more than enough accounts that pretty much matched mine, so with that knowledge, I started researching what kinds of stupefying agents caused those sort of adverse reactions. As I did so, I needed to focus especially on the ones that matched the effects I felt when it was combined with alcohol. My search for this mysterious substance brought me to a very knowledgeable woman by the name of Trinka Porrata.

This woman knew everything about date rape drugs and stupefying agents both past and present, and for good reason, too. She was a twenty-five-year veteran of the LAPD when she retired from the force in 1999 with the rank of Detective Supervisor in narcotics. While we never got to meet face to face, it only took a twenty-minute phone conversation with her to have her conclude with certainty exactly what Marcus had been using to render his victims comatose.

"Sounds exactly like GHB—technically called gamma-hydroxybutyric acid," she said without hesitating.

There was no way I was going to have a go at the word, so I asked politely, "Could you spell that for me please, Trinka?"

She obliged, then went on to confirm when consumed with alcohol, GHB can cause vomiting and a level of unconsciousness almost impossible to wake a person up from before the drug has run its course. I'd already known both of those details, so it came as no surprise, but the last thing she told me about it did. Apparently, when consumed with alcohol, it can be a potentially lethal combination. As if that wasn't enough, my whole body vibrated in anger as she went on to explain how GHB is a substance that settles to the bottom, making the doses more and more potent the further down into the bottle you get. A tiny dose could make a person pass out one time, then the next dose, pulled from the insufficiently mixed or unshaken bottom of the bottle, could cause respiratory arrest—a heart attack—and death. Essentially, a milligram extra could have possibly been my, or any of Marcus's other victim's, demise if he wasn't in the practice of shaking the bottle before dosing.

I still wasn't convinced he hadn't killed anyone, but I hadn't come across any proof that he had. (And I never did.)

"How long does it take for this GHB stuff to work its way out of the system?" I asked.

"Anywhere from one to seven hours. It's different for everyone and strongly dependent on the size of the person for the oral dose—and if it's taken with alcohol, it lasts longer. Women tend to take a little longer to get it out of their system. You're not likely to find it in urine after about the three-hour mark on anyone, which is a moot point because there isn't a rape kit out there that's testing for GHB yet. It's a trendy little bugger that's only just become an issue with regard to the party scene."

"Really?" Was my brilliant reply. "Lemme ask you this then—if it's gone outta the blood so fast, how the hell does the violent sickness it causes last almost two days?"

"Not everyone gets that sick. That's the by-product of an overdose. GHB makes it hard for your body to flush out toxins. So, when it's taken in combination with alcohol, the booze becomes concentrated in your liver and kidneys which can cause all sorts of terrible stuff to happen—vomiting and loss of consciousness, including the potential to become lethal. There's always the chance your organs will simply shut down, or you'll roll onto your back while unconscious and choke on your own vomit."

"Hmm," I said, too angry to muster any other response as I remembered back to the pile of vomit on, and down, the side of my couch. I finally mustered the ability to speak. "Trinka, if and when the time comes, could I get an official statement from you?"

"Of course, Investigator."

"Excellent. I'll be in touch," I said with confidence, then remembering my manners, I added, "Thanks for your time."

"My pleasure," Trinka replied. "I hate this GHB shit. It's scary as hell."

I couldn't agree more, but I couldn't do anything with the information she'd given me until I heard back from the crime lab. It didn't matter right then anyway. I didn't have time to sit on my haunches waiting for the information because on December 8, 2003, three days after Marcus's initial arrest, he made his first appearance in a courtroom, overseen by the honorable Judge Warpinski.

I couldn't have been more excited to be in that courtroom, and that excitement wasn't lessened any by the daggered looks from Marcus, who clearly wasn't at all pleased to be sharing the space with me. I suppose it goes without saying that he'd figured out I wasn't his *buddy* by then. I didn't care; that probably goes without saying, too.

As he stood beside his lawyer, rocking back and forth on feet donning prison-issued slip-on shoes, I couldn't help but swell with pride. And that was only the beginning…

Not much happened during that first visit to court. Judge Warpinski, through a steeled and practiced poker face, still managed to drive a glare down the bridge of his nose at Marcus as he informed him the bond for his release was set at $50,000. Marcus proceeded to set the judge straight on how unfair that amount was, then begged and pleaded in an effort to negotiate it down.

"Your Honor, sir, please, I can't afford that, really. I can come up with $10,000. I need to get out," he repeated ad nauseam.

It was clear Warpinski didn't give a shit what Marcus wanted. "There's a reason, Mr. Somerhalder, why these bonds are set where they are. Your request is denied; your bond remains at $50,000. Court dismissed."

With his request denied, he was ushered away looking dejected and on the verge of crying. I couldn't wipe the smile from my face as I exited the courtroom in the opposite direction. I knew I was going to enjoy each and every victory—big and small—throughout this case because he deserved absolutely everything coming to him.

Marcus was back in front of the judge once more before Christmas, on December 12, for the sole purpose of setting the date of his preliminary hearing. Of course, he had another agenda, and took this as a second opportunity to request his bond be lowered. Once again, it was denied. So, with that, we continued on with the reason we were all there—the preliminary hearing date—to which he waived his right to. Fine by me.

A preliminary hearing's sole purpose is to make sure there's sufficient evidence to keep the person in question under arrest. This typically happens when a criminal knows there's more than enough evidence against them, and their eventual plea isn't one of innocence. It's common enough to waive the right to a preliminary hearing, but, in Marcus's case, despite all the video evidence he must have known we were watching, his decision wasn't representative of an admission of guilt. I think he genuinely believed he'd be able to sweet talk himself out of the charges against him, because of course, he thought he was innocent.

Any opportunity to prove himself innocent was a long way off, so in the meantime, we continued plugging away at everything that contributed to his assured guilt, which included the video review and the finding of new victim after new victim. The publicity of the case right after Christmas sealed the guilt-riddled deal.

I had a really hard time enjoying that Christmas—it was an incredibly dark and busy time in my life. When I think back on it, I don't remember all that much about the holidays or ringing in 2004. If it wasn't for my two boys, I probably would've missed the season entirely. Other than them, there wasn't much that took my mind off the case for any amount of time.

With so many years now removing me from that dark time in my life, despite how awful it was, it was a small price to pay; my boys have no recollection of how vacant of holiday cheer I was. I spent years feeling guilty about it, but I had to forgive myself because the focus and dedication to my position throughout that time allowed me to amass more and more potential charges to be considered by the judge. I'm fairly confident with how hard I had been working, I could have easily presented the judge with anywhere from one to ten potential new victims daily if I'd been allowed.

Ultimately, by the time we got to his arraignment on January 5, 2004, the charges against Marcus officially included twelve counts of sexual assault and six counts of making a visual representation of nudity. We weren't done with the video review yet, so I was sure I'd have many more for the DA to consider by the time it went to trial. In other words, there was no possible way Marcus would be able to talk himself out of the charges against him.

It was during this court appearance that the official trial date was set for June 22, 2004, which might sound like it was a long time away, but every day within that less than six months' time would be integral to the case. I wondered if it would be *enough* time to pin every recorded victim to a living human being.

Would it be enough time if any of those women came up as missing persons?

Would I be able to get everything to the DA, a brilliant man by the name of John Zakowski, in time for him to get it organized for court?

We were so far away from being ready to bring this to trial and there was so much at stake. At that point, I think I would've felt the same if the judge would have set a trial date for a whole year later. Despite every worry and fear, all my team and I could do was keep plugging away between each and every appearance in front of the judge, so that's exactly what we did.

It was on January 22, 2004 at the Motion Hearing that the first of many inevitable stabs to my professionalism was included in the courtroom agenda. I say *inevitable* because I didn't have any doubt, from the very second I saw that first incriminating video, that Marcus would find a way to use the fact that we knew each other prior to his arrest to call bully on the whole thing.

So after his lawyer, Jackson Main, requested Marcus's money and wallet be returned to him, gained approval to change the venue on account of everyone in the Brown County area knowing who Marcus was (impartial jurors is a right even the worst scum get), and a second (denied) plea to have the $50,000 bond reduced, he began arguing that the affidavit I swore to be correct misrepresented Robert as an expert on sexual predators.

Basically, it was *strongly* suggested that I issued false information to the magistrate when I applied for the warrant—that I had maliciously added Robert's interpretation to justify searching Marcus's property with no legal grounds to do so. Furthermore, they continued on that line to try and convince the judge that the whole case was my personal vendetta against Marcus.

"It's of my educated opinion, Mr. Main," Judge Warpinski said looking over his specs at Marcus's council, "that Investigator Schermitzler, based on what we've *all* seen so far, was merely acting as a law enforcement officer assigned to investigate accusations of sexual assault. He professionally gathered information, as his position demands he does, and gained a certain body of information from the people alleging they were victims of your client."

That response wasn't good enough for Main. "Your Honor, despite what we've *all* seen, Robert is not a registered professional in the field of sexual predatory behavior, and thus, his report being given such legitimacy in the approval of the warrant to enter my client's home and businesses is highly suspect."

Main argued that the whole case should be thrown out, but the court ultimately agreed with me that Robert could be considered an expert based on the fact that he frequently worked with sexual predators. It was made clear that Robert was known by the courts as having a vast knowledge of sexual predator's actions and potential conquests.

"Your protest is noted, but this court believes Robert can be relied upon, and nothing suggests to the court that there was any falsehood perpetrated on the magistrate issuing the bench warrant." Warpinski cleared his throat and continued, "You'll note, Mr. Main, that Robert's report, without any personal knowledge of your client, was absolutely right about what he thought we would find hiding in Mr. Somerhalder's personal spaces."

And that was that. With no reason to dismiss the case, Marcus was once again ushered from the courtroom, and I returned to my chaotic job at the station.

By then, we'd finished our video review and sent twenty-four tapes off to the crime lab so they could carry out their own cataloging and assessment of the videos. With that giant burden lifted from my shoulders, I was spending my days continuing to sift through victim statements, both assured and potential, and fielding the odd call from women who'd had encounters with Marcus. Not many of the stragglers proved to have the kind of run-in with Marcus that I could use in court. Most of them just thought he was an asshole and wanted to see him behind bars. Still, I couldn't ignore a single one of them. I diligently listened to what they had to say, carefully logged their grievances, and encouraged them to come in to make official statements. Few of them did.

As I dedicated so much time to the case, my social life became hauntingly quiet. I didn't really go out and my latest female companion wasn't coming around nearly as much anymore. It was easier for me to maintain radio silence than it was to pretend I was happy to see anyone; I just didn't have it in me. I hadn't noticed how lonely and detached I'd become until I heard from Skinny in late January. I surprised myself when I realized I couldn't have been happier to hear his voice.

"Sherm, it's Skinny, how goes it man?" he asked.

It was the first time I'd talked to him since before Marcus's arrest, and I felt terrible that I hadn't been in contact with him sooner. I had strongly suspected the Washington Street Pub and the Velvet Room would be shut down in lieu of Marcus's arrest, but I couldn't be certain before the property searches happened. After that, things went a bit nuclear for me, so I didn't give the topic another thought until I was told both establishments had been closed.

So, maybe I had been too busy, or maybe it was how terrible I felt knowing it was ultimately my fault my old pal Skinny was currently without a job. At least, that's how I felt whether it was the case or not. Maybe Skinny blamed me, or maybe he blamed Marcus. I really was sorry Skinny was collateral damage, but it was unavoidable unless I had been willing to turn a blind-eye to Marcus's crimes. Either way, our conversation was long overdue, and as embarrassed as I was, I was extremely happy to hear from him.

"Yeah, yeah, good. How about you?"

"I'm good, man, yeah." He made a kind of groaning sound, then said, "Actually, Sherm, I've been better. Not gonna lie. I'm having a hell of a time finding good work." He sighed heavily into the phone. "I dunno, man, I can get my foot in the door if I wanna be a fry cook or sling drinks, but there's nothin' out there I can make a future out of." I echoed his sigh on my end.

When I'd went into this, I hadn't considered it might be difficult for Skinny to move forward after the arrest. In all honesty, I hadn't given a moment's thought to Skinny's future because, why would I? Not even I knew how utterly insane this would all end up.

Sadly, his enormous amount of skill and experience in the bar/ nightclub line of business wasn't even being considered as he applied for position after position. Any one of those bar-owning goons should have jumped at the opportunity to hire a man with Skinny's skillset but the work wasn't out there. I wondered briefly if my old pal had been blacklisted because of Marcus's arrest. No one suspected him of being involved in any way, still, no one was interested in being even loosely associated with a serial rapist. Skinny was considered more than a loose association. Everyone knew him as one of Marcus's guys, so yeah, I wondered if that was the reason.

"Aww, geez, sorry to hear that, Skinny. Are you getting grief because of Marcus's arrest?"

"Nah, if anything I'm getting interviews because of his arrest. They all know I worked for the guy, so everyone wants to hear the story, but none of 'em are hiring. One guy's interview of me was a bunch of questions about Marcus, then he told me he could schedule me in as a dishwasher. A *dishwasher*, Sherm!"

I could just picture the look of disgust on his face.

"Aw, shit," I said. I didn't think there was anything I could do for the guy, but... "Is there any way I can help?" I asked anyway, trying to be polite.

"As a matter of fact, I think you can," he said. Skinny went on to tell me about a business opportunity he'd come across. Resolved to the fact that he probably wasn't going to get hired for the kind of position he was qualified for unless he rode his dark horse out of the Green Bay area, he started looking into buying a place of his own to run.

The place was a small Mexican eatery and pub called El Toro, a nice little authentic joint about half-way down the block on Main Street in De Pere. It was in a great location situated in the middle of the peninsula between the East and Fox Rivers.

It was easy as hell to tell how excited he was about the place, and I'm not too manly to admit his enthusiasm pulled at the old heartstrings. I felt for the guy, I really did, so I heard him out.

"I talked to the dude who owns it, and he's motivated to get rid of it. I think I got him down to a pretty decent price, but I don't have the credit, or any capital for that matter, to buy the place on my own, so I was hoping you'd be interested in being my investor," he said, and made a sound like he was going to keep on talking but nothing but dead air followed. Clearly, the man was nervous. Maybe he was even holding his breath.

Sensing he was losing his confidence, I took the reins. "Look, Skinny, I have no doubt you could run a place of your own, and I might be able to help, so spit it out. What kinda money are you needing to get the title on this place?" No point in beating around the bush—I'm a brass tacks kind of guy.

"I got him down to $65,000 from $85,000. The guy's a dreamer. The location is great, but it's too small a venue in this market for an eighty-five grand price tag. The guy knew it, too. So...whaddya say?"

"That's still a lot. Get me some info, and we'll sit down, have a beer, and talk about it. If everything lines up, I think you're right. It might just be the best thing for you."

He thanked me profusely over and over again. I cut him off as my second telephone line blinker started blinking—another lass mad as hell with Marcus.

Skinny moved fast. Three days later, I was sitting across from him in a pub with papers spread out all over the table between us. He'd done his homework, and to my pleasure *and* chagrin, the whole crazy idea looked great on paper. So, I agreed to invest in my oldest friend and his *loco* idea.

In the midst of Skinny and I getting finances organized and prepping to sign the papers for El Toro, I was also finalizing the last of my findings and organizing victim statements so I could get them to DA Zakowski for consideration before the status hearing on February 17. It was important my timeline of offenses was accurate and my notes on my evidential findings were perfect and unquestionable, especially after the last day in court when my integrity was put into question. I doubted they would add any more charges against Marcus unless we found new, highly deplorable, and credible evidence, but I needed to make sure. If the DA wanted to, they'd have as much evidence as they'd ever need. I would've loved to see Marcus with a thousand-year sentence.

The status hearing was an in-and-out procedure, which was great because I had other things on my mind—El Toro to be exact, but that wasn't the only reason I was happy with it being such a quick thing. I was doubly pleased because with our required presence in the Brown County Circuit Court building being so brief, it meant Marcus's presence wasn't needed. I'd been having a good week and everything about him threatened to bring my lunch back up, so I was happy to hear his mug wouldn't ruin my rare, chipper mood.

The purpose of this sort of short and sweet hearing held in Judge Warpinski's office was simply to determine that the court should plan on needing two to three weeks for the trial. Easy-peasy. I didn't think it was going to take that long, not to mention, I was still doing everything I could on my own and with DA Zakowski to keep the women out of court.

With that over and done with, I went back to helping Skinny with his machinations, and by the end of February, 2004, we were the proud owners of a locally loved and well-maintained restaurante Mexicano. As a silent partner, I would leave him to handle the business. He was in charge of it all with the promise that I'd be assured unlimited access to on-the-house El Toro food; something I never really took advantage of because I loved putting money into the business.

I also loved the fact that I could help him because with El Toro's purchase, Skinny, and a large amount of my guilt regarding him, were sorted. I needed the weight of it off of my shoulders and the timing was just right—preparations to bring Marcus's case to trial were gearing up, so I needed to refocus all of my attention back to it.

The games began with Marcus on March 1, dragging Judge Warpinski away from his real judicial work once again for another attempt to amend his bond. We watched as he dropped crocodile tear bombs down the front of his pumpkin-colored jumper in an attempt to appear endearing. I can only assume he saw it as a clever ruse while he explained how appreciative he'd be if the judge honored his request.

"Your Honor, please. My family is rallying around me and have managed to get together $17,000. I'm certain we can come up with another $3,000 if you'd just reduce the bond down to $20,000. Please." He wiped at his nose with his sleeve.

"As I said the last time, Mr. Somerhalder, we have no reason to reduce your bond and find it perfectly appropriate," Judge Warpinski said. He seemed unmoved by the charade and didn't look the least bit impressed as he gave his reply.

I couldn't wrap my head around Marcus's thought process. For the life of me, I didn't understand how he saw himself as innocent. Even with so many people telling him he did a lot of *really* bad things, he still vehemently denied all of the accusations. He'd obviously convinced his family of his innocence as well, which I suppose, probably wasn't all that hard a feat.

Think about it. If you were in Marcus's family's shoes and of sound mind (of course), you would want to believe he was innocent as well. If it was your own son, daughter, brother, sister...you'd never want to think they were capable of the atrocities Marcus was being charged with. In fact, the stuff he was being accused of was so unbelievable, he probably had no trouble at all downplaying it. I could hear the hypothetical conversation in my head. "No, Mom, I swear I didn't do anything wrong! C'mon now, really? Drugged, raped, and videotaped dozens and dozens of women? Mom, you know I'm not that kinda guy, right?" His momma was probably crying and he probably had his arms wrapped around her. "It's a set-up, Mom. Someone's out to get me."

I wouldn't have been at all surprised if those were the exact damn words that came out of his mouth, too. It was sad to think about how crushed his family was going to be when the evidence proved Marcus to be the piece of shit most everyone else already knew he was. Thankfully for them, that was still a while off.

March 5, 2004, four days after the last appearance in court, we were all back in front of Judge Warpinski for another motion hearing. What could the problem possibly be? If you said, "An appeal to lower his $50,000 bond?" Well, you'd be wrong. Shocking, I know.

This particular jaunt into the Brown County Circuit Court building was to hear Jackson Main's motion to withdraw as Marcus's lawyer because Marcus was unable or unwilling (I'm not actually sure which) to pay Mr. Main for his services. Jackson Main declared, "Continuing to represent Marcus Somerhalder would cause an unreasonable financial burden on me."

And as if Main was pointing a finger and tattling on him, Marcus hurriedly said, "I am out of money, sir. I'm broke."

Wasting no time on the matter, the court assigned him a PD (public defender), and the motion was accepted. Well, accepted for the next ten days, at least.

On March 15, we were back in court to find out how Marcus had too much in valuable assets to even remotely qualify for a court appointed PD. This realization was merely a complication, because although Marcus was asset-rich, he still didn't have a single penny in his bank account. Had he been able to pay his lawyer in pubs, he'd have been set. Instead, to get access to a court appointed PD, he was ordered to liquidate his assets and individual retirement account (IRA).

Marcus agreed—it would have been a dullard's move not to—and on April 9, 2004, PD Shane Brabazon was officially assigned to Marcus.

A few weeks later, on May 5, 2004 in a Status Conference with DA Zakowski and Marcus's new lawyer, Brabazon, who was all caught up on the case—it was decided the trial would move from the original date of June 22 and be rescheduled for August 30, 2004. They were still confident the case wouldn't take more than three weeks, but I thought they were out of their minds.

District Attorney Zakowski, with my help, had amassed a list of approximately sixty state witnesses to bring in front of Warpinski and the jury, and Brabazon had thirty more witnesses of his own. Three weeks seemed ambitious, but there was a chance they wouldn't need to hear from many of them. I was hoping none of the state witnesses would have to show their faces in the courtroom—they'd suffered enough. As of that moment, there weren't any deals or plea bargains being worked out in honor of keeping those women off the stand, but it was still forefront in my mind, and Zakowski knew it.

If you can believe it, after May 5, I didn't have to roll my bones down to the Brown County Circuit Court building for over a month. It was June 14, approximately a week before the original court date had been set and we stood in front of Warpinski listening to Brabazon trying to convince the judge to have a trial for each count as opposed to having one big trial.

"So," Warpinski said, "you're asking me to hold eighteen separate trials? What would be your justification for this motion?"

"Your Honor, each case has its own extenuating circumstances. They are not the same, as the relationship with each woman was different, and my client has a right to respond to each woman individually."

"At the court's expense, Mr. Brabazon?" Warpinski wasn't going for it, and it was becoming obvious this might have been Marcus's idea, as even his lawyer didn't seem all that convinced that trying each charge separately was the best idea.

Brabazon didn't look a touch surprised when Warpinski, in a firm voice said, "Motion to sever charges denied. Dismissed." He smacked down his gavel and the lot of us turned on our heels to head out the back of the courtroom. Just another ridiculous waste of time and not the last time it would happen.

Exactly two weeks later, on Monday, June 28, 2004, I watched Marcus, dressed in his bright orange jumpsuit, stare disinterestedly at a fixed spot on the courtroom wall as I listened to his lawyer drone on. The topic of this motion hearing was how unfair, and more so, how unconstitutional it was to charge someone with something that occurred before it was officially against the law.

Back before December 3, 2001, the statute for visual depictions of nudity (2001 Wisconsin Act 33[4]) didn't exist in the great state of Wisconsin, which means that before that day in 2001, the act of filming someone naked and without their permission was only *frowned* upon. You still got nabbed and charged if you were sexually assaulting them because you were stupid enough to film yourself in the act, but you weren't penalized for the video representation itself.

Although I'm proud the state wised up, the statute's lack of existence before that time rendered counts 4, 5, 9, 10, and 18 on Marcus's menu of charges null and void in the eyes of the court. All five of those counts happened between 1997 and the enactment of the law. Sick and sad.

Considering how long personal cameras and video cameras have been around, I find it unbelievable a law like this didn't come to pass before 2001. I guess it just wasn't necessary before then.

First of all, not everyone had a camera like they do nowadays. Video and still-shot cameras have been a lot more accessible since the 1940s, but it was a long time before it became common place for every man, woman, and child to have such accessible video capabilities at their fingertips. Even back in 2001, there were no cameras on cell phones yet, so it wasn't nearly as common to find any kind of visual evidence of wrongdoing. People were more hush-hush about the things that would make others see them as weird. As an example, in the 1940s, if you were using your Bolex Paillard H16 Cinema Camera to record your woman sans knickers, you sure as hell weren't going to tell *anyone* you did it. It's true.

---

[4] http://docs.legis.wisconsin.gov/2001/related/acts/33

This brings me to my next point—even if I hate to say it—as we evolve technologically, our social de-evolution is becoming more and more obvious. We're a lot more okay with the stranger things in the world than we used to be. Maybe it's because there are a hell of a lot of lonely souls in this very "social" world. Maybe it's because with a video camera in every hand, there are so many more opportunities to be "caught in the act." Things that were once taboo are becoming more commonplace as it gets harder and harder to hide our kinks, habits, and tendencies.

We all have our place in this millennium, because with seven billion people on the planet, and internet access to all of it (with the exception of North Korea), it's a safe bet we'll find at least a handful of others who share a mutual love of even our most obscure hobbies, fetishes, and collections. Still, this age of internet is creating a people who are more alone than ever, and as police officers and first responders, we stand to wonder if that's why we're finding the things people do in the shadows so much weirder all the time.

As it was, Brabazon was right—no matter how much we hated the fact. The court had no choice but to dismiss charges 4, 5, 9, 10, and 18 without prejudice.

Sadly, that wasn't the end of the agenda that day. After a brief recess, Brabazon went on to argue that the garbage pull I did on Marcus in November of 2003 was illegal.

I swear to God, I thought for a moment that I was from another planet. Right in front of him was a sworn testimony on how many times I spoke with the apartment manager, Laurie, about how I collected the bags. What he should have also seen was the fact that I didn't find anything in his client's trash that was significant to the case anyway.

On closer inspection, he would have also seen the part of the report where I included what Laurie told me about how very seldom Marcus took his own garbage to the dumpster—opting, instead, to leave it on his patio for someone else to take.

Furthermore, had Brabazon turned another page or two, he would have found Laurie's sworn testimony that she had removed his rotting garbage from his patio at least ten times, despite the clear declaration in the apartment rules that tenants were required to take any and all of their refuse to the dumpster. Marcus didn't feel those rules applied to him, thus negating his expectation of privacy regarding his garbage.

The court eventually ruled there was no issue with the garbage pulls I conducted or the method in which I collected them.

Was Brabazon done with me then? Nay, he was not.

He continued to argue and question my experience in preparing search warrants.

"Investigator Schermitzler," he said, looking down at the notes in front of him. "Is it true there was a second woman at my client's home the evening Alisa Ryker alleges she was sexually assaulted?"

"Yes," was all I felt compelled to say.

"Is it true this second woman felt she had been assaulted but did not want to become involved in this case?"

"Again, yes," I replied.

Brabazon then turned to Judge Warpinski and said, "Your Honor, how are we expected to prepare ourselves for a case in which not all of the true and factual details are included?" He explained that because I left out that information, it could negatively reflect on Marcus, and it stood to question my credibility as an investigator. We argued back and forth between these newest points for some time, but the court eventually denied the motion.

The trial hadn't even officially started and already it felt like it was me under the microscope instead of Marcus. It had been a frustrating day in which I felt as though I'd done nothing but defend my honor, actions, and professionalism, so I was extremely relieved when court adjourned for the day.

*   *   *

The relief I felt was short-lived—my life, personal and professional, had been challenging since I first laid hands on the case back in August, 2003, but at about this point in the proceedings, summer of 2004, things started taking a turn for the worse. As the case really began to slow down from an office standpoint—there weren't any more victims to introduce into the case—things, for me at least, seemed to go into autopilot in the capable hands of DA Zakowski. This left me infinitely more time to mull over the past eleven months, but instead of it being a process of healing, it became the beginning of a slow descent into much darker days.

It started as minor insomnia; if I wasn't physically exhausted, I would have a hard time falling asleep. I couldn't seem to turn my brain off, and when I did manage to get deep into a REM mode, I would have terrible and sometimes all-too-vivid dreams. Some of those dreams were inspired by Marcus's case and the rest were from the many cases that had come before it. I guess it was probably the sticky residue left over from the years of horrors my mind had seen, tried to process, but ultimately just couldn't shake. There's no denying the impossible task for us public servants to sort through everything we see and hear.

So many times, I thought back on watching that movie from the 1990s, *Total Recall*, and just wished my mind could be wiped of all the shit I'd seen and then replaced with amazing memories of an imaginary vacation. Alas, the technology is a ways off yet, so goody for me, every single synapsis in my brain is firing just as it should to hold all of my memories, including the ones I hate, firmly in place.

The battle to get a good night's sleep was only the beginning. I was too close to it all to see how deeply the case had affected me; not only that—I knew I wasn't feeling like myself.

Unfortunately, I still had to keep my shit together as I was so often required to stand in front of a judge. I was also still working full-time as an investigator, so it served me better to push everything I was feeling deep down. Like so many times before, I'd deal with it later.

*   *   *

The motion hearing we'd begun earlier in the week—June 28 to be exact—picked up where it had left off promptly at 8:00 a.m. on July 1, 2004, and it was another doozy of a day.

Brabazon wasted no time getting down to one of the oddest arguments verbalized throughout the entire case.

He, and Marcus, of course, argued that the individuals (victims) involved in the videotaping didn't have an expectation of privacy because they were in Marcus's bedroom.

The court reporter's hands balanced over her Steno Machine, but you could have heard crickets chirping—no one in the courtroom spoke, opting instead to raise their eyebrows in surprise.

"So," Judge Warpinski began. Everyone looked to him as he spoke. "You're suggesting that people involved in sexual relations don't have an expectation of privacy?" Then, as I'd seen him do so many times over the last few months, he peered over his glasses and down his nose, awaiting Brabazon's response. We all slowly followed suit, shifting our gaze to the public defender.

"Correct, Your Honor." He looked and sounded confident as he said it, but it was hard to ignore his many attempts to swallow the lump in his throat. Brabazon must have known it was a ridiculous thing to say, but I couldn't blame him for trying every angle, no matter how far-fetched.

Thankfully, DA Zakowski wasn't going to stand by and allow bullshit like that to litter the minds within that courtroom. "Your Honor," he spoke to Judge Warpinski. "May I please respond to PD Brabazon?"

"Permission granted," the judge replied.

Zakowski shifted his stance to face Brabazon. "It's my job in a situation like this to agree with the State's opinion on matters regarding privacy. Furthermore, the State's opinion is the law—created by the people for the benefit of the people, and there are a whole lot of them in this here file," he said as he stabbed his finger down onto the thick manila folder I'd passed on to him, "who wouldn't have any right to find issue with what your client did if the law declared a person had no right to privacy the moment they darken the doorway of someone else's home." He chuckled a bit, then said, "Be damned ever leaving my house if that was the case, wouldn't you say?" He shrugged his shoulders as he looked down at Marcus, who sat beside Brabazon, then turned to give a quick nod of respect to Judge Warpinski before taking his seat.

The judge cleared his throat. "I'm in full agreement with DA Zakowski, and the State, of course, on this matter. One doesn't lose their expectation of privacy simply because they are in someone else's house." The judge went on to say, "It's my ruling that two people involved in sexual activity in a house, in a bedroom, behind closed doors, do not lose their expectation of privacy because the partner they're with may be videotaping. Consider please, it was for reasons such as this Wisconsin Act 33, a statute intended to prohibit exactly this kind of behavior, was created. You sir…" He pointed to Brabazon with his gavel, "…should know better than to try a stunt like this. Your motion is denied." The gavel hit the ornate sound block on his podium.

With that mess cleaned up, it was time to address the next motion on the list. I have to say, before this time in my life, I'd never experienced a motion hearing like this. Typically, things were settled or went to trial, and there would always be at least one motion hearing before either of those things happened, but never had any of those motion hearings been as intense as the ones I'd attended for Marcus's case, and none compared to this one. Not by a long shot.

Next on Brabazon's agenda was for me to address a number of arguments he was trying to make. Most of the questioning, which was the same as had happened in part one of this motion hearing on June 28, seemed to be in regard to the search warrant—in particular, how I wrote the affidavit for said search warrant.

It was his intention, like the previous DA had attempted, to prove to Judge Warpinski that I deliberately misled the magistrate—the judge who I presented my warrant application to—by giving him false information so he would sign my search warrant. The allegation was absolutely ludicrous and I venomously resented his malicious bid to paint me as a corrupt lawman.

He spoke the "facts" clearly, (as *he* saw them, at least) that there was no denying I *fabricated* most of the details within the warrant in an attempt to nail Marcus for something he didn't do.

I was simply listing the facts to the best of my knowledge, and I took no pleasure in it because everything about this case was awful and horrifying. It would have more than blacklisted me within the force if I'd fabricated the crap in that warrant; it would have meant, straight up, that *I* should've been the one in the orange jumpsuit and cuffs. Not to mention, why would anyone put in that much effort to frame someone? At the very least, it seemed a little too diabolical and nefarious for my personality.

This was one of the most stressful days in court I had ever had, and I really can't pin down why it had such a strong effect on me. I knew I hadn't done anything wrong, but it still seemed as if *I* was the one on trial. The consequences for not getting it right were extreme, though.

Maybe I *do* know why it was so stressful. Consider this: Brabazon wasn't spitting his sweet & savory lawyer-talk to a room of peers—otherwise known as a jury. No, it was custom-tailored to the one and only man who could shut this whole case down. If Brabazon somehow convinced Judge Warpinski that I did anything wrong in the writing and submission of the affidavit for the search warrant, DA Zakowski and I could potentially lose all of the evidence we had recovered from Marcus's apartment and bars. No matter how illegal Marcus's activities were; no matter how conclusively damaging the videos of Marcus having sex with unconscious women were, it would all be stricken from the record, rendering this case totally bunk.

So, yeah, I know what had my blood pressure through the roof. I couldn't help but be anxious to get this part over with, and I hadn't even taken the stand yet. That came next...

I was put under oath, sat down in the little booth reserved for those being questioned, and tried like hell to hide my anxiety and rage, both of which would have clawed their way out of me if I faltered in containing them. Marcus was the bum who should've been sitting in that booth, not me.

I waited for PD Brabazon to get his shit together and as I did, my mouth got so dry. My tongue stuck to the roof of my mouth and I couldn't even swallow—I had nothing to swallow! I reached for the pitcher conveniently placed near the witness stand, and as I lifted it to bring it to the plastic cup in my other hand, I noticed how badly I was shaking. It was amazing the falling water didn't slop all over my lap as it wobbled back and forth on its way into my cup. It's not often I suffer anxiety, so this was pretty extreme for me. I hoped nobody had seen me pouring that water, or I'm certain they would have assumed I had something to worry about while sitting on the witness stand.

It took me a few minutes, but eventually I settled down and took his inquisition in stride. He barraged me with questions about what I did and didn't put in the affidavit, why I left certain things out and included others. He also took issue with how I worded certain parts of the affidavit.

One of the things I had included in my affidavit was mention of the naked picture of Faith that Skinny and Mike had found on Marcus's camera. It really wasn't all that important a detail to the case to be honest.

Anyway, he inquired as to why I didn't indicate whether the naked picture Skinny had showed me was consensual or not. To me, it didn't matter if it was consensual or not; the fact that he had naked pictures on a camera that belonged to the Velvet Room and had left that camera in plain sight in the office of that establishment, was the only reason it was at all significant to the case.

Brabazon dug deep into the affidavit to question things I never would have considered questionable. It seemed to me he was grasping at straws; I knew this case inside and out and had taken it on originally with the fleeting intention of clearing my buddy's name, so I knew I didn't have to fabricate anything within the affidavit.

Then again, maybe Brabazon knew Judge Warpinski infinitely better than Zakowski and I did. Maybe he'd shared a courtroom with the judge enough times to know how to play him. It was definitely a possibility, and not knowing any better meant I really couldn't speculate, so all I could do was continue to keep my anxiety and anger tucked back and answer the PD's questions with the confidence I had been exuding. In the end, as the old phrase goes: the truth will out.

Brabazon had issue with some of my conclusions within the affidavit. One of the first he chose to bring up was my indication that Marcus got Theresa Martin intoxicated. Apparently, as he and Marcus saw it, I should have said she got *herself* intoxicated. There was no way I could have said it like that, though. I did infer that since Marcus was feeding Theresa shots that he was intentionally trying to get her drunk and seeing as this was exactly his modus operandi in most of the chargeable cases, I don't think it was misleading, especially when based on Theresa's statement. It had become apparent that the accusations of drugging were what Marcus hated the most, but I'd never said anything about Theresa being drugged, so why they chose to argue anything regarding her was beyond me. Whether she got herself drunk or whether he got her drunk was semantics—that he took advantage of her in an altered state was the *only* point needing consideration.

Brabazon then asked why I found it necessary to include the story about a woman named Paige in the affidavit. I had heard about Paige from Sarah Price, and although I never got a formal statement out of Paige, that didn't change the fact that she got ill enough at the Velvet Room to be transported away in an ambulance. I should also point out that when mentioning Paige, I didn't say she'd been drugged, just that she'd become violently ill.

It's notable that this event happened within the thickest timeframe of accusations against Marcus. It also happened the day before Sarah drank water all night, but somehow left her till at the Velvet Room uncounted, then was escorted out of the building by Marcus at 2:15 a.m., and has no memory of the four hours before she finally returned home at 4:30 a.m.

I included Paige as part of my testimony in an attempt to show this type of event was becoming a fairly regular occurrence at Marcus's establishments. When I brought up the point that whether Paige made an official statement or not wasn't important, but it *was* important to include her because her physical experience that night paralleled the signs and symptoms most of the women within my affidavit had experienced, I thought the frown on Brabazon's brow would surely reach his mustache. It was no secret I'd already made my suspicions of administering the unknown drug in alcohol to achieve the level of intoxication/drug effect known, so including Paige made perfect sense—so far, it seemed as if Judge Warpinski agreed.

Brabazon's counter to my justification?

"Investigator Schermitzler," he said through a firmly set jaw. "Is it not fact that the young woman in question was tested once she arrived in the ER at St. Vincent Hospital, and no date rape drug was discovered in her system?"

"I did my research on this and found they would have needed to complete a full panel urine test instead of a blood test to pick up any signs of most date rape drugs." I cleared my throat just to waste some time. "Furthermore, Mr. Brabazon, it's common knowledge in my line of business that the tests they run in the ER for the detection of stupefying agents don't always include some of new ones—the "designer" date rape drugs—if you will."

Brabazon huffed and was gearing up for a retort, when once again, I reminded the courtroom that nowhere in the affidavit did I claim Paige had been drugged. The reason it was important to include her information was to show a pattern of this type of event happening at an establishment that Marcus was ultimately responsible for.

Public Defender Brabazon didn't want to hear that information again— he cut me off mid-sentence to ask me why I didn't include the fact that Paige's blood alcohol concentration (BAC) was a whopping .15 when she was tested at the hospital. A person is fairly blitzed at that BAC.

I didn't get to respond to that statement because he had other things to say, but had I the opportunity to speak, I would have said, "That is a point completely moot to this case."

Instead, I listened as he dug further into the woman's hospital report to find that Paige told the hospital staff she had taken herbal supplements in the past.

Herbal supplements? Like, ginkgo biloba? Ginseng? I couldn't even fathom where he was going with this knowledge. Not true, I guess; I know for a fact that St. John's Wort can cause drowsiness when combined with boozy drinks, but that's a same-day use kind of interaction, and still wouldn't allude to the kind of reaction Paige had.

He continued on to justify his point by adding that Sarah, who had similar ill feelings the night after Paige, had probably been using herbal supplements as well. So, despite their incidents happening on different nights and there being no proof to suggest herbal supplements were capable of causing the women to suffer how they did, he still suggested, with unfounded confidence, that there was a strong possibility those herbal supplements reacted to the alcohol consumed, thus creating the adverse reactions both women experienced.

Every eye in the room glazed over—some eyes may have even rolled back into their owner's skulls. It's not that what he was saying was stupid, it was that it was so radically far-fetched... I remember thinking at the time Brabazon might be the one dabbling in herbals. How the hell could a few echinacea pills, for instance, taken "in the past" even be suggested as a suspect in a case like this? The man was reaching.

There was no way around it; none of what was being discussed could be connected to or blamed on herbal supplements. Furthermore, something that shouldn't have needed reiteration was the fact that Sarah—in her sworn affidavit, no less—clearly stated she didn't have much to drink that night. This proved to everyone else in the room that her memory loss had nothing to do with herbals or alcohol but did manage to bring focus on the fact that Marcus was the last one with her.

"Investigator Schermitzler, you're disregarding the fact that Sarah didn't count her till before she left the building, something she had never forgotten to do prior to my client walking her out to her car on the evening in question," said Brabazon with confidence. I honestly wondered where he mustered it from; I was impressed.

We all knew he was trying to show that none of what was in my affidavit, in any way, implicated Marcus of drugging anyone. I confirmed he was correct and said, once again, I was only trying to show a pattern of what was going on at Marcus's place of business.

Praise the lord, the court agreed with me that it was all relevant and appropriate to put in the affidavit. We could finally move on. Right?

CHAPTER 16

CASE #04CF841: PART 2. . .

AKA MARCUS B. SOMERHALDER'S LAWYER VS. ME AND MY AFFIDAVIT

No, no, no; not time to move on yet.

As much as the focus needed to shift from me to Marcus, Brabazon wasn't anywhere near being done with me. He had pulled so many tabs to try and illegitimize my affidavit that I was actually starting to worry one of them might pan out.

It was an odd feeling for me for two reasons. The first was that there was no question in my mind that everything found within my statement was fair, correct, and true. The second reason was I had no doubt about Marcus's guilt. Without even a whisper about him drugging those women, he was as guilty as a red right hand. It would have to be a fairly glaring infraction on my part for Judge Warpinski to throw out the thirteen charges currently resting on Marcus's shoulders. I worried nonetheless—what other tricks might Brabazon have up his sleeve?

The next item on Brabazon's "Why Schermitzler is a fraud and his little affidavit, too" agenda was the fact that Skinny and I were now business partners. Why was this pertinent to a case fully in regard to, and with proof of, his client raping unconscious women? Well, because he was trying to show I was somehow in cahoots with Skinny and had been all along.

Maybe I was naïve, or maybe I should've been used to it by this point, but I was so taken aback by the questioning of my integrity as an officer and detective. I knew Brabazon was only doing his job, and I probably shouldn't have been so butt-hurt about his accusations, but I was starting to hate the guy.

The truth had nothing to do with conspiracy or being in cahoots—it had everything to do with that guilt I felt for Skinny's situation. Leaving my friend without a decent job was bad enough, but how could I have said no to him and shut down his chance at a business opportunity in an industry he knew so well? I especially would never have forgiven myself if I *had* said no to his proposition of partnership just in case it came across as if we were colluding.

Not that I wanted the case thrown out because of it, either, but had I walked away and left him without any other employment options...

Honestly, up until Brabazon had brought it up, I hadn't even considered the possibility that the case could be thrown out based on me buying a restaurant with Skinny, but as Brabazon spit his fodder on the topic at Judge Warpinski, my mind drifted to the potential what-ifs.

What if I'd said no to Skinny and he ended up jobless, penniless, without a home, and all of it was my fault?

Alternately, what if buying El Toro with Skinny was eventually considered to be a big no-no by the courts? What if they saw it as grounds to throw out the case, rendering my hard work and suffering all for nothing, and Marcus walked free because of my enormous mistake? It would also mean I would have let down so many women entrusting me to fight for their rights.

A decision like that would have left me a broken-down husk of a man without any closure on the biggest case of my career, professionally shamed, and forever regretful of my actions...

Thank God—and I mean it—in the end, seeing as I was an entirely silent partner in Skinny's business, the court didn't agree that our professional situation was an issue. Brabazon was told to drop the whole thing, and that should have relieved me, but it had already rubbed me the wrong way.

That rubbing turned to chafing as soon as he opened his mouth again. This time, it was to twist Sasha's words on the transcribed audio file of my initial interview with her—the chat she and I had in the back room of the

Ten O'One Club. The interview that had allowed me to connect the dots in my own drug/Marcus experience.

It felt like the day would never end, and I was bordering on exhausted. "Could I get a break here?" I said as politely as I could. I didn't add that it was because my ass was killing me for sitting so long, but that was part of it. I needed to move around; I needed to not hear the PD's voice for just a few minutes, or I was going to crack.

"Absolutely," Warpinski said. "We'll take a twenty-minute break and pick up PD Brabazon's point on a one Sasha Colby after the recess." His gavel hit the block, and I felt like I could breathe again.

I shuffled my way out to the lobby and stood there for a moment. Rocking my head all the way back, as if unhinging it from my shoulders, I took a deep breath and looked up at the bright, high-ceilinged, echoing space above me. The beautifully painted murals brought me instant peace—this place of legal commerce was one of the most stunning I had ever seen, and I felt my pride in it begin to restore my confidence. I needed that.

Tearing myself from the view on the ceiling, I continued around the lobby to look at the paintings on the walls and read up on celebrated judges and historical cases. I realized I'd never really stopped to appreciate this space. It was awe-inspiring to be certain, and there was so much in there I'd never seen before. My mind had been desperate for a distraction—I thought about something other than Case #04CF841 for the first time in as long as I could remember, and it was incredible. Brief, but marvellously rejuvenating.

With the fastest twenty minutes of my whole life run out, I dragged my ass back into that court room and sat down to listen to what Brabazon had to say about Sasha Colby.

My restored energy and confidence hemorrhaged from my body as Brabazon read out the transcribed section of the tape he wanted us to hear. I replayed the conversation in my head, "So, Sasha, do you think Marcus drugged you that night?"

I was jolted back out of my head as Brabazon cleared his throat. "To which she answered, 'No.'" He paused for impact, then went on to complete her statement. "'It was something more than just alcohol.'"

Brabazon argued that because the first word of her response was "No," she was stating that she didn't think she had been drugged. His interpretation twisted her words totally out of context, and it had me absolutely seeing red.

Context is another cruel mistress in the law enforcement world, but it's one that doesn't only affect us; lawyers, judges—parents for that matter—suffer context all the time.

"Billy, did you, Chip, and Jim trick Mr. Potter into buying you beers on Saturday?" Momma asks her angel.

"Of course not, Momma! We wouldn't *all* go out drinking at eighteen years old!" he solemnly swears to her, because contextually it's true! Chip *was* with them but didn't have any beers that night, so Billy's statement is technically true when his mother is only given that much information. It's kind of the same way the media only puts snippets of video and audio so they can distribute the message they want to get across rather than the whole story of what happened or what was said.

Sadly, regarding anything that has to do with the law, "the whole truth, and nothing but the truth, so help me God" is an anomaly. Not me, or the lawyer, or even a perpetrator's momma will ever know the *whole* truth and nothing *but* the truth, so there's a lot of room for persuasion, personal opinions, and contextual interpretation when it comes down to sorting out the bits and pieces in a case. This is why *irrefutable proof*, like videotapes showing a crime in progress, are so damn important.

In this situation, the problem was Sasha's style of speech; I would compare it to kids using the word "like" constantly. They start every sentence with that word, and in Sasha's lingo, although she started the sentence with the word "no," it was still obvious her statement was clearly asserting that more than alcohol was involved…so yeah, Sasha thought she'd been drugged. Needless to say, Judge Warpinski agreed that was exactly what she was suggesting and didn't waste any more time in humoring Brabazon on the topic; it most certainly wasn't relevant as a reason why the search warrant shouldn't have been approved.

I felt sure there couldn't possibly be any more issues to be found with the affidavit. Onward and upward was necessary to get this incredibly important case moving—at least, that's what should have happened. Instead, Brabazon brought us back to the past to revisit an issue we'd already argued out of the courtroom months prior, back when Jackson Main was still Marcus's lawyer. This was a fact Brabazon would have assuredly been aware of once he brought himself up to speed on the case.

I agonized as I listened to PD Brabazon take a shot at me in regards to why I sought out and included Robert's opinion.

As much as I wanted to grab the man by the lapels and shake him silly while shouting, "Read the previous lawyer's notes!" I didn't. Instead, I vibrated in frustration as I explained it was at the recommendation of the DA's office that I find someone with knowledge and experience in sexual predators.

"In fact," I said calmly, "it was the DA's office who recommended Robert to me. I went over the case in detail with Robert, including each and every victim allegation and the details pertaining to them."

"And what did you conclude from your experience with Robert?" Brabazon asked.

"Basically, that there's no question the defendant is sick and undeniably in need of help." I shifted in my seat. I was so done with being there and it was becoming obvious in my tone. "Robert confidently states, as you can see in the report in front of you, that in his professional experience, Marcus has significant sexual problems and should be considered a marauding predator."

Robert's actual statement had titled Marcus as "marauding and predatory," not a "marauding predator" as I'd titled him, which, I presumed, was the fact Brabazon was trying to call attention to, but to me, it was tomato, tomahto—how it was stated didn't change either of those word's meanings or the impact they had on the case.

Thankfully, the court didn't seem interested in rehashing this topic further—it had already been ruled upon and as much as it seemed the court didn't mind this man wasting their time, they didn't want to deal with it again. I was happy about the decision, but it was still another ten minutes of my life I would never get back.

I could sense Brabazon was almost done with me. But, before I could be excused from the stand, he drilled me on what I knew about date rape drugs.

I genuinely began to wonder about the guy. He was irritating the hell out of me. Had he looked into me prior to this motion hearing, he probably would have saved us all a lot of time. Besides that, he could have asked Marcus about me—in fact, I refuse to think I wouldn't have been a subject discussed at length between the two of them. Marcus knew I was a copper, paramedic, firefighter, and he knew I'd been doing it all for a long time. I was highly qualified to come to the conclusions I did within the affidavit.

I logically referred to my medical training as a paramedic. Furthermore, I talked about the half-life of most of the date rape drugs being so short that it created difficulties in detecting them in a person. I also stated the body's ability to metabolize these sorts of drugs so quickly it was probably an attractive pro for anyone not wanting to get blamed for administering them.

With that, I shut up. There was nothing more that needed to be said.

Brabazon gave me a curt nod, then turned to Judge Warpinski, "No further questions, Your Honor."

Indeed.

I made to stand up but stopped short when I noticed DA Zakowski mirroring my movements. He straightened his back, taking the opportunity to stretch it out a bit, then said, "So sorry, Investigator Schermitzler, but it seems as if you're stuck in that seat a bit longer." He smiled at me through tired eyes, and I returned the gesture, nodded, and lowered my arse back down into my seat.

It was finally his chance to cross-examine me, and I had no doubt he was as motivated as I was to make short work of it.

He was able to reaffirm my credibility by talking me through the affidavit; he took a moment to respectfully recall every victim and their case details rather than simply rehashing only the ones Brabazon had picked out to argue. Zakowski knew they *all* mattered, and he knew what about this case was important.

The atmosphere in the room made an incredible shift; the curtness, resentment, and frustration seemed to melt away as soon as Zakowski began talking. Maybe it was only me who felt it, I really couldn't say, but even though I was just being honest about everything, I couldn't help but feel relieved to know I was now dealing with someone on my team. It was a lot easier to see Marcus's pattern of behavior and the picture I was trying to paint in the affidavit as Zakowski told each victim's story for Judge Warpinski to hear. The way the dedicated DA highlighted the information I had gathered as I knit my affidavit together for the search warrant was music to my ears.

Zakowski said everything that was required to be said by the DA's office for the benefit of the court in a quick forty-five minutes from start to finish. By the end, it felt like I'd earned back some of the time Brabazon had thieved from me.

From there, it was finally time to make final arguments. It was the longest day in a courtroom of my entire career, no competition.

Brabazon took this opportunity to reiterate his firm opinion that I'd intentionally twisted the facts and omitted things in order to get the magistrate to sign the warrant. He stated I based my affidavit on opinion vs. fact and took advantage of verbiage like "drugged into unconsciousness" to paint a dark and untrue picture of his client and deceive the magistrate.

DA Zakowski had a firm opinion of Brabazon's argument and wasted no time making his voice heard regarding it. "I ask the court to deny the motion and strongly take exception to the insinuation that Investigator Schermitzler tried to deceive the court or show any reckless disregard for the truth." He then looked directly at Brabazon as he continued to speak to the court in general. "It is obvious the defense is trying to paint a picture of deception by Investigator Schermitzler, but I feel, and I hope Your Honor agrees, that these women are undoubtedly saying 'I have been drunk before, but I have never felt like this before,' without any coaxing or leading by the investigator.

"Please, then juxtapose those facts with the truth that all of the women in question associate this never-before felt experience with Marcus Somerhalder, and Marcus Somerhalder alone. Furthermore, with the irrefutable evidence of sexual assault, it would be a heinous injustice to allow the defendant to walk free without accountability for his grievous actions."

To make it short, the court ruled in favor of the state and denied the motion to suppress evidence, which meant my affidavit was considered in good standing and without suspicion.

Judge Warpinski confirmed the defense didn't have a legitimate argument as there may have been some "wordsmithing" on my part, but they didn't feel there were any omitted facts, marred or misleading statements, or baseless accusations. So, despite the PD's attempt to draw Judge Warpinski's attention to tedious issues, he confirmed there was nothing that would have changed the magistrate's decision in accepting the affidavit and signing the search warrant.

For the last time that day, Judge Warpinksi's gavel hit the sound block. The muscles I hadn't realized I'd been holding tight in my shoulders relaxed and immediately began to ache from exhaustion. A long, hot shower was in order, but by the time I made it home after a short detour to the station, I was too exhausted to even peel my shoes off. I plunked myself down on the couch and tried to will my shoes to take themselves off. Moments after I leaned back into the cushions, I was out cold. With no more need to explain myself, defend the affidavit, or worry about whether the case would move forward or not, it was like I'd shrugged off a thousand burdens. So, as long of a day as the July 1 motion hearing was, it was a huge and defining day; the case, whether it went to trial or was settled out of court, was officially a success. Barring some terrible tragedy that I couldn't even fathom, my "buddy," Marcus Somerhalder was looking at a guaranteed stint in the clink.

I had the best sleep I'd had in an extremely long time. I'm glad I took advantage of it because it was the first real good sleep I'd had in months, and it was a long time before I slept that well again.

Still, many days in court were ahead, but I wasn't anxious about that anymore, so my lack of sleep didn't have anything to do with it. I was still managing to muddle through life, and I made it look like I was calm and collected, too. I was on time for work, crisp, clean, and ready to go; I still had my sons on a regular basis and we made the best of every moment we had together.

When I wasn't at work, when the girlfriend or kids weren't around, I simply couldn't turn my mind off. I continued to have terrible, vivid dreams. I remained severely disinterested in being intimate, which was really starting to affect my relationship with my girlfriend; I was either trying to wrap my mind around shit that was out of my control, staring at the TV with no real thoughts in my mind, or laying in bed, counting the bumps in the popcorn ceiling in an attempt to fall asleep. I couldn't shake the little demons in my head, but even then, I didn't think enough of it to seek help.

It's just a rough spot, I told myself. *I'll make it through,* and I genuinely believed that was true.

It was just a phase. So, I suffered it.

On August 24, 2004, nearly two months after the marathon motion hearing, I arrived back at the majestic Brown County Circuit Court building for Marcus's plea hearing.

First things first. While I'd been enjoying my return to the old-fashioned hum-drum of being an investigator for the Ashwaubenon Department of Public Safety (thirty cases spread in various states of completion on my desk), the lawyers, Brabazon and Zakowski, had been engaging in back and forth dialogue—Zakowski making offers and Brabazon countering them. It was their intention to come to an agreement on how to settle this mess without the use of a full trial by jury. One such letter was sent via fax to DA Zakowski on July 13, 2004. (I've changed the women's last names and removed a short paragraph, but it otherwise reads as seen below.)

> *Dear Attorney Zakowski:*
>
> *I reviewed your offer with my client. I was quite disappointed as it seems to have gotten worse rather than better. Where the last offer was prepared with the intent of taking out any drug charges, the new offer includes a drug charge read-in.*
>
> *In order to get this resolved, there has to be give/take on both sides. Marcus is willing to plea to the following assaults:*

1.	Serenity	Count VIII	2nd degree
2.	Faith	Count I	3rd degree
3.	Sasha	Count III	2nd degree
4.	Theresa	Count XVI	2nd degree
5.	Faith	Count II	Video
6.	Grace	New Complaint	Video
7.	Rose	New Complaint	2nd degree

My client is willing to read-in (or enter a plea to) any other video charges. This gives the State at least seven convictions and multiple video read-ins.

I feel that this is something both sides can live with. It offers the State seven convictions and ample culpability for the court to sentence the defendant to a lengthy period of initial confinement. It allows Mr. Somerhalder to feel as though the system has treated him fair (somewhat) and isn't concerned about being sentenced for crimes he is adamant he didn't commit.

In no way is my client happy with this plea. In some of these cases, he strongly believes that if the entire story were to come out, it would be better for him. In many respects, I agree.

But the reality of trial, John, as you and I know, is that a jury is unpredictable. My client is willing to accept such a plea to avoid any further litigation, and embarrassment to the alleged victims, himself, and his family.

He is willing to accept this plea agreement despite the Court's potential decision to server these matters.

I believe it is in the best interest of all parties to resolve this case. The way I have outlined, no one is probably very excited about it, which usually suggests it is fair.

Thank you for your consideration. I will await your response. If you have any questions, please call me.

Best Regards,
Shane Laughton Brabazon

By the time the August 24 plea hearing arrived, Marcus's fate, through a series of faxes between his PD and DA Zakowski, had been negotiated. Further to that, Marcus had put together an "apology letter" addressed to "The

Citizens of Northeastern Wisconsin." Please note, this letter was addressed to his community, not to his victims. For him, the women warranted no more than a partial mention in the closing paragraphs of his public plea to not be seen as a bad guy. I wouldn't even call it a real apology.

When he finished reading, the courtroom, I would assume in shock, remained silent for a moment. If they felt anything like I did, they were horrified by his complacency and utter disregard for his actions. It was a personal affront to me and my investigation and insulting to everyone else. Instead of admitting his crimes with the intention of apologizing to the women he had hurt so irreparably, he chose to inform every person in Northeast Wisconsin that he was sorry he brought such heavy, negative attention to them. Stating only "...to the women who are involved in this case, I have not treated them as I would want to be treated," is offensive, insincere, and far less than those women deserved to hear.

At least it made it so much easier to hear that it was agreed Marcus would make a plea of no contest to counts 1, 2, 3, 8, 16, and the two new complaints regarding Grace and a woman named Rose, so long as we dismissed the remaining charges listed in 03CF1161[5] with prejudice. In layman's terms, with prejudice meant that any other charges that arose out of the investigation could not be brought forth against Marcus.

Why the hell would we agree to this when there were so many more victims than the ones listed above? Well, because this bargain came included with the understanding that, although we wouldn't place any further charges against Marcus, we could "read-in" others. What does that mean exactly? Well, it means that even though we weren't allowed to add any new cases or charges to Marcus's laundry list, we could make the court aware of other cases *and* the details regarding them.

In other words, even though Marcus was responsible for *many* more cases of sexual assault, we weren't going to charge him for them; additional cases were simply going to be considered when it came down to sentencing. So, if he were to get anywhere from two to ten years for the sexual assault

---

[5] Twelve counts of second-degree sexual assault and six counts of making a visual representation of nudity.

of one woman, his sentence for that charge would be decided—up to the maximum of ten years—based on the courts' knowledge and consideration that Marcus had done the same thing to so many other victims.

While it seems like we were making quite a few concessions by allowing so many cases to be dismissed, we still felt it was the right thing to do. It was what we had to do in order to keep Marcus's victims out of the courtroom—and ultimately, out of his sight. Equally important was the fact that those brave women wouldn't have to sit in on video reviews that would force them to relive their traumatic experience in a room full of strangers.

We knew from the start it might be a cruel necessity to show a jury the terrible evidence, but it had been our intention to prevent it from the very beginning. Though some may not see it that way, this was an enormous victory for us. While each and every woman wouldn't see justice applied to their individual case, as a whole, they were victorious in throwing Marcus behind bars, possibly until the day he died.

Based on his violations, Marcus B. Somerhalder's no contest plea to those seven charges carried a total maximum sentence of 117 years. It wasn't the total of twenty charges we'd accumulated against him during this process, but I couldn't have been more pleased. He would never have lived to serve all 500+ years that came with the thirteen counts of sexual assault and seven counts involving videotaping. Heck, there was no way he was going to survive the 117 years he was accepting as consequence. So yeah, like I said, I couldn't have been more pleased.

I don't consider myself all that smug a guy. I think I'm pretty humble when it comes down to it, but on August 24, I couldn't contain how incredibly proud I was as I sat in the courtroom. Even as Judge Warpinski made it clear to Marcus what his plea meant and ensured he understood and was in full agreement with the consequences, I couldn't help but sit a little straighter, shoulders pushed back as I swelled with pride for how this case turned out. I kept any kind of smile from my face—his family was present and I could see they were suffering, but I had every right to feel good. I know Marcus wasn't at all happy about how things were going down. He seemed right out of his mind every time he looked my way. I could see his jaw clench and unclench as he shot quick glares in my direction as often as he could, while still trying to pay attention to the judge.

I admit, the smallest upward curl in the corner of my mouth may have been detectable, but it was subtle at best. I sobered up quick when Judge Warpinski turned his eyes to DA Zakowski and me to confirm that we were indeed happy with the plea.

"Yes, Your Honor, quite pleased," Zakowski said through a smile. "I've spoken directly with many of the victims and they feel, so long as Mr. Somerhalder is held accountable and still faces a strict sentence, they're also all right with the plea."

"Very good, DA Zakowski," said Judge Warpinski, then looked to me and nodded curtly with a half-smile. He turned his gaze back to Marcus, and staring down his nose as I'd seen him do many times throughout those court sessions, said "Marcus B. Somerhalder, the court accepts your plea of no contest. This plea stands as an admission of guilt, thus, you are hereby convicted of five counts of sexual assault and two counts of making a visual representation of nudity." He smacked his gavel down on the sound block, then placed the gavel down to scratch something into his notes. Finishing that, he looked back up to address Marcus and PD Brabazon, "The August 26 jury selection in Marathon County will be cancelled as this case will no longer be going to trial."

During this proceeding, they scheduled the sentencing date for June 24, 2005 (yup, ten months into the future for sentencing) and put in an official order for a pre-sentence investigation, typically called a PSI.

The purpose of the PSI in any case is to help the court determine what an appropriate sentence for the convicted would be. A pre-sentence investigator is charged by the state to bring everything having to do with the case before, during, and post sentencing together into a logical, unbiased timeline to ensure the convict's sentence is appropriate to their crime. It's important that they have access to absolutely everything pertaining to the case from both the plaintiff (in this case, the State of Wisconsin) and the defendant (Marcus) as reviewing every facet of the case is what's needed for a good PS investigator to make an unbiased report.

The PSI is an important step because it's also the PS investigator's intention in this process to consider which jailhouse facility will best be able to accommodate the kind of rehabilitation needed. For example, with Marcus being a sex offender, the PS investigator's job would be to find a facility that has the resources and staff best able to understand, aid, and rehabilitate him through counseling as he serves his time.

I had my own opinion on where he should be sent, which is probably why they didn't ask me for any suggestions regarding correctional programs and counseling for him.

The report is also used by the state to recommend how many years the convicted will spend in the clink, how many years of probation, and the conditions of that probation.

Despite what people think of our justice system, they really don't want dangerous people back out in society—there are so many programs out there for convicts to utilize while behind bars.

Now, the other point; found in a letter penned by Marcus and included in his plea of no contest, Marcus indicated that he denied every allegation that he used date rape drugs on any of his victims. The letter went on to indicate that the State "has agreed to acknowledge that no date rape drugs were ever found in my residence, business, vehicle, or anywhere for that matter."[6]

Sadly, it was a true statement. No matter how strongly I'd willed those dark shampoo bottles to be filled to the brim with sinister potions, it wasn't the case. The reports on the contents of those bottles came back from the crime lab listed as inconclusive. Inconclusive! They didn't know what was in them—I was baffled. How could they *not* know?

My theory? They didn't put all that much effort into it. Once they got through those videos, they knew we'd be able to nail Marcus with a lifetime of charges, so they probably shelved the shampoo bottles. But without that factual knowledge, we couldn't charge Marcus with drugging his victims.

---

[6] Point 7 in Court of Appeals Cir. Ct. Nos. 2003CF1161, State of Wisconsin V. Marcus B. Somerhalder. Filed October 16, 2007

This didn't sit at all well with me at the time. Who am I kidding? It still doesn't sit well with me to this day. How could it? No matter how pleased I was that the women would get the justice, and hopefully closure, they deserved, I wouldn't be getting mine.

Maybe that sounds selfish. Maybe it sounds ridiculous, but I don't say it with any desire to take the grand victory away from Sasha, Katie, Grace, or any of the rest of those incredible women. I say it because I could have very well met my demise that night of the golf tournament. If it was me who drove myself home while I was wigged out of my mind, someone could have lost their life. I could have lost my job because of Marcus's asshole move, and he'll never be held accountable for it.

I know, I know. Never suffer the "what-ifs," but I couldn't, and to this day, still can't forgive what terrible paths he could have sent me spiraling down that night.

The courts might not have found what they needed to prove his guilt regarding the drugging, and I couldn't prove it, either. Still, I had no doubt; there was no question in my mind that I had been drugged by Marcus, and I couldn't make him suffer it.

There was nothing I could do about it, so I tried not to wallow in it.

It was a different story once I got home that night, though. I couldn't take my mind off it and was so consumed in the thoughts swirling around in my head that before I knew it, I was six beers into a Tuesday night… Not at all how I roll.

I chalked it up to the frustration of the day. I'd already been having a heck of a time getting quality sleep, so much so that I had an appointment with my doctor to chat about sleeping pills, or something—anything. I just wanted to remember what it felt like to have a clear mind and a rested body. It was a step in the right direction, I thought.

Little did I know the momentum of frustration, anger, and bitterness would eventually thrust an accidental six-beer Tuesday into an intentional commonplace occurrence. I wasn't drinking every night by any means. I still had a job to do, but I found several beers infinitely helpful in washing away the images and suffering that kept me up every night.

CHAPTER 17

CASE #04CF841: PART 3. . .

AKA MARCUS B. SOMERHALDER
VS. HIS OWN LAWYER

I did my best to enjoy the rest of the summer before it was time to prep my boys for school—the youngest was finally on his way to kindergarten, a fact that made me very emotional. At least, far more emotional than I'd been about my eldest heading into full days of school.

Honestly, I seemed to be emotional about everything, which was not like me. I've always taken pride in being an eternal optimist, but I was truly in a funk. It wasn't all the time, but more often than ever before, I felt angry, frustrated, and sad. I felt dominated by the constant negative feelings. I was able to contain most of it. I still laughed and smiled, but my jaw ached at the end of every day from the tension of keeping it all tucked deep down. For whatever reason, I didn't want anyone to know what was crawling around in my head. I was the unbreakable Sherm.

I kept as busy as I could to hide all the shit going on with me, but even with so many distractions at both home and work, I still caught myself drudging through the details of Case #04CF841 in every unoccupied mental moment. I'm serious when I say I was beginning to drive myself crazy.

In an effort to find even more to distract my mind, I thought it might be a good idea to get back into the dating game. There was no shortage of women to choose from due to my status as a low-grade celebrity hero, but so many of them were shallow, and even more of them were just looking to climb into bed with me—a source of contention to be sure. I was still having a hell of a time getting interested in sex. I was in my prime, and despite knowing exactly what had brought me to my lack of sexual motivation, there didn't seem to be anything I could do to overcome it. Honestly, I'm not even sure I wanted to—it was a simple fact that I was somewhat repulsed by the idea of being intimate with a woman. I didn't want to be, though. Even after a few drinks for courage, the flashbacks of those videos would come roaring into my head.

I'd stop because my skin felt like it was crawling.

I'd push the girl away from me—gently, of course.

I'd escape to the bathroom to hide the cold sweat and shakes.

None of the above dissuaded me from seeking out female distractions, though, or having a few more drinks than necessary to get me through those nights. I needed it until the big day in 2005 when Marcus would be sentenced, and I could put the whole thing behind me. Then, I could heal. I'd no longer need an extra drink to sleep; my head would hit the pillow and I'd be out, just like I had my whole life before. Once it was over, I'd get my head on straight...

In mid-October, I got a call from DA Zakowski, who wasted no time in informing me that Marcus had gone through the PSI report and had found so much issue with the official paper that he was making a motion to withdraw his plea.

My surprise was non-existent.

So, on Tuesday, October 26, 2004, I stood to the left of Zakowski, exhausted and trying to hide a minor hangover, in front of Judge Warpinski as he brought the courtroom to order.

We then had the pleasure of listening to Marcus make a motion to withdraw his no contest plea based on three factors.

The first issue to be brought to the court's attention was the fact that I had spoken with the PS investigator, and apparently, I wasn't supposed to do that.

The investigator had called me, and when he did, I had asked him if it was even okay that I talked to him. He assured me the State had given him the right to do so because of his insistence that he needed me to clarify the chronology of the case. It sounded like a legit enough reason to me, and I wouldn't question the State's decision anyway, so I complied. I had no idea that a conversation with him was technically out of bounds, and I didn't tell the man anything he didn't already know anyway.

Marcus seemed as if he was always on the lookout for any old excuse to play the system in his favor, and this was just another in a long line of "breaches" he took advantage of.

The second reason was that he had discovered new evidence in his defense. What that evidence was, he didn't share with us because he and his counsel hadn't had enough time to prepare it and make a decision on how best to utilize it.

Sure, sure, champ. Sheesh.

The third, and final, reason we were in the courtroom that day was because Marcus insisted that he be allowed to withdraw his plea because he hadn't understood what was going on regarding the no contest plea he'd made or the consequences attached to it.

When Marcus finally stopped crying to Judge Warpinski, DA Zakowski sighed deeply, turned to me, and whispered, "I have the feeling this case is never going to end, Investigator, *ever*."

I chuckled without mirth because that's all I could do in my state of hangover.

When I glanced over at PD Brabazon, the down-turn of his lip and the brow resting on the bridge of his nose was proof he didn't agree with reason number three one bit. It was a dig at him, after all.

It was obvious to everyone in the room that Marcus had known exactly what was going on when he made his plea, he just didn't like the recommendations made by the PS investigator. I can only imagine they scared the shit out of him.

Beyond those recommendations (which I personally hadn't seen yet), Zakowski assured me there was plenty of negative shit against Marcus within the pages of that PSI report.

"There's more than enough mention of him drugging women. Most of it came straight from the mouths of his own victims," he whispered to me.

"That's probably got him madder than hell because I know he doesn't want the drugging talked about at all."

His only course of action was to attempt to stall sentencing by back-tracking into the case, hence the declaration of new evidence. Zakowski had also mentioned Marcus would likely be facing a long prison sentence if the court took the PS investigator's recommendations. I think I would've been able to reach that conclusion without being told based on everyone, especially Marcus's, reaction to the document.

Thankfully, on that morning, the court didn't see any legal reason to accept the withdrawal of the plea agreement, but humored Marcus by ordering a new presentence investigation; one in which I wasn't allowed to have any contact with the PS investigator no matter what.

They also agreed to schedule an evidentiary hearing for a month into the future, so Marcus would have time to organize his "new evidence," and the courts could determine if his accusation regarding his lawyer not properly informing him of what the hell was going on had any validity.

Court was adjourned for that day. I promptly made my way back to the station to have a nap at my desk.

*   *   *

It was nearly seven months before the new PSI report was in hand (May of 2005). Now, sentencing remained scheduled for June of 2005, so the new PS investigator had lots of time to put together their report. The investigator dug deep and covered every corner of the investigation from allegation to video spectacle, which is fantastic because half of the reason Marcus had fought so hard to get the first PSI report struck from the record was because of the many mentions of victims accusing him of drugging them. Another issue I assume he'd had with the first PS investigator was that it made him look like a psychopathic asshole.

The inclusion of these two tidbits of information was a problem for him because he thought neither of them were going to be included in the report; those drugging charges had been dropped, and he wasn't crazy—he was a well-adjusted man with sexual wants and desires just like every other man out there...

A laughable statement at best.

When the second PSI report was presented to the courts in May of 2005 and it included these two sections, I couldn't have been happier.

> "[Pg 13] Dr. Robert H. Gordon, licensed psychologist applied a number of tests to Marcus. Based on the evaluations, Marcus was diagnosed as having a paraphilia not otherwise specified, a personality disorder not otherwise specified with narcissistic features, and alcohol abuse enforced remission. It was judged that his sexual abuse of women was related to his opportunistic desire to satisfy his sexual arousal, his self-centeredness related to narcissistic personality features, and his abuse of alcohol. Although Marcus didn't see any particular need for counseling, it was judged that he would benefit from group counseling as a sex offender."

. . .

> "[Pg 14] One of the big questions that has come up, and that Marcus has adamantly denied, is that there was use of drugs with these women. In any event, if it was drugs or if it was alcohol, these women were in an unconscious state at the time he was having sex with them and they were not able to give permission for those sexual acts. It does appear very strange that so many women would all experience the same type of situation and react in this same manner from alcohol."

So, as you can see, me having contact with the PS investigator or not made no difference. He wasn't going to escape the drug allegations or declarations of him not being right in the head.

Zakowski informed me that both PSI reports had very similar opinions on the amount of recommended initial confinement, the post-sentence extended supervision, and pretty much everything else. So, in the end, the new report was only an enormous waste of time and taxpayer's money.

*   *   *

Fast forward a month to November 23, 2004 and Marcus's new motion/ evidentiary hearing.

What a joke, was the only thought circling around in my mind as I sat in the courtroom blinking incessantly in an attempt to train my eyes to the preposterously bright room. At 7 a.m. in November, it was dark everywhere else, so why not in the courtroom, too? Why were we not all still in bed?

Justice really doesn't sleep.

I had to shake myself out of it. It was only November and I was feeling the effects of the shorter days and less sunshine more than I ever had before, and my compromised mental state and crummy quality of sleep wasn't helping. I don't think I had gotten more than a couple of hours of good sleep the night before, but that wasn't justice's fault.

We listened as Brabazon and Marcus disagreed on what they had discussed when it had come down to Marcus's plea bargain. He was sticking to the fact that Brabazon had not sufficiently explained the repercussions of making such a plea. The mustachioed PD was saying otherwise; he insisted that he had shared every nugget of information Marcus needed to make an educated decision regarding his plea.

Thus, based on these mirrored opinions, it seemed most certain that Brabazon would need to be put on the stand and under oath to testify. To do that, he would be required by law to withdraw as Marcus's defense attorney. Turns out, you aren't allowed to testify *against* your own client. Go figure!

Before we could get down to that fun, the court had decided to put Marcus under oath to testify as to why he felt he should be able to withdraw his plea. Marcus argued that he was never told what "Truth in Sentencing"[7] meant and his perception of his sentencing based on the plea of no contest was that he would get good time, parole, and earned release.

Truth in Sentencing means that if they told Marcus his sentence was fifteen to seventeen years long, they wouldn't be able to release him before he'd served at least that first fifteen years. Furthermore, once he's released, there's an extended supervision imposed on him—it's Wisconsin's fancy word for parole

---

[7] https://en.wikipedia.org/wiki/Truth_in_sentencing

on probation. While their extended supervision is in place, if the convict breaks any of the many rules they're required to follow, or if their probation officer deems it necessary, the offender can find themselves back in the clink.

Since he'd been in jail, he'd made some jailhouse buddies, and those guys had told him that people will get sentenced five years prison and only need to serve two years. He said he'd heard jailhouse stories that made him think he wouldn't have to serve much time. Marcus claimed that Brabazon never informed him he would spend each and every PSI recommended year of his jail sentence behind bars. He swore he had no idea that it had been a long time since convicts only served partial sentences with the remainder served while out on probation. You'd think someone around him would have known that kind of information; he'd already spent almost a year behind bars and burned through one whole lawyer—someone must have known the truth.

No matter. He cried that the consequences as they related to the initial confinement (prison) weren't what he was expecting he would likely be facing if he made the plea. Oh, and that was apparently Brabazon's fault, of course.

The look on Brabazon's face told a different story, but we wouldn't get to hear that side unless he stepped down as Marcus's lawyer. We hadn't gotten to that part yet though.

We had to continue listening as Marcus went on to request that the new PSI report not be carried out essentially because it would be insufficient to cure the State's breach (which was allowing the PS investigator to talk to me). Marcus was also upset the PS investigator didn't talk to all the people he wanted him to speak to—they would have provided information that made it clear Marcus was a good guy.

News flash, *buddy*—you're anything but a good guy.

Onward, when he had entered his plea, he had thought the dismissed charges (and any suggestion that he had drugged anyone) would be buried deep. So, when the PSI report came back with interviews from victims *insisting* they'd been drugged, and the PS investigator's agreement with the courts that those accusations, although dismissed, should be read-in so they could be considered in sentencing, Marcus felt it was extremely unfair. He was adamant he'd been deceived and felt strongly that the mentions of drugging should be stricken from the presentence investigation report.

The court's response to that was that they had every right to include those dismissed charges as read-ins on his sentencing *and* they had no intention of cancelling the second PSI report.

This all led into Marcus's next argument, the one where he declared that he hadn't been properly informed what the difference between dismissals and read-ins were. He went on to explain that when he made the plea, he didn't understand that the court would allow read-ins or even what that meant to him. He said he thought every mention of drugging would be gone.

It seemed to me it was all utter bullshit, though; this stuff had been exactly what he, Brabazon, and Zakowski had discussed in the plea negotiations throughout the summer months.

Here's a quick guide to courtroom read-ins—don't be a Marcus. When one charge amongst many has been dismissed, it can't be brought back or included in sentencing, *but*, if the dismissed charge is read-in, the judge can consider the misconducts of that dismissed charge when sentencing other charges. It's used to reach the maximum sentence on a conviction.

The dialogue in the courtroom between Marcus and a frustrated Brabazon on the topic of the read-ins being discussed went like this:

[SOMERHALDER'S ATTORNEY] BRABAZON: I believe I was focusing on…the allegation that you administered drugs to one or more of these individuals?

[SOMERHALDER]: Correct.

[SOMERHALDER'S ATTORNEY] BRABAZON: And your concern with that fact as it relates to the PSI or sentencing is what?

[SOMERHALDER]: That [the mention of drugging] still exists…I thought that…by entering into this [plea] agreement that issue was put to rest. Obviously, it is not put to rest and I think the only way that it's going to be put to rest is if we go to trial.[8]

---

[8] Point [8] pulled verbatim from Court of Appeals State of Wisconsin V. Marcus B. Somerhalder - Appeal Nos. 2007AP155-CR & 2007AP155-CR. Filed October 16, 2007.

He wanted to make sure the court knew he didn't give anyone any drugs. He also wanted assurance that the "untrue" allegations of him drugging victims wasn't mentioned or considered during sentencing, which was absolutely ludicrous since the accusations were included in the vast majority of the cases he was being charged with. The charges were dropped, but there was no way their mention was going to be struck from the records.

In this place of justice, Marcus maintained his faux inability to grasp the concept that everything dropped to finalize his plea would still be talked about, written about, and considered in the sentencing of the remaining charges if it was read-in. Oh, and all of it was being read-in.

Marcus continued to claim ignorance and Judge Warpinski finally slammed him for it.

"Okay, Mr. Somerhalder, I think enough is enough." He shook his head as he stabbed a finger in Marcus's direction. "I find it hard to believe that a twenty-nine-year-old, successful, accomplished bar owner facing many years in prison, who, up until this point, seemed to be well-versed in most of the legal terms, did not talk to his own attorney about the consequences that come with making a plea such as the one we're discussing today."

Marcus wouldn't let up. "It was discussed, but not in depth enough for me to fully understand the plea or what would be included in the PSI and considered in my sentencing, Your Honor," was his retort. He'd said that about thirty times throughout the morning.

Brabazon piped up to continue the argument from earlier in which Marcus claimed he did not fully understand "Truth in Sentencing" and the difference between extended supervision and initial confinement. "There's so much to our legal process, Your Honor. I must not have described the consequences and processes as clearly as I thought I had to my client."

I couldn't understand why Brabazon was carrying on with this. He must have known it was all bullshit—he knew how smart Marcus was. His own client was trying to throw him under the bus by claiming he hadn't explained any of what was going on, and it seemed as if he was joining forces with Marcus to convince the judge of the same thing.

Mayhap Brabazon was sick to the teeth of working for Marcus Somer-halder but that's just speculation. It could have been that Brabazon was ready to step down as Marcus's lawyer. I can't imagine it was easy working for a narcissistic sociopath.

The fact of the matter was, to make a proper decision as to whether or not Brabazon properly informed his client of Truth in Sentencing specifics and Marcus's every other claim to ignorance, the lawyer would have to step down.

DA Zakowski cleared his throat to address the court and when he did, I turned to see him red in the face. "Your Honor," he began to say through gritted teeth before finally relaxing into an exacerbated tone. "Mr. Somerhalder is one of the more intelligent defendants that the court is going to come across, and his testimony is just not believable." He pointed to Marcus as he continued to address Judge Warpinski. "I don't think there's any doubt that this man is the driving force behind this attempt to withdraw his plea based entirely on the fact that he doesn't like the negative light the *true and unbiased* PSI report shines on him."

Warpinski concurred with the DA and accused Marcus of playing the semantics game, but they also couldn't determine with any surety that he was telling the truth in all this. The courts' confusion on the matter was moot; they had to take the appropriate and ethical legal action by giving him the benefit of the doubt; Marcus would be granted the right to withdraw his plea. The only stipulation to this was that he would need to get himself a new attorney; a necessity so Brabazon could be put on the stand to testify as to what he had told Marcus.

Marcus was pleased by the outcome. I could see it on his face and hear it in his voice as he kissed Judge Warpinski's ass. "Thank you, Your Honor. This is true and fair justice, thank you."

It was a frustrating outcome because we all knew, including Marcus, every time he changed attorneys they would need several months to review and understand the case fully.

First, with the controlling and manipulation of many dozens of women, and now, even convicted and behind bars, Marcus was holding the reins on his own case; controlling barristers, magistrates, and judges all the same. The man was a master puppeteer.

I looked to Zakowski, still red-faced and flustered, and wished I could unplug the man; he'd clearly hit his boiling point. He probably wished he could be kicked from the case like Brabazon. Poor guy.

I was upset, too, but not more upset than I was ready to clear out of the painfully bright courtroom and retreat to my low-lit office—the exhaustion of the late night before had caught up to me with a vengeance.

Unfortunately, we weren't *quite* done for the day. The conclusion of the hearing sewed up the seams mentioned above: the court took Somerhalder's plea withdrawal motion under advisement and allowed Brabazon to withdraw as his attorney. When court next reconvened, we would hear his testimony in which, under oath, he would state that he had informed and educated Marcus to the best of his ability before he'd made his plea.

Lastly, Somerhalder was appointed another attorney.

I shuffled my exhausted ass out of the courtroom and had almost made it through the lobby to the front doors when I heard my name being called from behind.

I stopped, looked up to the incredible mural on the ceiling of the great copper dome because it sounded like that's where the voice came from—it hadn't, of course, but the lobby of the courthouse does weird things with sound. Anyway, I turned slowly to locate the source of the voice and was pleased to find who it belonged to.

"Schermitzler!" I heard Investigator Lawler say again as she continued toward me.

She caught up, and like a shot of adrenaline to the heart, I immediately attempted to perk up as she stopped a few feet away from me.

"Lawler, yeah, how are yah?" I closed the gap to clap her on the shoulder.

"Good, good; I thought I'd sit in on the proceedings today. I haven't made it to all of the sessions, but this one was early, before shift, so I figured I'd see how all this stuff was going down. What a pile of shit, by the way." She'd said it through a laugh, but her smile quickly shifted to a look of concern. "So, uh, how're you?"

There was no denying I looked worse for wear.

"I caught you closing your eyes a few times in there," she said.

"Oh yeah, I'm good. Just such an early session, and I had my boys last night. Couldn't get the youngest to settle, so I didn't get my usual eight hours, you know?" I lied, not wanting to share the reason for my lack of sleep. They were tucked in on time at their mother's house.

Lawler was close enough to see the dark rings around my eyes, I'm sure, but she didn't comment on how exhausted I looked. She simply said, "Yeah, I know how that is. You'll probably crash early tonight."

It was a nice idea, and I don't remember if I did crash early or not, but I appreciated her concern.

"Anyway, you need a ride back to the station?"

"Thanks, Lawler, I'm good," I said and started to turn away. "I'm gonna stop off at home before I head into the office."

She grabbed my arm before I could walk away. "I know this has been tough on you, but you need to know I'm available to talk it through if you need it. I saw those videos, too. I know how you feel."

"Okay, Lawler, thanks. I'm fine but I appreciate your concern." I shot her a smile because things were just fine. Super fine, in fact. I was dealing with it in my own way. I'd never let myself down before and I wouldn't this time, either. I was a foundation rock; I held everyone else up because I was so well put together that I could.

Super fine.

*   *   *

Now, if you can believe it, the day before that scheduled hearing where Marcus would withdraw his plea, just like he wanted, he withdrew the motion.

After all that, he decided to walk away from his hard-earned right to try again with a new lawyer and a new plea.

By this point in the case, it wasn't important that Zakowski keep me up-to-date on what the hell was going on with it. He was a busy guy, and I just didn't care anymore, so I can only speculate as to why Marcus would withdraw his motion.

Maybe it had everything to do with his new lawyer telling him it was time to pull his head out of his ass. We all knew Brabazon had worked out a hell of a deal for him, and Marcus had to face facts. He had done a lot of terrible shit. Whether he thought he was guilty of it, or it was wrong at all, didn't matter one bit—the people who needed to believe he was guilty did. If we took into consideration the opinions of criminals regarding the crimes they committed, they'd all be walking free. I could only hope the new lawyer opened Marcus's eyes to the fact that he wasn't going to get a better sentence than the one coming to him.

Either way, the matter was settled, and the only remaining step was his sentencing—six months down the road.

No problem, I could start taking the time I needed to work through all the stupid shit I'd suffered through those last fourteen months or so. At least, that's what I told myself.

I missed DA Zakwoski's first call to fill me in on Marcus's plea withdrawal because I'd left work early on account of a pounding headache. I was really starting to suffer the lack of sleep. When he tried to get a hold of me a second time a few days later, he called my cell phone, but I was in the shower, prepping for my second of three dinner and drinks dates that week.

I'd been missing a lot of stuff lately, and to put it bluntly, I just didn't fucking care.

Except for the sentencing, there was nothing left to do in Marcus's case. I finally had time to get back to normal. Things started to wiggle into place for a while, when in February I got promoted to lieutenant. It meant I could shake off sitting at a desk full of unsolved investigations and get back into the nitty-gritty duties of an active officer. It also meant I was now responsible for a whole shift of officers.

It was a completely different role for me; it created a whole new gamut of stress. I really should have utilized the counseling resources available to me. I was so used to just taking care of myself as a detective, and before that as an officer. Having to deal with other people's problems and issues on top of my own wasn't something I had experience with, and I initially found it incredibly challenging, especially at this juncture in my life. I needed to quickly figure out how to be a good leader, how to make them feel safe, and I had to do it while keeping my scattered head on straight.

Instead of taking the time to talk to the right people and put the effort into working through the stuff going on in my head properly, I wallowed in it when I was alone and ignored it while I was working. I put absolutely everything I had into my job, while I continued to numb my feelings and forget about the thoughts driving me mad as they rolled around in my brain.

The guy who only drank once or twice a month had turned into the guy who started having a couple of beers at least a few nights a week before bed because it helped me get some rest. Occasionally, on really bad days, I'd toss back a 6-pack before kicking off the sheets. Please, don't get me wrong. I never became an alcoholic. I never drank the day before work, because despite what was going on in my head, I knew how to keep my shit together. No matter how little sleep I got the night before work, I managed to keep myself as crisp and clean as I could.

That being said, with Marcus's case technically over, and my promotion to lieutenant, my career was blossoming. I was in my prime! I was receiving a lot of attention from old friends, new friends, local cops, single women, the media, and the general public. I was the investigator that dug into a very dark world and put a dangerous predator in prison, and that was enough to afford me offers for appearances on national and local talk shows. If you can believe it, I even got a call from the Maury Povich Show—they wanted me as a guest. I had speaking engagements lined up at schools, church youth organizations, and anywhere else they wanted me.

The community was safer, and people admired me for my commitment and vigilance. They showered me with respect, compliments, gifts, and often, food and booze, so it was a frequent occurrence that if I was having drinks, I wasn't cracking beer tabs alone. I'd had to see and experience a psychotic criminal's terrible, ugly underbelly to earn such glories, but…it was worth it, right?

I have no doubt it was, but at that time in my life, I wasn't thinking straight and didn't feel quite the same way as I do now. I felt like I had given more to the case than everyone else—which was true enough, but I also felt that I'd suffered more than everyone else, too.

It was total bullshit, but my addled brain had me convinced I deserved the celebrity status, so I embraced the marred and obtuse idea as fuel for my excuse to revel in the spotlight. Furthering my ignorance, I denied the obvious truth that the pedestal I stood upon was made of and encouraged by power and influence—for the benefit of others—void of any true regard for what I'd done and devoid of any sincerity or love for me. None of those new friends, reporters, or anyone else from my newfound fame cared about me. They were using me to their benefit while I was a hot topic, but I was happy to oblige so long as I could get back to my new "don't give a damn" lifestyle when they were done with me.

People seemed to think my career and life were just peachy, and sure, on the outside, everything *seemed* great. But boy, add all the attention and outward distractions to what was going on in my head—I had never seen such atrocities before this case, and it didn't sit well inside. It was more than a guy like me could handle.

The aftermath of any case was always sorting through the shit in my head, but I had no time, and I didn't want to make time because, like the victims I'd fought so hard for, I didn't want to relive any of it.

Unfortunately, the beloved public attention waned, and when it did, all the supressed emotions began to trickle out of the cracks in my psyche. Less company meant fewer chances to excuse my drinking as social. Once again, I wasn't an alcoholic; I wasn't relying on booze. I rarely felt good, happy, or at ease, and when I was at my best, I was usually surrounded by people, food, and more alcohol than I'd typically drink. When the opportunities for that lessened, I simply continued to have drinks more often without companions. It didn't help. Nothing helped.

I finally came to terms with the fact that I was at the bottom of a chasm I couldn't imagine how to climb out of. I couldn't stop thinking about the case and it was making me miserable. I felt depressed and ashamed. I felt I had let all of those women down. Never mind that Marcus was going to jail, I couldn't shake off the shadows of doubt that loomed over me. Sure, we kept them off the stand and yeah, they appreciated that, but I felt like I should have fought even harder for them.

I hated that Marcus was getting away with drugging the women, and even more so, guilty that I had let him get *me* with that *fucking* coma drug. Those women were unsuspecting, trusting, and just looking to have a nice time with who they thought was a respectable, successful, and handsome (I guess) guy. They didn't see what was coming, but *I* should have.

The seasoned cop should always be on guard, because even out of our uniforms we can't help but want law and order to rule. Like a superhero, we are ever-vigilant; it suits us and we're good at it—usually.

I'd often get flashbacks of the faces in Marcus's video files: Sasha, Theresa, Faith…their eyes glazed over or closed completely as Marcus's movements rocked their limp bodies, and those visions haunted me. It made the cowardice of not revealing my story chew at me viciously. God, was I angry. At Marcus, at myself, and sometimes, even at the innocent women I'd helped simply for being more brave than me. They were better people than me. I expected and encouraged all of them to spill their most personal, sexual (not all of the women were raped), traumatic experiences as I hid behind my little wall of shame. But no matter how much it ate at me, I didn't feel like anyone would believe the lead investigator was, in a sense, also a victim of Marcus's. I was experiencing some of the trauma the women described feeling during and after their assaults, but in a much *different* way. I hid it; I was in a great place from the outside looking in.

I was not in a good place internally. I was just so goddamned angry!

What happened to me: the hours forgotten, the scary possibility that I made a black-out jaunt home in my car, the fear that I might've maimed or killed someone if it was me that had driven home, the shame of knowing that me, the hero, the big, tough, smart-as-a-whip cop had also been drugged had worn down my thick skin. I hid behind my secret wall of shame, but it didn't matter how much it ate at me, how angry I was, or how violated *I* felt, my story didn't compare to what those women had gone through. I knew that, so I kept on shutting up.

I didn't feel like anyone would ever consider the lead investigator a victim of Marcus's, and if anyone did, I could hear them respond with, "Were you videotaped while he raped you?" And when I said "No," they'd wonder what the hell I was complaining about. There would be no need for them to make that compassionate connection.

It was the shame that he had got to me at all that angered me. My reasons were sound—the ones I gave above—and now add to that list the fact he could have *killed* me…and he would never be answerable for it. In no courtroom, or on any official document, affidavit, warrant, or in an apology letter from the man himself, would a word of what he did to me ever be said or written. I fought so hard for those women, suffered so much to get them justice and see Marcus pay for his crimes, and I really was proud of that, but I didn't get my own closure. In my fucked-up state, it was one more thing that slowly chewed at my mental health.

"Another beer over here!" *Buddy*—my MO for months, even when no one else was drinking. Alcohol is a powerful, mind-numbing agent, and at the time, I could *almost* understand why trying to get women fall-down, pass-out drunk was one of Marcus's initial diabolical steps. Like me, he should have only used it on himself. We'd all have been better off if he'd drank himself into a stupor every time he felt the urge to rape another woman.

Despite the drop off in public interest, I was still getting a lot of attention from the ladies—my dating opportunities seemed endless and more random than ever. Women who wouldn't have ever given me a second look were all of a sudden cloying for my attention. Not that they needed to try all that hard; just like the alcohol, they were a welcome distraction. Of course, I say that, but that wasn't really the case… I wasn't actually interested in any of them no matter how badly I wanted to be. Beyond that, I didn't have any mojo, so to speak, and no amount of talking myself into intimacy seemed to work. I damn near needed to force myself into the mood, and my efforts backfired all the time. Sometimes, it took as little as a woman pressing her chest against mine as she leaned in for a kiss to trigger flashbacks of the video review from Marcus's case. It was out of control. I was broken.

No. It was more like I was haunted. That seems more fitting.

I don't consider myself anything like a Casanova, but I've never had any problem building up and enjoying relationships with women. I like monogamy and the companionship that comes with it; I'd always been confident enough to think I was a pretty darn good catch for any woman, too, but that was before the case. The post-case Scott Schermitzler thought he wanted to find a quality relationship because he was convinced a good woman would be the remedy to all that ailed him. But, how do you settle into intimate companionship when you can't even fathom being intimate? Could I get past the vulgar horrors my eyes had seen? Not if the woman I was hoping to help me do so couldn't touch me without making me nauseous.

None of the women looking to date me were interested in who I *really* was anyway, so I just dated for the sake of dating; a new woman every night so I could avoid the awkwardness of forced intimacy. Dinner and drinks for her, and dinner and drinks for her, and for her, and her, and her, too.

I remember vividly a time, as I plummeted toward my rock bottom, when I dated three women in the same day. Less vivid by the end of that day were their names, as I cracked a beer and propped my feet up on my coffee table that evening. I'd already forgotten two out of three of them—one of them had slipped my mind while we were still on the date. She wasn't all that impressed when she was forced to remind me. I didn't care. There was a severe lackluster regarding pretty much everything in my life—nothing meant all that much.

I should've sought help. Instead, when I was sober, at work, or with my kids, I took it out on myself and blamed myself for the way I felt. When I was drunk, cavorting, canceling weekends with my sons to party with strangers, I was numb and entirely unfocused. Anything in my life that I didn't like needed to go away; not sorted in a healthy way, just gone. My terrible disregard for self-care manifested into me becoming someone I didn't know and frankly, despised.

I needed a wakeup call…and fast.

It was April 14, 2005. I was on the tail-end of my public popularity/usefulness, so I'd jumped at the invitation to attend the grand opening dedication event of the new emergency room at St. Mary's Hospital on the west side of Green Bay. It was kind of a big deal, so every media outlet was going to be in attendance and everybody who was anybody in the community had been invited. Thankfully, the who's who of Green Bay still included me, but to my disappointment, it also included my recent nemesis who had worked for a local newspaper and loyal friend to Somerhalder, Andy Nelesen.

I'm not going to get too deep into an explanation on Andy Nelesen. Beyond him being a long-time friend of Marcus's, Andy had used his position at the newspaper to spearhead the smear campaign on the case.

He was smart about it—not seeming to pick sides, but still managing to make me, and everyone on Marcus's case, look like a pack of roving idiots. I had to take everything he wrote with a grain of salt. It was difficult when he'd mentioned to Skinny and I that we were terrible friends for throwing Marcus under the bus. Maybe that made Skinny feel bad, but I'm a cop—Marcus threw himself under a bus.

Back to the fancy party. I had brought along my current girlfriend, Kelly, who was easily seven years younger than me and a bit of a party animal, which was a huge part of my attraction to her. Admittedly, she was one of the many women I dated knowing there wasn't likely any future with them, but they were fun and refreshing to be around. Looking back, she definitely wasn't a suitable mate for a divorced father of two young boys working as a law enforcement officer. Don't get me wrong. Kelly was a beautiful young lady that I really enjoyed spending time with, but neither of us were in it for the right reasons. Both of us were in drastically different places in our lives. At any rate, she was my date for the evening.

We enjoyed the party: the plentiful array of food, interesting and influential people, an excuse to celebrate, and alcoholic drinks to amplify the cheer. We cavorted for the better part of the evening, sipping through a few glasses of spiked punch, and thus far, all had been well. It was a wonderful event for everyone from doctors, medics, nurses, all the way to local politicians.

Many people at the bash had learned I'd recently purchased El Toro (I mean, I was bragging about it), and a posse of about a dozen people looking to shrug off the properly stuffy current venue requested that the party continue at my new establishment. I wasn't opposed to the idea, but something about it didn't feel right. It was a Thursday after all, so that alone should have been reason enough to call it a night and head home, but it was the idea in general that nagged at me. I couldn't pin down what was truly chewing at me. Kelly had already encouraged the posse plus many others to meet us at El Toro, so I ignored the mysterious red flag and conceded to the fact that it would be an excellent opportunity to get people into the doors of my new business.

When we arrived at El Toro, I sponsored some beer for the entire group, and it soon became clear that several of them wanted to repay me with shots.

I've never been good at doing shots, and these days, I still avoid them at all costs. I never liked the idea of drinking just to get wasted, which is what shots are designed to do. However, that night, for whatever reason—maybe it was me reveling in the spotlight once again—I obliged and threw back everything that was handed to me.

Kelly and I had a great time as we made our way around to the tables filled by our new friends, but by 11 p.m. it was time to go home. I gathered up Kelly, who was gushing over some woman's sequined dress and tried to shuffle her toward the door, but she was having fun and didn't want to leave.

"You're just being a party pooper, Sherm." She pouted at me, grabbed me by the tie, and tried to drag me away from the entrance.

I resisted as she persisted, "C'mon! It's *so* early. Tomorrow's Friday; you can have a nap at your desk or something. Please," she said as she dropped my tie and turned to head back to the party. She probably wouldn't have cared if I'd left, but I caved and made my way to the bar to order another beer.

I didn't drink that beer. I held it and peeled at the label a bit as I watched Kelly do a round of shots with the tailor-suited men at the table in the corner by the window. I couldn't hold back my annoyance any longer; I left the still-full bottle sitting on the bar and made my way to Kelly. Enough was enough, we were leaving.

Frustrated, I marched out to the parking lot with Kelly, who was close on my heels and stubbornly protesting our early exit. I only lived about three miles away, and being as completely done with the night as I was, I went against my better judgement and recklessly climbed behind the steering wheel of my Lincoln LS.

"It's not even that late, Sherm!" said Kelly as she stood outside of the car, bent over to shout through the closed window at me.

"Seriously." I heard her huff as she pulled the door open. "Like, another hour is gonna kill you? Tomorrow is Friday, it might as well be another day of the weekend." She plopped herself down into the seat and slammed the door shut before continuing her protest. "I dunno about you—" She cut herself off to roll down the window and spit her gum into the parking lot. "But Friday is a wash. I don't do any work on Friday—no one does! Why can't you be like everybody else?"

I waited for her to shut up, then said, "Look, if you wanna stay, stay. I'm not going to force you to leave." I started the car but left it in park. "I'm not your keeper or anything, but we only met some of these people tonight. I'm not comfortable leaving you in their care." I did up my own seatbelt then turned in my seat to look at her. "You know the case I'm on and it would be naïve to think that because someone like Marcus Somerhalder is in jail the streets are now safe for women everywhere."

"I can take care of myself, Sherm," she said with her face down as she started digging through her purse.

"I know you can, Kelly—are you staying then?" I sighed in resolve. I wasn't angry anymore.

"No." She threw a fresh piece of gum into her mouth, rolled the foil wrapper between her fingers, and flicked it to the floor of the car. I frowned at the action, but she refused to look at me, so she missed my disapproval.

I threw the car into drive, and as soon as we started to roll forward, she picked up again. I had to ignore her. I'd won, and no matter if she liked it or not, she was safe, so I could sleep sound.

I calmly listened to her yammer on as we drove south toward the Brown County Fairgrounds. Less than a mile from home, I noticed a car parked on the right side of the road. I couldn't tell if the car was running, but the brake lights were on. I didn't think anything of it—why would I? It was a parked car, and not in my way. Just as I approached, the vehicle jetted out in front of me. I jerked my wheel to the left as I slammed on my brakes and narrowly avoided contact with the rear driver's side door.

The vehicle swerved a bit, then took a quick left into the parking lot opposite to where he had been stopped on the side of the road.

"Goddamn it," I barked as I quickly checked for oncoming traffic, then turned left, following the car very closely into the busy parking lot of one of the local taverns.

"Holy shit!" I said, frazzled and out of breath. "What's this guy thinking? He must be drunk."

There was no question in my mind that alcohol was involved in what had just happened, and I was right, but not how I thought.

The car drove about thirty meters into the lot, then stopped abruptly—an action I wasn't at all prepared for. I braked, but not fast enough, and bumped into the back of the vehicle.

I glanced over at Kelly, her eyes the size of dinner plates and her mouth was open in shock. It didn't last; clacking her jaw shut, she unbuckled, threw her shoulder into the door to get it open, and nearly vaulted out of the car. She didn't look at either vehicle, just rounded my Lincoln at a march to confront the driver. He hadn't even exited his car yet and she was yelling, "Just what the hell do you think you're doing! Are you drunk?"

The driver got out, and ignoring Kelly, he stepped around her to look over at me still sitting in my car and said, "I know who you are, and I know *you're* drunk." He then held up his cellphone. "I've called the cops, so you might as well just sit tight."

My efforts were audible as I poured myself out of the driver's seat, ready to confront him, when I realized he was absolutely right... I was the drunk.

Almost as if to prove it right then and there, as I lifted my foot off the break to fully exit the car, it lurched backward a foot before I immediately and without grace plopped back down to put it in park. I guess, in the excitement of Kelly jumping out of the car and confronting the driver, I inadvertently had put the vehicle into reverse instead of park.

Unlike with the golf outing where I drank little and forgot everything, I remember this night like it happened yesterday, despite my heavy inebriation. It's probably because I hadn't been drugged, but also, because it was at that very defining moment I knew everything in my life was going to come crashing down; I was about to learn a major life lesson.

I had always been the good guy, the fixer of all the problems, and now, to my complete disgust, I was undeniably the problem.

By the time the De Pere police responded, my head had sobered, but I knew my blood alcohol content would betray me. I took a personal inventory of how intoxicated I thought I was, and was ashamed at just how much alcohol I could recall consuming that night.

I was sitting on a concrete parking curb with my head in my hands. Kelly had gone to sit in the car; it was warmer in there and she wasn't having any fun. I'd told her to call a cab, but I'm not sure if she did or not. I admit, I kind of lost track of her once the cops arrived.

The man in the other car jumped into action as soon as the first officer's boot hit the pavement. "I want that man arrested. I know for a fact that he's drunk!"

He was absolutely correct. I had made a terrible mistake, and I needed to take responsibility for my actions.

The officers on scene knew who I was and came over to talk to me.

"You can smell it on him, can't you?" the man said.

The officer stopped dead in his tracks and pivoted on his heel to face the guy. "Sir, I'm going to have to ask you to return to your vehicle. One of the other officers will be over shortly to take your statement." He turned back to me, offered me a hand and pulled me up to my feet. "Good evening, Investigator Schermitzler. How are you tonight?" He shined his flashlight into my eyes for a quick second, and while I blinked through the pain of it, he slipped his pen and notepad out of his front shirt pocket, flipping to the first blank page.

"Yeah, uh, yeah; it's lieutenant now—I've been better," was all I could muster as I rubbed my eyes. I was so horrified at the situation I found myself in that I almost wished they'd have slapped the cuffs on me and thrown me in the back of the patrol car. I wanted it all to be over with.

"Lieutenant, have you had anything to drink since the incident?" he asked.

"No." I sighed. I knew what he was trying to do.

"Are you sure?" He hadn't written my response in his little book yet. Why? Because most officers know that if someone says they've downed a bottle of liquor since the accident happened it would be difficult to convict the person of drinking and driving prior to that moment. This guy was clearly offering me an out. "I really think you must have been drinking since you had your fender-bender, right?" The officer urged me to answer yes, and I appreciated what he was trying to do for me, but I couldn't get myself to lie about it. I was frustrated with myself and knew how important it was that I take responsibility, not that I'd made a habit of it, but I'd driven home after a few drinks once or twice more than I'd like to admit—which should be *never*. I recognized this development was a long time in coming and I needed an eye-opening experience to bring me back to Earth.

After the third or fourth time the officer asked me, I started to get upset with him. Of course, I wanted to say, "Yes, I just slammed a pint of whiskey and threw the bottle in a bush!" I would've loved to get off without consequences. How great is special treatment? Right?

How would I ever live it down, though? I wouldn't. It's not in my character to be a crooked cop. I'd think about it constantly until I was either driven into confession or utter madness by it. No—there was no choice; I was drunk, and my only peace of mind would be found in getting treated like everyone else that makes this same shitty mistake. I was fortunate I didn't hurt or kill anyone, so how bad could the consequences be? I needed to take my lumps.

Sadly, and with a great deal of remorse, I had no idea how wrong I was about getting treated the same as others. I was made an example of and punished much worse than the average offender.

I think what made it all that much worse for me was, to my surprise and disgust, Andy Nelesen had my name and the story of my debacle in the paper before sunrise. How could he have known what happened that quickly? Maybe it was his way of getting me back for shining such a bright light on his best bud and Marcus's love for destroying lives through rape? Who knows, but there were a lot of people who suggested Andy tracked me that night and set me up. It was plausible, but didn't matter, because what I did was careless and wrong whether I had been set up or caught legitimately.

The rundown on the whole thing was massive. I was the shameful recipient of:

- Two weeks unpaid leave
- A six-month suspension from the SWAT team
- Over $2,000 in forfeitures and several thousand in attorney fees
- Mandatory counseling sessions
- A six-month suspension on my driver's license

All of it terrible, and difficult, but most of all, I had lost the admiration I had worked so hard to earn from so many people for so many years. It was extremely embarrassing and shameful to be "that cop," but what I hated more than anything was that they now questioned my integrity.

The entire ordeal was covered by every single media outlet throughout Northeast Wisconsin and delivered in various formats for all to see. I was officially back on top of the news, but I'd had to officially hit rock bottom to get there.

I've known of many others—even a few officers—that have made the same stupid mistake as me, but none of them have been so publicly ridiculed for their actions. I think I understand the reasoning though; this mistake didn't only reflect negatively on me. Messing up when I did, before Marcus had even been sentenced, drew a lot of terribly negative attention to the Ashwaubenon Public Safety Department. It was wondered why my department hadn't taken better care of an obviously traumatized agent, but my superiors and I knew I'd denied help many times. They never said it to me, but I'm certain they resented how it all went down, hence the counseling sessions being mandatory.

Since then, I've had to try twice as hard and work twice as diligently to regain the respect and admiration of my fellow officers. It took a long time, but I was humbled by the event and never quit, so I came out a stronger person because of the experience.

Ten weeks after my big event, June 24, 2005, I walked into the Brown County Circuit Court building a new man; excited and proud to be in such a good place on Marcus Somerhalder's day of reckoning.

As I looked up to the mural on the ceiling of Green Bay's old legal building—something I'd never done before this case but had done so many times throughout it—a sob tightened my chest. It had been such a long haul. I held back the tears threatening to escape my eyes. I couldn't help but let the feelings wash through me—good God was I ever glad to be there. Good God was I ever glad I could shut the manila folder on this case forever.

In the time since my own arrest, I'd worked through most of the issues brought on by the case, the ones that had clawed their way into my psyche and mutated like a cancer to slowly sicken and debilitate me. I even managed to work through shit that was buried even deeper down—stuff I didn't even know was bothering me—and now I felt great. I'd shaken off the anger at how I'd been treated by the safety department, the public, and the media after my arrest, which was important because I had no intention of changing my career. I still wasn't up to snuff or full duty, but I was feeling the best I had in years.

I brought my hands up to the solid knot on the tie at my throat, made sure it was centered below my Adam's apple, and took a deep breath; it was time to head into the courtroom. I was merely a spectator for this event as DA Zakowski had no need for me at his side.

Despite the shortness of the event, the courtroom was full. I saw a few of Marcus's victims scattered discreetly throughout the courtroom, which was fine by me; all the more power to them for being there. Beyond those brave enough to face their abuser, the room overflowed with reporters clutching cameras close to their chests, uninvolved but still finely dressed lawyers, some interested members of the general public, and the magistrate who signed my search warrant; bless his heart. Marcus stood beside a lawyer I didn't recognize. I guess Brabazon had either been fired or was smart enough to wash his hands of the whole thing. I hoped the latter was the answer.

Warpinski's gavel hit the sound block; he called the court to order and got right down to the good stuff. "It's important that I state *this* has not been treated or sentenced as a date rape drug case, because despite popular belief," he glanced quickly to me, "there weren't any facts to support that."

I disagreed, and I think most of the victims would have, too, but they weren't in there to protest. I knew we'd made our concessions no matter how frustrating they were.

Warpinski looked down to Marcus, and said something like, "This court, myself included of course, cannot in good conscience ignore the alleged crimes against you that we were forced to dismiss as part of your plea."

Which I'm certain encompassed the drug allegations as much as it did the visual representations we had to throw out, but I admit that's just conjecture on my part.

Warpinski went on to say, "You know you apologized to a series of women who were the victims in this case, but there are a group of other women out there who deserve that apology just as much. I'm not dealing here with a case where this happened once and it was over. I have a situation here where over a period of three years that we know about, that you were raping women.[9]

"Your offenses are serious, the effect your crimes had on your victims are substantial, and the conduct depicted on the videotapes found in your possession are sick and horrible. We need to deter others from committing crimes such as this. So, while you're being made an example of..." I knew exactly how he felt, "...we did take into consideration that you spared your victims from testifying and you have no offenses on record prior to the events we're sentencing you for today.

"It's with this in mind," Warpinski continued, "that I now impose the following sentence on you, Marcus B. Somerhalder..."

The court saw fit to mention that Marcus was facing a possible sentence of over 100 years, but felt comfortable in committing his maximum to sixty-six years under their supervision. This included a total of twenty consecutive years of incarceration and forty-six years of extended supervision.

Furthermore, there were several conditions that went along with that sixty-six years. To start, because Marcus had committed crimes of sexual assault, which are offenses that fall within Chapter 940 of the Wisconsin State Legislature,[10] he wasn't eligible for early release. Another requirement of joining the Chapter 940 club was the need to declare himself as a registered sex offender, which is a federal list offenders remain on until they die. I assure you though, if an offender is on the federal sex offender's list, no one in history who talks about them post-mortem will ever forget to mention their inclusion on that list—except, respectfully, maybe at the funeral.

People can change, though. I've seen it. I've seen many convicts turn their lives around to create legacies they and their families are proud of... I suspected that wasn't likely for Marcus; a man who still insisted he'd been set up by his victims and me.

---

[9] Point [9] pulled in part as verbatim from Court of Appeals State of Wisconsin V. Marcus B. Somerhalder - Appeal Nos. 2007AP155-CR & 2007AP155-CR. Filed October 16, 2007.
[10] Chapter 940 – Wisconsin State Legislature: https://docs.legis.wisconsin.gov/statutes/statutes/940 with reference to Subchapter II: Bodily Security reference number 940.225 – Sexual Assault

He would have a lot of time to rethink that as the continuation of his restrictions after release included not having any contact with his victims *ever*, a lot of treatment for his sexual deviancy, no use of drugs or alcohol, and he wasn't allowed to be in possession of any pornographic materials.

Lastly, my favorite consequence, because I feel it's the most important, is Marcus must disclose the fact that he's a registered sex offender to any woman he's interested in spending time with. Further to that, if Marcus wants to pursue a romantic relationship with a woman, he must ensure his probation officer knows about it, and the probation officer must give Marcus permission before he can proceed with said relationship.

Whether Marcus follows the rules or not is up to him, but I sure as hell hope he does. I worry every single day that he's incapable of remorse for what he's done and that scares the shit out of me. I have a hard enough time processing the fact that there are others out there who are constantly doing the same as what he did. My heart hurts, and I choke-up every time I think about the reality of my world—it isn't just women who suffer at the hands of men like Marcus—children too, little boys and girls. Sometimes, in my line of work, I run into situations as such, and it takes such a long time to shake the feelings that come with them. Sometimes it's crippling, but at least I know how to handle things these days.

Still, I can't help but wish Marcus had been the only sexual predator on the entire planet and once he was thrown in jail, no one ever had to suffer the kind of pain he brought his victims ever again.

Ah, the stuff dreams are made of.

INDOMITABLE AND STALWART. . .

AKA THE HEROIC BUT HAUNTED

Now, as I begin to bring this whole chronicle to a close, please know, I'm so proud to have been such a big part of getting Marcus Somerhalder under the microscope and off the streets, but I'm not the real hero here, I assure you.

It was important to tell this story for many reasons, but foremost in my mind was if I didn't, Marcus would remain the smug winner in all this. He would remain the man who thought he was innocent, the man who thought he did no wrong. He would go through life telling everyone he met that he'd been set up, and that's not fair. It's not fair to me or the officers who worked the case with me. Never mind that though, first and foremost, it wouldn't be fair to the many women who made the sacrifices needed to help me take down Marcus Somerhalder.

I know I've said it before, but with more dedicated space to declare it—a chapter all for them—their lives could have gone very sideways if the case would have gone to trial. They would have had to suffer court date after court date and being in the same room as Marcus wouldn't have even been the worst of it. So many other eyes would have watched those videos, they would have had to sit on the stand, under oath, and talk about the absolute worst and most violating experience of their whole lives. In the most haunting of those scenarios, they would have had to identify themselves as their respective videos played in that courtroom.

I can assure you, many of them wouldn't have coped very well under those conditions.

Still, even with no assurance that I could keep them or their vicious assaults caught on tape out of the courtroom, each and every one, through terrible fear of consequence and humiliation, agreed to help me stop Marcus.

For some of them, it took explaining that his behavior was becoming more aggressive—we were seeing swift evolution in his sexual process and the natural progression of his psychosis could be necrophilia. For others, it took cries of compassion or assurances of protection and support—everything we said to convince them was the truth, but each woman responded to different truths and for different reasons. In the end, they agreed to help because they were so sure they didn't want anyone else to suffer what they had gone through.

As I began writing this book, I made every effort to contact the heroines of Case #04CF841 and was even fortunate enough to sit down with a few of them. Of those I met, most had found their way to healing enough to lead happy lives, but every single one of them still felt the effects of what Marcus did to them. I could see how they suffered still; I could hear it in their voices and the way they talked about their lives, and I could see it in their movements and demeanors...

There was one exception, though. One woman I know I won't ever have an opportunity to sit down with and who, at great cost, I know isn't suffering anymore.

It's with the deepest condolences that I share news of Katie DeNiel's passing on June 2, 2014—she was only thirty years old.

It broke my heart to learn Katie wasn't able to shake the trauma she suffered at the hands of Marcus Somerhalder and I could relate. I've thought dozens of times about how I could have ended up like Katie when I hit my ground zero—when I was incapable of figuring out where broken me ended and healthy me started... So yeah, I understand, but I wish it would have been different for her especially.

I thought the world of each of the women that stepped up to help me build the case against Marcus, but Katie was special. She was young, but so full of ambition. I honestly worried less about her than the more than hundred other women I talked to throughout the case. I thought she would be able to deal with being a victim, pick up the pieces, and move on to lead a successful and happy life. I was horrified and terribly sad to find out just how wrong I was.

I was moved to contact Katie's family and was honored to sit and have a chat with them. They talked about how desperately hard Katie fought against her demons. She had incredible things to live for, and she knew that, so she did everything in her power to heal…*but* you need to understand just how difficult a process it is. To say everyone is able to succeed at moving on after going through what Katie did isn't realistic, but I desperately wish she had.

At the end of our chat, I asked them if they would consider writing something about Katie that I could include in the book, and they didn't hesitate to say yes. They did a lovely job of it.

Katie was an incredible, caring, and intelligent person who lit up the room with her beauty and contagious laugh. She was passionate about many things, but graduating from the University of Wisconsin-Green Bay with a bachelor's degree in history with dreams of pursuing law school was at the top of that list. Those dreams changed forever when Katie began working for Marcus Somerhalder.

Like many college students, Katie took a job as a cocktail waitress to help pay her way through school. She was only eighteen when Marcus hired her on at the Velvet Room, and it was there that he, the owner of the bar and her employer, gained her trust, only to take advantage of it.

Marcus spiked Katie's cocktail with drugs and raped her several times—making sure to videotape it all. The very essence of her character was irrevocably shattered. Marcus's actions have had a profound ripple effect on both our family and Katie, with the ultimate cost being her life.

Some people have drawn their own conclusions and assumptions regarding the case and the life and death of Katie, and they're entitled to their opinions, but they don't know what was done to her, and didn't know Katie like we did. The resounding truth is that she experienced something horrific and traumatizing at the young age of eighteen, and that experience soon became a high-profile case that was sensationalized by the media over several years. Furthermore, the case was prosecuted by the Brown County District Attorney's office, the same office where Katie had just finished an internship; she was humiliated, ashamed, and traumatized anytime the case was discussed. Every time the videotapes were viewed as evidence, she was revictimized. She received no resources to support her in her healing and recovery. Still, Katie—being the brave, selfless, and courageous person we knew her to be—came forward to speak out against her attacker, to bring Marcus to justice, and ensure no one else would be victimized by him.

Ultimately, the system failed Katie.

The community doubted the victims. Whispers of "those women got what they deserved," were heard in grocery stores, at gas stations, in schools. After her testimony, Katie was left to deal with the trauma alone. She was expected to be her own advocate. When she did try to reach out, wait times for therapy appointments and insurance roadblocks stood in the way of her getting the help she needed. The trauma and lack of help became insurmountable.

Paralyzed by her guilt, shame, and pain, Katie struggled to tell her family what had happened. Alone in her suffering, she dealt with depression, anxiety, poor self-esteem, and PTSD all so severe that she was never able to overcome it all. In desperation, she turned to prescription drugs and alcohol to escape the trauma she had endured.

Her depression, and subsequent addiction, led to stays in crisis centers and hospitals. She struggled to make meaningful relationships and became a victim of domestic abuse.

For twelve years, her family lived in a state of hypervigilance. Amid the constant worry, they tried to get her help, but without being able to address the root cause of her pain, Katie was unable to recover. She died at the age of thirty of an accidental interaction of her prescription medications, which caused her to stop breathing. Katie died in her sleep.

Yet, through the darkness, there were spots of light including the birth of her son, Kaiden. While she struggled—physically, mentally, and emotionally—to care for him, she loved him with of all her heart. She did the best she could and was there for him when she was able to be. When Katie came to the realization that she was unable to care for him, she selflessly gave her parents guardianship, knowing Kaiden would be better for it. As he continues to grow, he will learn how much his mother struggled and the reason why.

Katie was shattered and irrevocably traumatized by the nights Marcus assaulted her. In the shadow of that trauma, Katie left behind a family, a son, and her potential. The aftershock remains amidst her family, who will grieve the lifelong loss of being left with the heart-wrenching reality of who Katie could have been, and what her life would have been had this not happened.

Katie's life is the collateral damage of Marcus's crimes.

The DeNiel Family

*   *   *

Another woman I was pleased to sit down with was the ground zero gal— Hope Alby. I'm sure you remember Hope, but if you need a recap—she honored this book by writing the foreword for it.

More than that, Hope wasn't the first of Marcus's victims, nor was she the last, but if not for *her*, there's a really good chance that none of this would have come to pass.

When Investigator Lawler gave me the go-ahead to look into Marcus based on Alisa's complaint against him, Hope's name and her report accusing Marcus as the man who had assaulted her was the history I drudged up.

The case had been thrown out, but the fact that it existed at all confirmed there was a need to start digging deeper into Marcus Somerhalder.

I had thought about her often as I moved through writing this book but hadn't had any luck in finding her. Fortunately, Hope shot back onto my radar in August of 2018 in the weirdest of ways.

My wife, bless her heart, (yes, I finally found love again and am happily married) strongly suggested I attend a five-year-old's birthday party with her and my daughter. I couldn't fathom why my presence was necessary, but sometimes, it's best not to wonder (at least, not out loud), so with very little complaint, I complied.

Upon our arrival, it was obvious I was one of very few dads in attendance, and I didn't recognize any of the guys who were there, so of course, I made my way over to the food table. I'd eventually mingle, but that's easier to do on a full stomach.

As I picked through kindergartener-approved, allergen and gluten void snacks, I overheard a few women chatting to my right. I caught bits and pieces of their conversation as I chomped on rice crackers topped with dairy-free cheese, but really started to pay attention when I heard one of the women mention a friend of hers, Hope Alby. I wondered if it was the same Hope Alby who I'd been hoping to talk about this book project with.

I'm smooth and not the least bit bashful, so I sidled over and asked. They confirmed it was her and that she still lived in the Green Bay area. I was pretty excited and made an extra-special point of trying to find her after that.

As with many facets of this case, God has had a way of putting me in the right place at the right time. I truly believe in divine intervention, and I'm blessed to have been the consistent recipient of his grace. On this case, I needed all the help I could get, so, thank God I didn't fight my darling wife on attending that party because less than a month later, Hope and I were chatting over a coffee. It was amazing to see her.

That first sit-down with her was great. We talked about the case and how her life had been since, which was incredible because the last time I had talked to her about it, I was an investigator. Now, with the case being a personal interest, it was astonishing to be able to listen and respond as myself as opposed to a professional.

I asked her if she would want to write an impact statement for the book, and I'm pleased to say she didn't hesitate in saying yes. Once I read it, there was no doubt in my mind that her words were exactly what I needed to kick off my story. It fully encompasses one of the key reasons why I had to write this book. It's an honest and true declaration of how deeply carved into the hearts and minds of his victims Marcus's actions were.

When I first read Hope and the DeNiel family's statements, they dredged up a lot of the feelings I'd lovingly tucked away—all important parts of my past and carefully dealt with a long time ago. In fact, throughout this whole book writing process, I've had to revisit so many demons from this time in my life, and I've noticed those feelings don't have nearly as big an impact on me as they once had.

Reading these statements and speaking with other victims confirmed what I hadn't truly realized for myself: Case #04CF841, Marcus Somerhalder, and everything I was forced to endure to put him in jail are now just memories. Knowing this reiterates one of the main reasons why I wrote this book in the first place, which is, if I didn't write it, Marcus wins and the sacrifices made by everyone involved in this case will have been in vain. This is especially true for his victims; the emotional pain and anguish they had to endure—continue to endure—would be for nothing.

It's my hope that the glorious heroines of Case #04CF841 feel their voices and calamitous stories have been heard in a respectful way, so they can rest a little easier, and the eternal optimist in me can feel like something truly good has come out of this terrible tale.

Everyone is deserving of closure, and while I don't believe I've achieved this fully, and may never, I feel like I have some hope that it's attainable. Time will tell, I guess, but I think it's all in my own hands because I still suffer one regret regarding this case, and that's the fact that I was never able to locate or identify the specific drug/chemical Marcus used on all of us.

Way back on warrant day, we pulled several items from his residence and establishments that we suspected *might be* the "secret potion," but none were ever identified as a date rape drug. In retrospect, we should have seized every single liquid we found. Every bottle found in his bars; empty, full, sealed, opened should have been bagged and tagged. Maybe we should have seized every powdery substance we came across, too… Hindsight is always 20/20. It would have likely been several hundred pieces of evidence needing to be sent to the crime lab. I'm certain they wouldn't have been all that excited that they were required to test every questionable bit we had located, but maybe it would have made it so there was no possible way Marcus could deny drugging his victims, and I'd have total closure.

I'm confident, had I continued to follow-up and investigate further into this case, it would have led me to the supplier or origin of the drug and potentially many, many more victims. I can't even imagine how it would have opened up the case. I shudder to think how this case would have gone had we found accomplices who had provided Marcus with the product. There was never any indication that anyone else was involved, and at that time, everyone was focused on Marcus and preventing any further victimization. I still can't help but think I could have dug deeper.

Or maybe I'm giving myself a hard time, and how the case went was as good as the case was going to go because we reached a point during proceedings when Judge Warpinski requested we stop sending forth new charges and give Marcus an opportunity to make a plea on the current charges. After that, unfortunately, we no longer did much more follow-up on the drugging issue and left well-enough alone. We had a mountain of evidence against him, so what was the sense in piling more on? It was also my contention that surely Marcus would take responsibility for his actions if he was going to wave the white flag and make a plea. At that point, with all the evidence, I couldn't imagine any possible scenario where Marcus wouldn't just admit to slipping drugs into women's drinks and having his way with them. We all know how wrong I was.

In 2015, I attempted to contact Marcus in the Dodge County Prison; he'd been incarcerated for about twelve years by then. I hoped he was doing all right and more importantly, I was expecting he'd accepted the fate he was serving was the necessary consequence of his actions. I was cautiously optimistic that he'd taken responsibility for his actions.

I requested a visit, and although I knew we weren't friends after what had gone on, I'd hoped he didn't see me as his enemy. He was quick to refuse seeing me.

I settled for speaking with Marcus's case agent to find out more about his decision not to meet with me, and to learn more about his demeanor. The case agent explained that Marcus felt if we met it would just be a yelling match, and besides, he had nothing to say to me—a pretty clear indication that he still held a grudge toward me.

I shouldn't have been, but I was disappointed and dumbfounded because as I once explained to him, I originally took the case to make sure he wasn't getting railroaded or framed. I had no idea what strange and mysterious skeletons were hidden in his very large closet. He could hardly blame *me* for finding his trail of breadcrumbs.

Throughout the ordeal, I had never raised my voice to him, and I was always completely honest to him, his defense team, and his family about the specific allegations against him. With all the evidence and corroborating stories, there was absolutely no reason to hide anything or play any games with him. His inability to accept responsibility leads me to believe that his sociopathic behaviors are still very much in play—not surprising, seeing as there really isn't any way to truly medicate or cure antisocial personality disorder. Marcus is terribly defined by this psychosis.

For his sake and the sake of his victims, I still like to believe that someday, he'll accept his fate and be apologetic for what he's done no matter how farfetched the idea truly might be.

I would probably be equally as happy if he at least dropped the fictitious belief that he's a completely innocent man who's been framed by me and my faux victims. Then again, even I know that if you live a lie long enough, it will eventually, in your mind, become your truth. The problem in Marcus's case is, those video recordings don't lie, the many tears he caused were never fake, and the scars of his victimization have not gone away for many of these women; they might be affected until the day they die.

With Katie as proof, some women ended up walking a hopeless road of minimal self-worth, succumbing to depression and drugs because it was the only coping method they felt would work at easing the pain. That's the real truth. That's the truth that Marcus chooses not to see. He doesn't know how the heroines who proved who he really is continue to flail and fight to lead the comfortable lives so many others enjoy easily. Or maybe he does know, and simply fails to accept his actions had anything to do with the alteration of so many bright futures.

Lessons can be learned and healing can take place if Marcus chooses to accept one hundred percent accountability. Unfortunately, that won't likely be the case. It only took one request to speak with Marcus in prison to determine he still wants to push blame in the opposite direction and make feeble attempts to minimize and downplay his deplorable actions.

In the end, he'll have to answer to the big guy upstairs, but for right now, these women deserve their voices to not only be *heard*, but also *believed*. The fact is, the general public never heard the tragic real stories of duplicity the women endured. The people behind these stories are not simply inconsequential numbers or insignificant property stolen off a shelf, they're human beings with legitimate and undeniable grief and internal torment. They were not simply boozed up, imagining things, or fabricating fictitious stories where they lost periods of time; all of them had enough experience with alcohol to understand what its effects subjectively do to them.

Furthermore, none of them have ever experienced again that complete lapse of memory since Marcus has been out of their lives. If it's never happened to you, I could understand your skepticism and ease in writing this off as alcohol induced, but this is so much more distinctive and extraordinarily scary a feeling than alcohol can produce, I promise.

Despite Marcus knowing how to use "the drunk girl" excuse in his defense and shift blame to these poor ladies, we know it's a ruse. He'll continue to stand behind his curtain of lies and deceit, and he may have been able to tiptoe around the real story in the court proceedings, but he can't hide from the veracity and unvarnished truth forever.

So, I suppose I'm forcing his hand.

In a few short years, he'll get out of jail and be allowed to wander back into public. He'll have all sorts of correctional services' eyes on him all the time, but Marcus Somerhalder is one of the darkest, most surreptitious criminals I have ever known...and now, the public will know, too. This is what I can do to prevent him from ever hurting anyone ever again, because, like Hope and all of the other women he hurt, I don't ever want this guy to live near me or my family, and I want all of you to be safe as well.

No matter the precaution, there's one thing for certain. God will be the ultimate judge and jury on this matter, and Marcus will not be able to manipulate the truth with the almighty.

To those going out to the bar to drink with friends, I remind you of this: never stop thinking the wolf is out there and certainly *never* drop your guard. Don't live in paranoia or fear, but rather, be hypervigilant in remaining aware of yourself and your surroundings in social atmospheres. Although we're fighting for a world where these measures aren't necessary, we're still a long way off, so please don't leave your drinks unattended, and tell your friends the same. Make a pact with the people you go out with that just as you arrived somewhere together, you're going to leave that place together as well. This stuff doesn't just happen to other people... It happens all the time to all sorts of people and the statistics are not biased.

Know and understand how these things can happen, and don't ever ignore or write off the unexplainable "black-out" type incident. There's probably something more to the story and a very dark motivation to what happened if things just don't make sense. If you know or suspect you've been sexually assaulted, your body is essentially the evidence, so don't shower or bathe, just go directly to the emergency room, tell them what your suspicions are, and request a Sexual Assault Nurse Examiner (SANE), who is a registered nurse specifically trained to help rape victims. They'll work with you in whatever way you need, including doing what's required to complete a rape kit, which, you should know, isn't given to police without your permission and doesn't include your name if you don't want it to. Also, it's best to request an immediate urine test for stupefying agents. Keep in mind, they're still difficult to detect, but the sooner you can get a urine sample, the higher probability it can be detected and identified.

Don't ever feel guilty, think you "put yourself in that situation," or feel you did something to deserve being sexually assaulted—you are *never* to blame—ever.

Offenders are very sly, and even when confronted or caught will predictably make excuses or shift blame toward their victim. The decision to harm you was their own, not yours; you were merely a pawn in their repugnant quest for control and power. Guilt and shame will only put you in a dark and lonely place. Don't give your aggressor any power—hold them accountable by speaking out against their deplorable actions.

I don't remember details, what if I am wrong? I would hate to blame someone for something they didn't do. I know I had sex, but I just have no recollection. These are all common lines of thought and reasons why so many fail to report sexual assaults. Not knowing the answers or details might make the situation easier to deny, but it isn't good for you, and *is* exactly what your offender wants to happen. That's pretty much the entire modus operandi of drug-facilitated rape. It's time to change that, and, at the very least, file an information only report with the local police department to get the event on file. This will allow for the information to be retained but not immediately acted on if you so wish.

In Marcus's case, finding out this sort of file existed on him because of Hope's allegation proved to be a great motivation for me to dig deeper into him. It also proved to make Alisa's allegation more credible. Without the courageous actions of those two women, it could have been a lot longer before Marcus was caught, which would have turned into even more rape victims or worse.

Don't make things up because only the facts and why you feel the way you do matter. If you were truly violated, I can very nearly guarantee your offender will do so again, and probably do almost exactly what they did to you to the next person. Your story, no matter how few details you recall, can still be enough to hold them accountable for their crimes. I would think the guilt of not reporting something and finding out that person continued to victimize others would be just as devastating down the road.

When enjoying time out, be aware and report anything that seems suspicious. For example, there's absolutely no reason for anyone to be loitering or adding anything to an unattended drink, even if you know for certain that person is there *with* the drink's owner. Don't overlook the obvious, because anytime you see someone put something in a drink that's not theirs, it's a screaming red flag.

There's no exception for bartenders, either—this book is about one, don't forget. If you see the bartender reach for an unusual container, a bottle hidden off to the side or pulled from under the counter, don't fail to imagine what they might be up to. Marcus thought he had the perfect scheme because his job was to make drinks for women. The most trusted person in the bar is the bartender, right?

No. Never assume, just always be smart, vigilant, and take care of each other. Typically, offenders of drug-facilitated rape will put whatever they're looking to dose with into a drink that's sweet or strong. If it's your drink, you won't taste it or notice the drink tastes off in time to protect yourself; if it's your friend's drink, you won't have any idea until it's too late. When you see something that makes the hair on the back of your neck stand up or otherwise just doesn't make sense, *do not disregard* that feeling. Discard the drink and ask for a bottled or canned drink that you can observe them open and deliver to you.

So, yeah, take care of yourself and each other. There have been developments with coasters, straws, nail polishes, and small, portable testers that can detect common date rape drugs, which is a start, but none of it points to whodunit. Further to that, most of it isn't available for purchase, but at least there are efforts being made. Always remember, by reporting something, you could prevent others from becoming victims or quantify and support the credibility of others that reported past encounters. You could potentially save a life.

The good news is that GHB, the drug I strongly suspect Marcus used on his victims, is now on every date rape drug list in North America.

And, finally, to the women of the past, present, and future…I'm sorry and yet, I'm not. Let me explain.

I can't pretend to know how it came about—brute strength, maybe— but it's been millennia since men assumed they had a right to dominate over women, and I'm sorry at how fully we've taken advantage of it.

I'm sorry women have to live guarded and cautious. I'm sorry you have to watch your drinks when you're out. I'm sorry you can't walk or run alone, especially after dark. I'm sorry the assaults of Marcus Somerhalder ever happened, because it made it so terribly obvious to me that victims consider backlash and consequences of calling out their aggressors over knowing it's their right to get someone who's hurting them arrested. Protecting yourself should never be a consideration—it's a right.

More than anything, I'm sorry I have to say any of this, but I'm not sorry because I have hope things are going to change drastically, and for the better, soon.

So much media about sexual assault in the last few years especially, has created an incredible amount of necessary dialogue. I've seen, after years of repression, women finally speaking out, respectfully and without shame about the terrible things they've endured and been subjected to. I'm finally seeing those who do speak out get the deserved reactions, understanding, and compassion they would have found infinitely useful when they were first assaulted. I hope it's helped them find closure; I hope it was another step in their healing.

I'm also blown away at how responsive so many men have been—so many listening to and understanding for the first time what the women they love have gone through. It didn't used to be this way—we men didn't always care to listen. Maybe it made us uncomfortable? I honestly don't know, but I'm so glad for this change. I've fought for so long to create a world that's fair, united, and safer for everyone. I teach understanding and mutual respect daily through my work, and I want everyone I encounter to follow suit; despite my efforts, I know the works needing to be done are colossal, but if no one ever tried to change the world...

Still, I have so much more hope than I ever did before...that my daughter will grow up in the midst of the movement where women declared, without compromise, that they won't take any more shit from their masculine counterparts. I know many of you have suffered, do suffer, and might suffer at the hands of a man in the future, but I can't tell you how incredible it is to see you all rise up.

One thing I know for certain is this: women of the world, you are the essence of compassion, patience, and perseverance. You are the world's best examples of inner strength and tenacity—demand the world gives you what you need to feel safe in it. Fight for change, and please know, there is an incredible amount of men in this world who respect you and what you're fighting for—we support you, we won't think twice about helping you, and we know change is possible.

AUTHOR'S NOTE

I am telling this story from my point of view as a police investigator and as an acquaintance of Marcus. It is solely about my role and the things I did during the several months' investigation. There were certainly several other people that assisted me in the investigation and prosecution of Marcus Somerhalder. Although the information generated was a direct result of pounding the pavement and building personal contacts, this case would not have been successfully resolved without the diligent group of officers, investigators, and prosecutors that assisted me in this endeavor.

This is my best recollection of the case from my investigative perspective. Throughout the entire investigation, I remained honest and open to the victims, to the witnesses, to Marcus's supportive family, and most surprisingly to Marcus. I did not ever need to play any mind games to hide what I had uncovered in Marcus's dark and dangerous world. It was what it was, and no one could change the truth.

I think it is an important story to be told in the hopes that people can understand and be cautious that opportunistic sociopaths roam the world in cities big and small. We must stay vigilant and demonstrate situational awareness at all times in order to protect ourselves and loved ones from becoming victims of drug-facilitated rape.

The women involved in this case did not deserve to be violated, nor did they ask to endure the emotional, mental, and sometimes physical pain inflicted on them. The women were mere pawns in Marcus's crazy, dangerous game to control their every breath and steal their most intimate and personal attributes against their will. It is my hope this story will encourage and build strength for victims of similar circumstances to come forth and break the silence.

And please, if you or someone you know has been sexually assaulted, contact your local police department or find resources at RAINN (Rape, Assault & Incest National Network). Call 1-800-656-HOPE (4673) or visit https://www.rainn.org.

ACKNOWLEDGEMENTS

To my wife, my daughter, and my sons who might have wives and daughters in their futures—to all of you—your incredible, confident outrage and unyielding demand for equality is what humanity needs. Thank you for your support and understanding my need to get this story out.